FOREVER SHOWTIME

OTHER BOOKS BY PHIL BERGER

Miracle on 33rd Street: The NY Knickerbockers' Championship Season

The Last Laugh: The World of the Stand-Up Comics

Blood Season: Mike Tyson and the World of Boxing

Punch Lines: Berger on Boxing

Twisted Genius: Confessions of a $10 Million Scam Man
   (with Craig Jacob)

*Smokin' Joe: The Autobiography of a Heavyweight Champion
   of the World* (with Joe Frazier)

Larry Holmes: Against the Odds
   (with Larry Holmes)

The New York Knicks: The Official 50th Anniversary Celebration

Aerobox: A High Performance Fitness Program
   (with Michael Olajide Jr.)

Mickey Mantle

Deadly Kisses (a novel)

Big Time (a novel)

FOREVER SHOWTIME

The Checkered Life of Pistol Pete Maravich

PHIL BERGER

TAYLOR PUBLISHING COMPANY
DALLAS, TEXAS

Book design and composition by Mark McGarry
Set in Goudy

Published by Taylor Publishing Company
1550 West Mockingbird Lane
Dallas, Texas 75235
www.taylorpub.com

Library of Congess Cataloging-in-Publication Data
Berger, Phil
   Forever showtime : the checkered life of Pistol Pete Maravich / by
Phil Berger.
     p.   cm.
   ISBN 0-87833-237-5
   1. Maravich, Pete, 1948– 2. Basketball players—United States—
Biography. I. Title.
GV884.M195B47   1999
796.323'092—dc21
[B]   99-042597

10 9 8 7 6 5 4 3 2 1

Printed in the United States of America

To the three ladies of my life—
my mother, my daughter Julia, and Miss V.

CONTENTS

ACKNOWLEDGMENTS

IN 1985, after a magazine article I'd written on Pete Maravich appeared, I got a call from a stranger—a woman—who told me, "Nice piece on Maravich, but you don't know the half of it."

The woman's name was Sharon Danovich, and her father had played for Pete's dad, Press, at West Virginia Wesleyan and had maintained a friendship with him the rest of his life. As a result, Ms. Danovich knew quite a lot about the Maraviches.

What she told me teased my imagination; the idea of a book on Pete Maravich incubated there. When, finally, I got around to signing a deal to write the book, I called Sharon and told her. She volunteered to help with the myriad chores that such an enterprise brings. Her assistance has been invaluable.

In 1972, my friend Bill Gutman wrote *The Making of a Basketball Superstar, Pistol Pete Maravich*. My thanks to him for making available transcripts of interviews he did with Press Maravich and others in researching the book and for allowing me to excerpt material from the book.

In 1982, I wrote a series on the NBA's first season, 1946–47, in the course of which I did taped interviews with Press Maravich, his Pittsburgh Ironmen teammates, and his coach, Paul Birch. Many of the quotes attributed to Press are from that session.

Thanks to Linda Ronan and Linda Wachtel at the *Sports Illustrated* library for permitting me access to pertinent research materials.

Special thanks to Norb Garrett, editor of *Sport Magazine*, for permission to quote from articles on Maravich that appeared in the magazine. Copyrighted *Sport Magazine*. Reprinted with permission.

Many individuals were interviewed for this book, and to all of them I am grateful. Note: The job descriptions given pertain to that period when those mentioned were involved with the Maraviches.

From Press Maravich's formative years in Aliquippa, Pennsylvania: his half-brother, Sam Kosanovich; his distant cousin, Lazo Maravich; his next-door neighbor, Sarah (Marovich) Kostal.

Walt Miller and Peter Lalich recounted their experiences playing pro basketball with Press.

For information on Pete's boyhood years in Clemson, South Carolina, and Raleigh, North Carolina, I am indebted to Bob Bradley, sports information director at Clemson, and his wife, Louise; Pete's high school coaches Howard Bagwell, Dr. Billy Hunter, Pete Carlisle, Olin Broadway, and Ed McLean; teammates Tommy Peele, Jimmy Broadway, and Jim Sutherland; boyhood friend Sam Hunter; Clemson varsity basketball player Jim Brennan; North Carolina State varsity players Hal Blondeau, Joe Serdich, and Eddie Biedenbach; North Carolina State sports information director Frank Weedon; North Carolina State assistant coach Charlie Bryant; North Carolina State freshman coach Les Robinson; and reporter Paul Phillips of the *Raleigh Times*.

For the Maraviches' years at LSU, my thanks to Pete's teammates Jeff Tribbett, Rich Hickman, Ralph Jukkola, and Rusty Bergman; LSU sports information director Bud Johnson; LSU team manager David

Tate; reporter Sam King of the *Baton Rouge State-Times*; and Bud Montet, sports editor of the *Baton Rouge Morning Advocate*.

Those interviewed regarding Pete's years with the Atlanta Hawks included teammates Herb White, Jim Washington, and Walt Bellamy, rival player Bill Hosket, coaches Richie Guerin and Cotton Fitzsimmons, team publicity man Tom McCollister, reporters Frank Hyland and Mike McKenzie of the *Atlanta Journal*, columnist Furman Bisher of the *Atlanta Constitution*, team business manager Irv Gack, Hawks general manager Pat Williams, Hawks broadcaster Skip Caray, attorney Les Zittrain, and past Hawks executive Marty Blake.

For their help regarding Pete's years with the New Orleans (and Utah) Jazz and the Boston Celtics, I thank teammates Rich Kelley, Neal Walk, Paul Griffin, Andy Walker, and Mel Counts; coaches Butch van Breda Kolff, Elgin Baylor, and Tom Nissalke; Jazz trainer Don Sparks; again to Bud Johnson, first publicity man for the Jazz, and to Dave Fredman, who succeeded him; Jazz owner Sam Battisone; Jazz broadcaster Rod Hundley; Marty Mule and Jimmy Smith of the *New Orleans Times-Picayune*; Lt. William Watson, Boone, North Carolina, Police Department; Johnnie Fox, assistant to Jazz executive Barry Mendelson; Jazz season-ticket holder Richard Katz; and Hollywood producer Arthur Friedman.

John Lotz, assistant athletic director at the University of North Carolina, and Gary Lydic, director of ministry services for *Focus on the Family*, provided insights on Pete Maravich's religious awakening, and Charley Rosen, coach of the Savanna Spirits of the Continental Basketball Association, shared an anecdote from that period.

"Maravich was unbelievable. I think he was, like, sort of ahead of his time in the things he did."
—Magic Johnson

"He could do things with a basketball I've never seen anybody do."
—Rick Barry

"The best showman of all time? I'd probably have to say Pistol Pete."
—Isiah Thomas

PROLOGUE

THE THUMPING SOUND awakened the boy, who rubbed sleep from his eyes and raised the window shade a few inches. Rolling onto his stomach, he peeked into the backyard.

There in the macadam driveway, his father was at it again.

His father—a robust 6-footer with dark eyes and a coal-black crew cut—had a basketball in his hands, his back toward the metal rim and wooden board that were mounted on the garage.

As the boy watched, his father feinted to his right, then turned abruptly the other way and, with a sweeping motion, let the ball go, watching it catch a sweet spot on the backboard—that thumping sound again—and carom smartly into the orange hoop.

"Maravich with the hook!" shouted his father, raising a clenched fist and shaking it several times before he retrieved the ball.

The screen door at the back of the house flew open, and the boy's mother—a slender, pretty brunette—hurried out.

"Really, Press," Helen Maravich scolded. "Little Pete's not up yet."

"Sure he is," said Press Maravich, pointing toward the bedroom window and smiling. "I see you, you little rascal. Get your lazy bones moving."

And then, a step farther from the basket, Press again arced the ball off the board and into the basket, as deftly as George Mikan, the broad-beamed dominator of the Minneapolis Lakers, did it.

It was 1953, and the Maraviches were living in a small, wood-frame house on a tree-lined street in Elkins, West Virginia. Elkins, population 8,000, sat in the eastern corner of the state—a quiet place in the heart of the Appalachian Mountains.

Press had come to Elkins to coach the basketball team out at the college, a four-year Presbyterian school called Davis & Elkins. He was consumed by the game and liked nothing better than to hunker down at the kitchen table after dinner and talk basketball with coaches from neighboring towns or, if they were busy, sit by himself and scribble diagrams full of Xs and Os and directional arrows well into the night.

Yet when morning came he'd be up early and out there again by the garage with his basketball, making a ruckus.

Little Pete, who was six years old, knew that these shows were meant for him—he was just not sure why. He suspected that his father wanted to draw him into playing with the ball. But the boy hadn't decided yet whether he really wanted to. What if he were to throw the ball into the air, and it didn't fall through the metal circle, which seemed to be the object of the game? In that case, what would his father do?

On this morning, Pete watched, as he usually did, peeking around the side of the house while Press, pretending not to notice his son's equivocal body language, continued shooting one-handers, hook shots on the run, and reverse layups, whooping it up each time the ball dropped through the net.

Then suddenly he lowered his voice to the magisterial baritone of a sports announcer: "Eight seconds to go. Score tied 63–63. Maravich with the ball. Drives to his right. Oh nooooo."

At that moment Press took a calculated misstep that caused him to "stumble" while the ball rolled free, toward the boy.

"Six seconds, five seconds," Press croaked. "Get the ball, Pete! Time's running out!"

After Press had baited his son for weeks, now finally the boy reacted, swept up in the contrived emergency. Little Pete retrieved the ball and, squatting before the basket—the ball held with two hands at the side of his chest, his eyes fixed on the rim so high above—launched himself upward. The ball—a knuckler—floated part way to the rim and then came plummeting back to earth.

"Ohhhhh, just short," crooned Press. "Maravich misses. Game over."

Little Pete scowled as he chased down the ball so that he might try again. As the boy lined up the shot, Press fell silent, watching his big-eyed son gather himself before pushing the ball into the air. The look on the kid's face—his pursed lips, the gleaming eyes—was all Press Maravich needed to see.

"I've got him," he told himself as the ball fluttered short of the rim again. "He's hooked."

"Hooked" on a game that long ago had become the father's passion, imbuing him with this overwhelming desire—need, really—to invest all he knew and felt about basketball in this skinny, almost frail boy. A Geppeto bent on sculpting a prodigy.

Today would be the jumping-off point in the father's master plan for what the son might one day be. And as the years passed and the boy got caught up in this vision, for both of them the dream would become an obsession—and the obsession would become what obsessions often turn into—a pursuit fraught with complications.

But that—that was a long way from where this craziness about Dr. Naismith's game had begun.

I

PRESS MARAVICH grew up in a Pennsylvania steel town whose skyline was dominated by the blast-furnace snouts of the Jones & Laughlin mill.

Aliquippa was a city of foul air and troubled skies—an industrial landscape 26 miles southwest of Pittsburgh. The mill sat on 1,500 acres on the west bank of the Ohio River, its behemoth furnaces and Bessemer converters churning 24 hours a day, turning iron ore to steel—products as diverse as pipes, ingots, nails, seamless and welded tubes, and tin sheets.

The men who ministered to these hulking industrial creatures, who stoked and swept the furnaces, were recruited from the immigrant tide that brought millions of newcomers to these shores at the turn of the century.

Whereas the bosses at mills everywhere in those days tended to be Irish or Scotch, the men who worked up close to those raging furnaces were Italians, Greeks, Slavs, Russians, Poles, Ukrainians, Croatians and, like Press' father Vajo, Serbs.

The first blast furnace in Aliquippa began operating in 1909, and by 1912 there were four more of them going full tilt. As J&L prospered, Aliquippa's population rose, hitting a peak of 27,000 in 1930. A good third of the citizenry ended up working in the mill.

From the beginning, Aliquippa was a company town, dominated by the long reach of Jones & Laughlin. When you bought your house, it was from the J&L Land Company. The town's prime department store, Pittsburgh Mercantile—"P-M" to the locals—was owned by J&L. The schools were built by J&L, the library was named after Benjamin Franklin Jones, who had founded the Jones & Laughlin Steel Corporation in 1850 in Pittsburgh. In Aliquippa, the company owned the real estate, the water system, the buses. The company even built a swimming pool for the workers, and when blacks wanted to use it, the company built them a separate pool.

Where other, earlier steel communities had been maligned for their companies' indifference to the living conditions of their working stiffs, image-conscious J&L created housing with indoor plumbing for its un-skilled immigrant workers that was deemed more than adequate by so-cial critics. The company created separate neighborhoods that were designated by numbered "plans" for various ethnic groups, native-born Americans, skilled workers, and managers. Even though the workers lived in box-like affairs, crowded one against the other, whereas the bosses lived in bigger dwellings fortified by the company's steel beams (Plan 6), in an era when unions were struggling for their place in the American fabric this was considered progress.

When Press was two, his father—a locomotive engineer in the steel mills—was killed in an accident in Clairton, Pennsylvania. After Press' mother, Sarah, remarried and moved from Pittsburgh to Aliquippa, the family settled into an attached house at 418 Hopewell Avenue, in what was called the Logstown section (Plan 2). Logstown was in the northern part of Aliquippa, hard by the mill's blast furnaces and basic steel-mak-ing divisions and buffered by only the railroad tracks, along which the Pittsburgh & Lake Erie Railroad transported iron ore from the Great Lakes region.

All day long the tumults of the mill assailed its Logstown neighbors. At any hour of the day, the cacophony of this fire-eating, chemical-spuming industry resounded—be it in the rumble of those Pittsburgh & Lake Erie trains or the boom-bang of the ever-blowing furnaces or even in a tugboat's whistle. There was no escaping the existence of that mill. Its sulfuric fumes flew into the night, offending the nostrils even as they left a carpet of soot on cars, porches, and on the collar of any man bold enough to wear a white shirt.

But for those who were newly settled in this land, the Aliquippa Works, as the mill was known, offered opportunities far greater than existed in the countries they had abandoned. Still, it didn't take keen insight for an unskilled immigrant worker to know that he was a bottom feeder in the J&L hierarchy. Show up in the company employment office and you might linger for hours until a company man would appear to say: "Any Dagos, niggers, or Serbs wants greasers or wipers jobs, c'mon in."

The contempt of the bosses—known as "cake eaters" to their hired hands—was built into a system that merely played at being paternalistic. Push come to shove, J&L hewed to the bottom line. The company's security force, in conjunction with the local police and a network of informers, kept labor organizers from unionizing the mill, resorting to violence when necessary. Mill hands who showed interest in the labor movement might find themselves out of a job in the blink of an eye. In union circles, Aliquippa became known as "Little Siberia."

The conditions in the mill—the hours, the pay, the perils involved in working close to hot metal—made a case for change. The job, as writer Armen Keteyian has described it, was a hard, grinding affair:

Steelworkers are known as "hot-metal" men because steel in its natural state runs as hot as 3,000 degrees Fahrenheit, painful to the eyes, fluid as a flag rippling in the breeze. Most men today wouldn't last ten minutes in a steel mill. Rocked by the sound of red-hot strips of steel being shaped . . . *ba-boom, ba-boom, ba-boom* . . . in rolling machines . . . standing a few feet from bubbling baths of live liquid . . . blinded by a blast furnace hot enough to fry your face in seconds.

No wonder that when Friday came and a man stepped from the tunnel that led out of the mill, he might be tempted to leave more than a little of the cash from his pay envelope at the many bars on Franklin Avenue, the main drag of the town.

A quaint local custom rose up on those paydays, with the more budget-conscious wives of these men with big thirsts standing just outside the tunnel, where Franklin and Hopewell converged, waiting to snatch the pay envelopes from their spouses before the poor bastards could blow the money in bars like Zernich Grill, Diane's Tavern, Mill City Inn, Mars Grill. But, of course, the men drank because their lives were hard and there wasn't much chance that things would change. Not in the steel mill. If you were a tin flopper, you were a tin flopper the rest of your life. A pipe threader—same thing. And back then, there were no EPA standards in the mill. No protective gear. In an environment where steel in its natural state could run as hot as the ninth circle of hell, accidents happened. Men died. A shot and a beer anesthetized a steel worker.

As a boy, Maravich—Christian name Peter—got the nickname "Press" because he always had an opinion on every topic. His cousin, Bob Maravich, told him he was like the *Pittsburgh Press* newspaper: never at a loss for words. The nickname stuck.

Press was a popular boy, part of a Logstown crowd that hung out at Albert Friedman's candy store, where a card game was always going in the back room and the older guys would show young fellows like Press the latest dance steps, to music on Friedman's record player.

Friedman sponsored teams in football and in an Aliquippa version of softball called "mushball." Though Press was an all-around athlete, he soon enough was concentrating on basketball. He began playing in the 1920s on a street corner where an old peach basket was nailed to a telephone pole, and the ball was made from a tin can weighted with a rock and wrapped in newspaper and electrical tape. That fabricated "ball" was capable of no more than a single bounce, but it didn't deter Press and his friends. Under a night sky that was perpetually orange from the smoke blasting up the chimneys of the Jones & Laughlin mill, Press and his buddies would play until a local policeman, Officer Jimmy Istock, would chase them at the city's nine o'clock curfew.

When a neighborhood clergyman, Reverend Ernest Anderson of the Woodlawn Mission, observed the boys' dilemma, he offered them the use of his Presbyterian church gym so long as they agreed to attend church services.

"There were two baskets right in the church, real baskets with a net, rims, a wooden backboard, the whole thing," Press recalled. "And when we saw those baskets in the church, it was like a professional hall to us. It was so exciting, a real thrill to see it. I must have been somewhere between seven and nine years old then.

"So that's how it started. We attended the bible classes faithfully and listened to everything Reverend Anderson had to say. And when he was finished, we'd go play ball for hours on end."

Through the Woodlawn Mission, Maravich got his first taste of age-level organized competition—against church teams from nearby communities. The game struck a chord in him. He had an unquenchable desire to learn the fine points of basketball, not easy with a sport so relatively new and unsophisticated.

At Woodlawn Mission, Press watched the older boys to see what he could learn from them, but they were greenhorns themselves at the game. A far better opportunity came whenever the preeminent professional team of the era, a barnstorming New York-based group known as the Original Celtics, played at Duquesne University in Pittsburgh. Press would make it a point to be there to savor the slick passing and constant-motion offense of players like Nat Holman, Davey Banks, Joe Lapchick, Nat Hickey, and the man credited with originating pivot play, Henry G. (Dutch) Dehnert.

"We knew then that the Celtics were a great team," said Press. "What I liked most about them was that although they had individual stars they were a magnificent outfit from the standpoint of team play. They meshed so beautifully together . . . When I'd see them play, I'd say to myself, 'Gee whiz, if I could just be like one of those guys.' They were really my idols in those days."

Press' infatuation with the game was not shared at home. To his step-father, George Kosanovich, and his mother, Sarah—both from the old country—the boy's devotion to basketball seemed a time-waster—and pointless. In fact, when Press began playing for coach Nate Lippe's Aliquippa High team as an eighth-grader, he did it on the sly, with his half-brother, Sam Kosanovich, acting as a collaborator.

"It was pretty simple," said Sam. "Press would walk out of the house. I'd throw him his uniform out the window, and then his gym bag."

Still, Press' pursuit of the game was complicated by his stepfather's Plan B—a desire to make a musician out of the boy.

"My stepfather," said Press, "was a big man, must have weighed 250 pounds. And he had three cousins who were built just like him. We used to call them 'The Four Tons.' They all loved music and a lot of nights they would come home from the mills, have dinner and then sit around drinking wine and singing Yugoslavian songs. They were hearty men, strong as bulls and never missed work no matter what they did. But any-way . . . there were these traveling salesmen back then who timed it so that they showed up on payday at the steel mill. One of them shows up with a violin. He played it for my stepfather and his cousins, and they all fell in love with it. The guy had some deal where you take lessons for something like a dollar a week and at the end of a year you get to keep the violin. So I took lessons for a whole year until my brother sold the violin finally. He needed some money, so he sold it for five dollars. And by then I was kind of happy he did.

"Another time a guy came around, on payday, and sold my stepfather a banjo. So I took banjo lessons for a while, which I enjoyed. But by then basketball was really creeping into it. And looking back, I think I became a prisoner of basketball. There was something about the game that challenged me."

Love of the game, though, was tempered by the exigencies of a De-pression era economy. By the time Press was a freshman in high school, he had begun working the midnight-to-eight shift in the mill, lying about his age to get a pipe threader's job.

"That tunnel that went into and out of the mill—I remember these old Indians used to be just inside there, selling snake medicines for all ailments," Press said. "They'd set up their teepees in the tunnel and we'd go down and watch them do their dances. Then they'd sell us the snake oil and tell us how strong it was and how it would cure rheumatism, arthritis and a lot of other things.

"With the job at the mill, I was going 'round the clock. I'd go to school after maybe sleeping a couple of hours in the mill, then I'd practice basketball, go home, sleep a little more until it was time to go to work again. Funny thing, though. With all that other stuff—the banjo and violin lessons, and having to work all night in the mills—there was never any thought of giving up basketball. That was in me to stay."

Clippings from the mid-1930s sports pages of *The Daily Times*, a Beaver County newspaper, refer to Press as "a high-scoring forward" for coach Lippe's Aliquippa High team. Of course, compared to now, scoring back then was relative in an era when a jump ball occurred after every basket. Take this item from *The Daily Times*:

In one of the most thrilling cage games of the current scholastic campaign, Nate Lippe's Aliquippa high passers dropped their first Section 3 contest to the New Castle high quintet by a 25–24 score at New Castle Tuesday night.

From another *Daily Times* report:

Before a capacity throng of cheering students and fans the Ambridge high cagers defeated Aliquippa high 20 to 16 . . . and thereby clinched the Section IV, and Beaver County floor championships for the 1933 season.

In a curious tangent to that article, Aliquippa coach Lippe soon after lodged a protest, claiming that two Ambridge players had competed against professionals, an infraction that could have cost them their eligibility and caused their team to forfeit its title. However, the Ambridge coach asserted that the players had been assured that the tournament in which the alleged violation occurred was sanctioned by the Amateur Athletic Union, and the Ambridge coach was upheld by the Western Pennsylvania Interscholastic Athletic Association.

The irony was that in those days capable high school players from impoverished areas routinely moonlighted for professional teams under assumed names, including Lippe's very own "high-scoring forward," Press Maravich. Press played as "Peter Munnell" as often as the chance to pick up 10 bucks a game arose.

"Back then, they had tournaments all over, and my friends and I would play whenever we could," said Press. "We played in Ohio and West Virginia, up at Pitt and Duquesne. We traveled like a bunch of gypsies and all this while we were still in high school. We took trains and buses and sometimes we'd all pile into a car."

As captain of the Aliquippa quintet in his junior and senior years, Maravich was the model of the clean-cut athlete—a handsome crew-cut lad who took seriously the constraints on a ballplayer's life. He did not smoke and did not drink. His next-door neighbor, Sarah Kostal (nee Marovich), remembered him as "pure, pure, pure. He just went according to Hoyle, like bridge. He did everything coach Lippe told him."

Well, maybe not *everything*. Growing up in Logstown, Press had acquired the neighborhood habit of chewing tobacco.

"All of us did," said Lazo Maravich, a distant cousin who grew up with Press. "By the time we were 12, 13, we'd be chewing tobacco. Most of the boys started on Copenhagen. Copenhagen is snuff. You put it inside your lip and teeth. Press preferred Mail Pouch, which you chewed on like food and then spit out the juice."

By his senior year, in 1935, Press was known for his accurate two-hand set shot. Under Lippe, he'd become a dominant player, in one game scoring 28 points—remarkable for that time.

When Maravich graduated from Aliquippa High, the Depression was still generating bread lines, and in Aliquippa mill jobs were at a premium. Among the measures that President Franklin D. Roosevelt tried to jumpstart the economy was the creation of the Civilian Conservation Corps (CCC), which offered outdoor work to young men at minimum wage. Maravich worked in the CCC for six months in the hills of West Virginia and Pennsylvania.

Eventually jobs opened at the Aliquippa Works, and Press went into the blooming mill. While there he was part of the blooming mill team that beat the tin plate team to win the J&L League. Among Press' team-mates was Pete (Pecky) Suder, who would go on to play 13 years as a major league baseball player.

In high school, Press had taken a vocational curriculum, shunted there by a school system that tended to regard east Europeans like him as mill fodder. That academic background would have severely limited his chances for a college education had it not been for basketball. Even so, many of the schools that expressed interest in him—LIU, Duke, Pittsburgh—could offer only partial scholarships. Basketball hadn't the economic clout then that football did, and for a while it looked as though Maravich's life might be bound to the mill—he simply hadn't the means to cover what the scholarship offers wouldn't.

But then an opportunity arose.

"There was a kid by the name of Mike Winne, who was a guard on the Davis & Elkins basketball team," said Press. "He was from Ambridge, which was not far from Aliquippa, and we knew each other. He told me they had a good ballclub down there and I had a good chance of playing as a freshman."

Davis & Elkins coach Bud Shelton offered Maravich a full scholarship. In the fall of 1937, he landed at the picturesque campus nestled in the Appalachian Mountains and was soon debunking the Aliquippa school system's idea that he was academically inept.

Press learned to take class notes in shorthand and then would type them up. By this method he was able to succeed in his course work. And though he was an athlete, he did not confine himself to the playing field, taking an active role in student life: in his senior year he was elected student body president, *and* for the second straight year he was voted "best looking man on campus."

His scholarship obliged him to play football as well as basketball, and he did so as a pass-catching end. But it was on the basketball court that Maravich made his reputation. As captain of the squad, he was also its scoring dynamo, as this news article from back then attests:

Point-a-minute Man!
That pretty much describes Capt. Pete "Press" Maravich.

Davis-Elkins' one-man basketball team. . . . Many teams find it hard enough to score as many as 36 points in a game, but that's just what Maravich, former Aliquippa High player, did all on his own against Salem (W.Va.) Teachers last Saturday.

It was a new district one-game record, bettering the former mark of 34 held jointly by Mel Cratsley and Bill Laughlin.

Press flipped 16 field goals and four fouls to rack up his 36 point total, but it still wasn't enough to prevent D-E from dropping a 73–59 decision to Salem.

Maravich ranks with the leading point-getters in the nation. On a recent Eastern trip, he scored 27 points against Long Island U and the next night collected 30 against LaSalle, but D and E lost both games.

In four seasons as a varsity player, 1937–41, Press scored 1,635 points and was named to the All-West Virginia Conference team.

"I handled the ball most of the time," he said. "And we played pretty much of a passing game. Mainly we controlled the ball, split the posts, did a lot of weaving, backdoor cuts and ended up with drive shots and sets."

While matriculating at Davis & Elkins, Press was always at loose ends for money. The scholarship did not cover room and board, so he was obliged to work odd jobs to keep his belly full. That constant pressure to cover expenses drove him to continue to moonlight as "Peter Munnell."

"During my junior and senior years in college, we had very little to eat," he said. "So when Joe Stydahar, a great football player for the Chicago Bears, got up a semi-pro basketball team, the Clarksburg Pure Oilers, and called me and asked if I'd like to make a hundred bucks a game, I'd say, 'Joe, we're starving here.' This would be right after Jumbo Joe [6-foot-4, 233 pounds] finished football season.

"Joe was a helluva basketball player. And the Oilers had another guy, Babe Barna, who played baseball with the New York Giants, and there was a guy named Phares who'd played with the old House of David team where all the guys had beards. And we'd barnstorm against other barnstorming teams. We'd go up to Rochester, for instance, and play the Original Celtics, or the [all-black] New York Renaissance or the Globe-trotters. As Peter Munnell, I'd get my hundred bucks and come back and share what I'd made with some of the other athletes.

"One time I almost got caught. I played in Rochester against the Celtics and then came back to play with Davis & Elkins against LaSalle in Philadelphia. Well, the referee for both games turned out to be Pat Kennedy, a famous official. I was captain of the Davis & Elkins team and, when I came out to meet the captain of the LaSalle team, Pat Kennedy said, 'Hey, haven't I seen you before?'

"'No sir,' I said, but I was shaking like a leaf and breaking out in a cold sweat. I was scared to death, never so frightened in my life.

"Kennedy said, 'Are you sure I haven't seen you some place before?' he said, again.

"'No sir. I'm from West Virginia.'

"Then he asked, 'Do you know Joe Stydahar?'

"'Never heard of him,' I said.

"But he had me pegged. I just refused to buckle, but I was scared to death. If I'd been caught I guess I would have been declared ineligible. But I had to make the money so we could eat."

AFTER GRADUATING from Davis & Elkins in 1941, Press worked that summer at the J&L mill and that winter continued playing weekend games with the Clarksburg Pure Oilers.

As an Oiler, he caught the attention of the famed Dutch Dehnert. At the time Dehnert was the coach of the Detroit Eagles. The Eagles had just beaten the Oshkosh All-Stars 39–37 to win the 1941 "World Championship" that was played each year in Chicago and was sponsored by that city's *Herald-American* newspaper.

From 1939 to 1941, the Eagles also played an abbreviated schedule in the National Basketball League, an early pro league that rose up in the Midwest, with teams sponsored by industrial entities. Fred Zollner owned a piston factory in Fort Wayne. Frank Kautsky, who owned the

Indianapolis Kautskys, ran two grocery stores. Goodyear Tire and Rubber sponsored the Akron Wingfoots. And so on. Against the Eagles Press scored 30 points and was recruited on the spot by Dehnert, who offered him a one-year contract to barnstorm with the Eagles.

"My salary," said Press, "was somewhere in the neighborhood of $3,000 that year and for me that was pretty good money. Because they had won the championship in Chicago, people wanted to see the Eagles. We must have played about three hundred games that year, 1941–42.

"There were six players on the team, including Buddy Jeannette, Jake Ahearn from St. Johns, Ed Perry, Paul Widowitz and one other guy from Darby, Pennsylvania—I can't remember his name. Dutch was the coach and we traveled in an old touring car. We put all the equipment on top and piled in. We played and we traveled. That's all we did, maybe five, six or seven games a week. Sometimes we'd play in the morning against maybe some faculty team, and in the afternoon we'd be up against some other club. We played against good and bad teams— just so long as we got games. We slept mostly in hotels, but they weren't the best places in the world. And traveling in that car could be a harrowing experience."

A barnstorming team's schedule was often incredibly tight, and all-night drives after playing three games in a day were not unusual. One player would take his turn at the wheel while the others slept. Although Press had no driver's license and had never taken a lesson behind the wheel, when a weary Jeannette asked Maravich if he could drive, Press assured him he could.

The trip was from Davenport, Iowa, to New Orleans, and it was on a dark country road that a cow stepped onto the road, into the path of the Eagles' speeding touring car. Press was unable to stop in time but, given the urgency of the team's schedule and the fact that none of his teammates had been awakened by the impact, he just continued on to New Orleans.

For Press, the hoops tour would come abruptly to a halt when, arriving in New Orleans with the Eagles, he found a telegram awaiting him at the hotel's front desk. With war having been declared, and Press having taken naval flight training at Davis & Elkins, he was ordered to report to Anacostia Naval Base in Washington, D.C.

"When I was at Anacostia, they saw my records and asked me to coach the basketball team," he said. "So I coached while I was doing my preflight training, then went on to Pensacola for flight training. From there it was to San Diego and on to the Pacific, and the war against the Japanese.

"For 32 months, I was a flyer, a Black Cat operator stationed in Guadalcanal. I flew the old DVY5As, bombing at night and saving pilots in the open seas. We always went up at night and were shot at quite a few times. I still managed to play a little ball, right on the sand, but just little pickup games, three on three, stuff like that."

Returning stateside while still on active duty, Press enjoyed a stopover in Aliquippa that occasioned this write-up in *American Srbobran*, a Pittsburgh-based Serbian newspaper:

Lt. (j.g.) Press Maravich, veteran of 40 bombing missions in the South Pacific, is home for a well-deserved rest, his first in 16 months of actual warfare.

Despite the grueling pace of crowding in 1450 hours in the air as a pilot, friends report he's looking better than ever, is huskier, more supple and tanned to a beautiful Hawaiian brown.

The former Aliquippa hi, Davis-Elkins College and Detroit Eagle pro basketball star, whose unerring eye earned for him the tag "dead-eye Dick," is carrying over that tradition. While no actual figures are permissible, his crew's bag of Nippon planes is known to be considerable. In one engagement alone, the standout of Press' career, his gunners shot down nine Jap planes. Press recalls the episode with the casual nonchalance of a typical athlete whose team has just pulled through in the dying seconds, but who harkens back on the affair as just another game.

Their own landing gear shot away and the wings and fuselage riddled with holes, it was nip-and-tuck whether they'd live to see another day again. But no sooner had Press miraculously grounded the plane on its belly than the visions of shaking hands with St. Peter gave way to the business of claiming their bag.

"They stripped the [Japanese] plane and occupants of everything," Press chortled. "It was a 'santy-grab'—as if someone had tossed a score of pennies in the air and invited kids that finder's was keeper's. Me? I salvaged a flag, rifle, dog tag, identification bracelet, laundry slip, coins, bullets and an officer's cap."

Press, who was commissioned an Ensign and given wings at Pensacola, Fla., September, 1942, upholds the view that sports is a No. 1 advantage to precision action in warfare. The shiftiness absorbed in basketball, he said, definitely aided in learning to maneuver a plane and the split-second thinking that comes with when to shoot and take advantage of an opening held just as good in readying a pilot or gunner for the "kill." In Press' opinion and that of "most of the boys out there" the Japs have had nothing in the way of preparation that comes with American competition on gridirons, floors, diamonds, parks and fairways.

Following his leave, Press expects to take over somewhere in the States for training on a four-motor job. Then, he hopes, it's "good-bye Tojo, hello Hitler." But whichever salutation, it's certain to spell curtains for the Axis dictators.

FINISHING UP his stint as an active pilot, Press became a flight instructor in Pensacola, also coaching the base's basketball team. When Paul Birch, the coach of the Youngstown Bears in the same National Basketball League in which the Eagles had played, heard that Maravich was nearing the end of his duty, he offered him a spot on the Bears' 1945–46 roster. Meanwhile, the Army was trying to get Press to re-up and go to China to instruct pilots there. For Press Maravich, the choice was a no-brainer. He traded in his lieutenant's government-issued apparel for a Youngstown Bear uniform.

2

AT WAR'S END, basketball as a pro spectacle was only a few steps removed from the game played decades before in ballrooms on whose slippery floors patrons danced afterward. The game was a mere adjunct of folks' social life.

Pro leagues were transient entities back then, chronically going under from financial shortfall. By 1945, the best-known leagues were the American League, a weekend operation with teams in New York, Philadelphia, Wilmington, Paterson, and Trenton; and the National Basketball League (NBL), an organization with teams largely in Midwest cities like Fort Wayne, Sheboygan, Oshkosh, Chicago, and Indianapolis.

It was in that NBL that the Youngstown Bears operated, giving returning servicemen like Maravich a chance to make a modest wage while playing a boy's game. In that 1945–46 season, Press would earn

$3,500, suiting up for 32 of the team's 33 games for 35-year-old player-coach Paul Birch.

"The game then was a little faster and the passing a little bit sharper than it had been before the war," said Press. "There was more bounce-passing, overhead passing and one-hand passing now, as opposed to the old two-hand chest pass. Shooting was a little bit better, too, because instead of shooting from down around the knees, players were shooting from the chin up—they could get their shot off much quicker that way."

Still, the game was a long way from the big-time operation it would become. A Youngstown teammate of Press', Peter Lalich, recalled the Bears' home games being played in a high school gym and the officials determining which ball to use by rolling them along the floor to find the one that wobbled the least.

"And most of us had other jobs," said Lalich. "The games were for the most part on weekends—Friday, Saturday, Sunday. I worked for White Motor Company in Cleveland, and would drive to Youngstown to play. Back in those days, 'cause there was not much money to be made, it was nothing for guys like Press to play with other teams during the week, even during that NBL season."

Lalich had played against Press before the war in an annual Serbian tournament and now saw the rust in Maravich's game that the war years had brought.

"Before the war, he had the zip," said Lalich. "He reminded me of a rubber ball. He'd bounce into a spot and shoot. He had great rhythm. Now he was older and slowing up."

The Bears listed Press' age as 25, but when he died his tombstone would indicate he was born in 1915. That would have made him 30 years old at the start of the 1945–46 season. No matter. For Press, it was a chance to play the game he loved.

"I remember playing in small towns like Oshkosh and Sheboygan," he said. "Sometimes the crowds were as big as three, four or five thousand, but the arenas were something else. There was one place where the hoop was hooked directly over a stage. The kids sitting on the stage had these toy popguns that shot some kind of pellets. Every time one of our players drove to the hoop, the little bastards would hit him in the face with the pellets. And no one did anything about it."

As primitive as conditions were, for men who had been to war and had had the good fortune to survive, life in the pros was as good as it got.

"Yes, it was a challenging life," Maravich said. "But the players were much closer than they are today. We had our share of laughs. Like those overnight train rides. We played a lot of cards, a lot of poker. Frankie Baumholtz [a future major league baseball player] was a teammate of mine and we used to cheat on our coach, Paul Birch. We only played for nickels, dimes, and quarters, so it was all in good fun. But we'd get Birch in the game and I would sit next to him all the time. Whenever I folded, I'd turn to Birch and say, 'What do you got, coach?' He'd say, 'None of your business.' I'd say, 'Aw, come on.' And take a peek. He'd bet and I'd sing in Serbian, 'He has a king in the hole.' *Un ima kral.* Frankie would sit there with that poker face, wouldn't smile. And Birch: 'Cut out that Yugo singing.' I'd say, 'I'm happy. Why shouldn't I sing?' And Frankie: 'Yeah, I like to listen to his songs. He's got a good voice.'"

Press was popular with teammates, and his gregarious personality made an impression on the ladies, too. Maravich had met 21-year-old Helen Montini, a onetime Aliquippa High School cheerleader, now working in that city as a taxi dispatcher. Like Press, she was the child of a former steel worker, Nicholas, and she was a Serb. The two of them hit it off.

In the midst of a year in which Press played for the Bears and moonlighted in exhibition games in West Virginia and Pennsylvania for the extra buck, Helen had caught his fancy. She was a war widow—her husband, Veo Montini, had been with General George Patton's Third Army and had died in the D-Day invasion of France. Even though Helen had a three-year-old son, Ronnie, Press viewed that as no obstacle to their future together. After a whirlwind courtship, the two of them were married in June 1946 at St. Elijah Serbian Orthodox Church in Aliquippa, in a wedding that brought out more than 700 guests, including Navy and basketball buddies of Press. The tab for the wedding would amount to $7,000, an enormous sum in the postwar economy. But through donations of the invited guests, the Maraviches would not have to go into pocket.

By then, the NBL season had run its course. The class of the league that year was the Rochester Royal team, whose roster included back-court stars like William (Red) Holzman, Bobby Davies, Al Cervi, and Otto Graham, better known as the future quarterback of Paul Brown's Cleveland Browns dynasty. Royals big men included 6-foot-6 George Glamack, 6-foot-8 John Mahnken, and 6-foot-7 Chuck Connors, who found lasting fame as television's "Rifleman."

"I played against them," said Press, "and against a few other guys who could really play. Like big George Mikan, who was with the Chicago American Gears that year. George was a great ole shooter in close with that hook shot. And he could use his body beautifully, roll with it, like rolling with the punch. You know, the more body you put into him, the more effective he became as a hook shooter. It gave him rhythm."

The undersized Bears were easy prey for teams with legitimate big men, finishing with a 13–20 record. Press managed to average 5.6 points a game and showed enough talent—rust or not—to be recruited by the Pittsburgh Ironmen the next year when a new league, the Basketball Association of America (BAA), was founded.

THE BAA, renamed the National Basketball Association in 1949, would prove to be *the* league of the pro game, although it would have taken a prophet of some magnitude to foresee that back then.

The impetus for its formation came from a group made up mostly of members of the Arena Managers Association of America. These men controlled indoor stadiums in many major American cities, and their past experience in professional sport had been with hockey. Most of them saw pro basketball as just another event to keep their calendars filled and their profits flowing through winters previously given over to hockey, ice shows, rodeos, and college basketball.

The BAA was officially founded on June 6, 1946, and set a regular-season schedule of 60 games, with a championship playoff to begin less than five months later. In contrast with the 40-minute college games, BAA games were to run 48 minutes, on the overly optimistic notion that the public would feel it was getting more for its money.

There were to be 11 franchises in two divisions: the Boston Celtics, New York Knickerbockers, Philadelphia Warriors, Providence Steamrollers, Toronto Huskies, and Washington Capitols in the East; the Cleveland Rebels, Detroit Falcons, St. Louis Bombers, Chicago Stags, and the Pittsburg Ironmen in the West. Each team paid the league a $10,000 franchise fee, the money going for operating expenses, which included the salary of the BAA president, Maurice Podoloff, who, like the arena owners who had hired him, was a hockey man first. In fact, he was president of the American Hockey League at the same time he was president of the BAA. The owners saw nothing odd in this.

Once the league was established, each franchise set out to fill its roster, trying to lure players with salary offers generally ranging from $3,500 to $6,500. That was decent money for the time, though not enough to keep most BAA players from needing off-season jobs. The approach that teams took to secure talent varied. Arnold (Red) Auerbach, the 29-year-old coach at Washington, had coached the Norfolk Naval Training Station team during World War II, and he worked the phones that summer to sign up players who had impressed him during intramilitary competitions. It didn't trouble him that these men lived all over the country. For other teams, though, geography was a factor. The Providence franchise relied heavily on Rhode Island College players; the Knicks were top-heavy with talent from New York-area colleges; Pittsburgh chose its men mostly from within a hundred miles of the city.

As the teams sorted out their personnel that summer, salaries were quibbled over and contracts signed. In one instance, that of the Detroit Falcons' Tom King, the job category was expanded. King, who would average 5.1 points per game in 58 contests that season, later recalled: "When I reported to the Falcons' training camp, it was obvious to me they had a coach and a gym and the uniforms were ordered. What they didn't have was a publicity director or business manager. I had a B.S. in business administration. I knew how to write and type, and I knew how to keep the books. So I asked for the job of publicity director and business manager of the Falcons and was hired by Arthur Wirtz and James Norris [who owned not only the Falcons' Olympia Stadium but also Chicago Stadium and St. Louis Arena, the home courts of the Stags and Bombers]." With a deal worth $16,500, King, who later became president of the Merchandise Mart and Apparel Center in Chicago—the largest wholesale-buying complex of its kind in the world—made more than any other player in the league that season.

During the season, King would file game stories for the wire services while still in his uniform. In the chaos and confusion of the new league's launching, that kind of accommodation was possible. The NBA that is today an established league with multimillion-dollar television contracts and popularity so widespread that its players are recognized merely by nicknames—the Mailman, Sir Charles, the Admiral—arose from humble beginnings.

For the BAA in its first season, it was a question of survival—a matter of keeping the league afloat game by game, at a time of only lukewarm public interest and an economic squeeze so keen that the BAA's front office would quibble over laundry charges on referees' expense vouchers, insisting that the whistle-blowers absorb the expense.

Nowhere were the circumstances more dire than in Pittsburgh. Just as the Youngstown Bears lacked height, so did the Ironmen, with the result reflected in the standings. Pittsburgh was a loser from the outset.

When the team's 6-foot-3 pivot man, John (Brooms) Abramovic—his father owned a broom factory—was injured early in the year, a Pittsburgh sportswriter, Bob Drum, contacted a 6-foot-5 war vet, Coulby Gunther, to see if he wanted to play. Gunther, recognizing the leverage he had, negotiated a $5,500 contract and joined the Pittsburgh squad. It made little difference. The Ironmen—in spite of coach Paul Birch's intensity—remained a hard-core loser.

Birch, who had been a star at Duquesne in the mid-1930s and then toured with the Original Celtics—was a fire-breathing hoops-o-maniac. At Youngstown, his competitive urges on occasion ran to extremes,

Maravich recalling how more than once Birch, while sitting on the bench, had stuck his foot out and tripped an opposing dribbler.

"And then," said Press, "he'd make an excuse that it was the ballplayer's fault for coming that close to the sidelines."

At Youngstown, Press had had the misfortune of running into a George Mikan elbow, which knocked him to the floor and had enough impact to split his lip. "In fact," said Press, "I could put my finger right through my lip and touch my teeth. So I was laying on the floor grabbing my mouth . . . because of the shock of the blow. Birch came over and looked at me. 'Get up. You're okay, you're okay. We'll worry about that later.' So he told the trainer: 'Just put a bandage on it. Hell, the Celtics played with broken hands, broken feet, broke noses, black eyes.' It was always the Celtics this, the Celtics that."

By Maravich's account, Birch was a split personality—a raconteur and fun guy removed from the arena but a raging martinet in game time, even more so at Pittsburgh, where he was a full-time coach rather than that hyphenated creature, the "player-coach."

"He was so bent on winning," said Maravich. "Many times he'd scream at us at halftime. We knew the meaning, knew he wanted us to play harder, but it was difficult on us as players. At halftime, Birch would be steaming like a bull. And we'd stick both hands—if you can just picture this—cup our hands on our foreheads with our fingers half an inch apart . . . so it looked like you had a baseball mask. And we'd hold our hands like that real tight in front of us and watch him—you know, look through those fingers because when Birch came by he'd just hit you with his left hand or right hand—just bang you right in the face. But since we had that, like mask on, our heads would just bounce back. He loved to compete. God, how Paul Birch loved to compete. I mean, even if a fan would get on one of the players—'Get him out, Paulie'—Birch would challenge the fan: 'Why don't you come down here? We'll play you.' Or go up in the stands after them. He was very intense."

In the heat of battle, Birch would insult officials—one news account reported his incurring his second fine of the '46–47 season for arguing too strenuously with a referee—and even throw chairs during halftime talks. The coach once needled Washington's Irv Torgoff from the bench, with words that included "kike." This precipitated a fight between Torgoff and him and so incensed one of Birch's own players, Moe Becker, that Becker tried to have at Birch after the game and had to be pulled away and held under a cold shower by teammates.

As charming as Birch could be hours removed from a game, he was usually in high dudgeon immediately after a loss. Sid Borgia, a smallish BAA referee, recalled the night the Ironmen played the Knicks in New York's 69th Regiment Armory: "I was working the game with Chuck Solodare. At the end of the game, Paul Birch came after me and Solodare interfered. Solodare was my protector. And Birch said something to Chuck that was more or less a challenge: 'Knock you on your ass you don't get out of the way.' Solodare and I go back to the dressing room. Next thing I know, Solodare has his knuckles wrapped up with hankies and he's going over to the dressing room after Paul Birch. Of course, the players broke it up."

Though to a man his players commended Birch for his knowledge of the game, his combustible personality had an adverse effect on them. "It got to the point where you were so intense on winning that sometimes you couldn't do your best," said Maravich. "You were always afraid of making a mistake."

The Ironmen made their share of mistakes and quickly sank to the bottom of the Western Division. Birch tried strategic moves. He had his undersized squad play a zone defense, even though it was prohibited by the league's rules. When Washington's Auerbach protested to the BAA front office, Podoloff sent a cease-and-desist telegram to the Ironmen.

Nothing worked. Gunther, by his own admission, was not into sharing the ball, in an era when pivot players were geared to sustaining the flow of perpetual-motion weaves. This produced some grumbling among teammates, and even a team meeting dedicated to the subject of Gunther's me-first approach. But neither reasonable discussions nor Birch's outbursts changed the Ironmen's predicament. They were just not good enough, and it galled Birch no end.

"He was a perfectionist," said Maravich. "He loved basketball. He was deeply dedicated to it. And he couldn't stand to lose. I remember once I was in the shower room after we had lost a ballgame in overtime. I was soaping up when Birch finally came in. I hadn't played that badly. But he was mad that we had lost. And he always took it out on me because I never talked back to him. As a kid, Birch was my idol and I deeply respected him. When he was playing at Duquesne University, I used to comb my hair like he did—down the middle. I used to walk like him. I was absolutely enthralled by his basketball. Even had pictures of Paul Birch from the Pittsburgh *Press* and *Post-Gazette* all over my room. No matter where I turned I could see Paul Birch, shooting, passing and so forth.

"Anyway, I had all this soap on me and he told me if I came out of the shower, or even ran the water, it was gonna cost me $100. And Moe Becker came over, said, 'Come on, Paulie, let him go.' But Birch said, 'He comes out, it's a $100 fine.' So I just stayed there till Birch cooled down. I didn't put no water on my body. I didn't take the soap off. I just stood there and waited in the shower room. When he left, I finished up my shower, which was about an hour-and-a-half."

So much for the behind-the-scenes lunacy of the BAA's first season. There was also competitive basketball to see—and for as little as a dollar a ticket in some places. The game that the admission price commanded was still largely earthbound, its perfect expression the now-defunct two-hand set shot. The shot often was taken 25 to 35 feet from the basket— well beyond today's three-point goal range, and the shooter's feet were planted when he let the ball fly.

Because the shooter needed more time and room than, say, jump shooters need today, teams ran a weave around the perimeter of the floor that kept men in constant motion, and that was calculated to free a player for the two-hander or an easy layup. The distinctions common to the modern game, of power and small forward, of point and off guard, did not apply then. With the weave, all but the pivot man were interchangeable.

Bear in mind, though, that the BAA pivotman was no more apt to hang on rims than anybody else. Photographs and rare film footage from '46–47 reveal a game conducted well below the iron and often with players at close quarters in the six-foot lane then in use. Today's NBA lane is 16 feet across.

The newfangled leaping shot that a few pros—Philadelphia's Joe Fulks foremost among them—took would change basketball completely. But like the one-hand push shooters before them, jump shooters were occasionally met by skepticism.

"I played in one game," recalled the Knicks' Bud Palmer, who later became a TV performer, "where I took a jump shot and missed, missed two more and got pulled out of the game by the coach, Neil Cohalan. He asked me, 'What the hell kind of shot is that?' I told him it's a shot I use most of the time. He said, 'Well, don't use it any more on my club. Sit down.' The rest of the game, all I could use were hook shots. A while later—we had a couple days off—I convinced him in a practice it was a pretty good shot."

In the context of those times, a scene like that was apt. Because the BAA was, after all, a league that was making it up as it went. In its struggle to exist, circumstances arose that could not have occurred in the pro game as we know it today. In Pittsburgh, for instance, the Ironmen's 6-foot-5 forward, Harry (Hank) Zeller, was going to med school even as he managed to suit up for 48 of the 60 Pittsburgh games. Walt Miller, 6-foot-3, shuttled between his high school coaching job and the occasional home game before deciding there wasn't enough future in the BAA. After nine games, he left the Ironmen.

Those who remained, in Pittsburgh and the rest of the league, carried on. A few were bothered by inequities in pay, usually caused by franchises that had been desperate to fill out their rosters in the weeks just prior to the start of the season. As a result, a star who had signed early in the summer might find himself making much less than a reserve who'd signed in October.

But the mood among players then was more serene about playing conditions. With the war only recently ended and a peacetime optimism prevalent, the players—many of them ex-GIs—felt lucky to be earning money for merely playing a game. Yet some of them were not whole-heartedly in the basketball business. For instance, Frankie Baumholtz, Press' card-playing collaborator at Youngstown, would cut short his sea-son as a Cleveland Rebel, in spite of being among the league's top scor-ers, to report to the Cincinnati Reds spring training camp. He was one of at least half a dozen baseball players in the BAA. St. Louis had George Munroe, a Phi Beta Kappa from Dartmouth who was taking a few semesters off from Harvard Law School to earn tuition through the pro game. Providence coach Robert Morris had taken accrued sick leave from his Pawtucket, Rhode Island, high school job to coach the Steam-rollers, not wanting to risk losing his pension in case the BAA did not catch on.

The early returns suggested the wisdom of Morris' preternatural cau-tion. The public was not storming doors to get into the arenas. Cleve-land general manager Roy Clifford was at the turnstiles the night a patron turned up with four complimentary tickets and was advised there was a 60-cent tax on each. Incredulous, the fan told the gate employee: "Sixty cents? The hell with you. Keep your tickets."

The game was proving to be a hard sell. Attendance in BAA cities was a disappointment. Auerbach's Capitols, the best team over regular-season play with a 49–11 record, averaged only 3,000 fans a game in Uline Arena, whose capacity was 5,500. Not surprisingly, Press' Iron-men—with a 15–45 record, worst in the league—couldn't draw flies to a dump. One night in Pittsburgh only 819 paying customers materialized, and another night only 917 showed.

The BAA struggled to promote its product. In league meetings, own-ers discussed ways to excite fan interest. There was talk of playing dou-bleheaders—four BAA teams in two games—to build up the gate. The idea was tabled, but the league agreed to experiment with longer games. In Chicago—whose owners were pushing the concept—some 60-minute games (four 15-minute quarters) were played. The thinking was that it would give fans more entertainment for their dollar.

Other gimmicks were tried. Tom King, the player-executive at De-troit, agreed to admit free any party of 12 that had an individual in it named Miasek, the surname of the Falcons' high-scoring center. When no Miasek appeared, he made the same offer for fans whose last name was that of another Falcon, Bob Dille, and this time he found takers. In Pittsburgh, women were let in free on some nights. The admission fee on ladies nights in Washington was 50 cents, though they could be summarily called off for games that attracted large crowds. Scorecards contained a "lucky number" that could win a fan 10 free lubrications at any Lincoln-Mercury dealer in Detroit (with a later chance at a 1946 Mercury), or a cigarette box, hat, chocolates, or a $10 clothing certificate if a fan's number came up in Philadelphia.

The season wound down. For the Ironmen, it was proving to be a hard go without the height and muscle to match up against other squads. Not that capable big men were plentiful back then. That year BAA teams billed two players as 7-footers—height that was rare enough to entice customers into the arena then. One of the big men, Elmore Morganthaler, was probably a couple of inches under 7 feet and could not go at the pace his Providence team played—"Civil War basketball," Steamroller coach Morris called it: "We shoot and run." Morganthaler is remembered less for his pivot play than for his peculiar way with a stick of chewing gum. Elmore would keep it balled behind his ear, from time to time retrieving it to chew. He played only 11 games at Providence and averaged 1.4 points per game. Ralph Siewert, 7-foot-1, was called "Timber" by St. Louis Bomber fans for his resemblance to a felled tree when he capsized during the action. He played seven games with St. Louis and was sent on to Toronto, finishing the season with a 1.0 scoring average in 21 games.

For players of any size, the BAA's road life was taking its toll in the final months of the season. Teams flew then, but not as extensively as they do now. Rail was the common mode of transportation. In fact, when a team did travel by air it was considered a kind of feat, as shown by this item from a Philadelphia Warriors late-season game program:

> The Philadelphia Warriors have the distinction of having traveled more
> regular-season air miles than any other athletic team in the world. The

Warriors used the air lanes for every trip in excess of 100 miles and since December it is estimated the squad flew in excess of 15,000 air miles in touring the Association of America's 11-city circuit.

For players raised on the weekend schedules of the American League, or the shorter season of the collegians, life on the road took getting used to. As Bones McKinney of the Washington Caps would put it: "We would travel in what we called 1,000-miler shirts. That was a shirt you could wrench out and hang over a bathtub. You didn't take but two with you on the road. You didn't have room in your suitcase. You only had one uniform. And say you'd play in St. Louis on Saturday and Sunday afternoon in Chicago. Your uniform would stand tall in the corner . . . it was so full of salt. I mean, you just got the jock itch early in the year so you wouldn't have to worry about it—just kept it for the rest of the year."

The regular season ended with Auerbach's Capitols winning the Eastern Division by 14 games, their margin of victory nearly 10 points a contest. By contrast, Chicago—the winner in the Western Division—had an average margin of victory under four points a game.

But in that cockeyed first season, what else would the fates decree but for Washington to be eliminated from the playoffs in the opening round? For the record, the Warriors—led by jump shooter Fulks—won the BAA title.

That, too, was as it should be. Because in the first season nothing added up. Things were always just a bit out of whack. Measured against seasons in the distant future—in terms of monetary and artistic success—1946–47 could properly be viewed as a colossal failure.

But 1946–47 would be connected in time to all basketball, linked past-to-present by men like Paul Birch, who stood for the two-fisted approach of an earlier game, and by Auerbach, who was already out front of the new game.

But in Pittsburgh, the failure of the Ironmen would void an NBA future. The Ironmen had had the second-worst attendance in the league: 40,970 paid admissions for net receipts of $56,005. The franchise folded after the '46–47 season.

"I had a chance," said Press, "to go to the St. Louis Bombers, where Kenny Loeffler was coaching or a chance to go with the [new franchise] Baltimore Bullets."

Instead, weary of the travel and aware he was no longer the player he had been—he'd averaged 4.5 points a game in 51 contests for the Ironmen—Press retired.

With his experience as a naval pilot, he figured he'd have no problem landing a position as a commercial airline pilot—a job that not only paid well but also would, he thought, reassure Helen, now pregnant with the couple's first child, that she had a responsible husband. Much to his surprise, she was vehemently opposed to his flying. She feared the dangers of the job—and more.

Helen's father had deserted the family when she was a child, and her mother, Anna, passed away not longer after, leaving Helen to be raised by an aunt. That history, compounded by the loss of her husband in the war, had created a kind of separation anxiety in the former Helen Gravor. She told Press that if he chose to become a pilot, he would do so at the cost of his marriage.

That threat was enough to coax a discussion of which line of work would keep peace and harmony in the household. Helen, like anybody who'd spent time with Press, knew that her husband was most passionate about basketball. Nothing rivaled the game in Press' heart of hearts. When she suggested he try coaching, he readily agreed.

Press quickly found an assistant coaching job at his alma mater, Davis & Elkins. But before he tooled down the road to the campus there, the couple's first child, Peter Press Maravich, was born on June 22, 1947.

Although Press would coach many teams over the years that followed—high school and college, here and in Europe—no assignment would be more consuming than that of making his and Helen's first born—the future "Pistol Pete"—into a hoops magician.

3

PRESS MARAVICH was a man with a plan.

From the moment he baited six-year-old Pete into shooting a basketball, he intended to make him into a player. To Press, that meant the boy needed to be focused, exclusively, on Dr. Naismith's game.

Early on, though, Pete's attention was diverted by baseball in the spring and by football in the fall. Press tried to dissuade him from squandering time on these games and eventually succeeded. The result? The boy became as rabid for basketball as his father—he played the game year around and all day long during summers.

Through Pete's early years, the family was on the move, hunkering down in the various college towns where Press found work: assistant coach at Davis & Elkins (1947–48); assistant coach at the University of West Virginia while receiving his master's degree in recreation and health education (1948–49); head coach at West Virginia Wesleyan (1949–50); and then back to Davis & Elkins as head coach (1950–52).

None of these jobs paid much, and most of them required Press to take on other chores—as assistant football coach or, at Davis & Elkins, as a typing and shorthand teacher. Wherever he went, Maravich would recruit players from the Aliquippa area, more often than not the elite of the Serbian talent pool. Maravich knew these young men because he had worked out in the Aliquippa High School gym even as he was playing professionally and, as late as 1950 at age 35, was player-coach for the Aliquippa team that won the annual national Serbian tournament.

In all of these coaching stops, Press was proving himself an original, publishing his master's thesis on basketball scouting in 1950, using a psychiatrist to evaluate his players at West Virginia Wesleyan, and, as head coach at Davis & Elkins, creating a gym where none had previously existed.

Until Press assumed the head coaching position in 1950, Davis & Elkins had played its home games in a local high school gym.

"I figured," said Press, "we couldn't go on without a gym and if no one else was going to do anything about it, I would."

Press borrowed a tractor and cleared a stand of trees. Then he called the local paper and had it send a photographer to shoot the future site of the school's gymnasium. "Ground Cleared for Gymnasium," the headline read in the next day's paper.

"Then," said Press, "I looked for retired carpenters. I remember promising one old fellow that I'd build him a monument if he'd help get some more volunteers. Anyway, with the help of my experts, some students and anyone else who wanted to pitch in, we had our gym within a year. It wasn't much. There was a tin roof that leaked. But we fixed that by stringing burlap sacks on the ceiling."

He applied the same ingenuity to making a hoops prodigy of little Pete.

"Sometimes I'd go out in the backyard and start shooting," said Press. "When I knew Pete was watching me I'd go into my act."

The act consisted of a variety of trick shots—behind the back, over the head, or bounced off the floor and into the hoop.

"I really made like I was enjoying myself," said Press, "like I was having the time of my life. And I could see he was going for it. This is how I first got him interested. Plus I would talk to him about how great the game was and, since I was coaching college then, I would take him to the games with me when he was just a little kid. I'd let him sit on the bench while I was coaching. He had a ball there and, when he got rest-less, I'd let him play with the ball on the side by himself."

Even though Press had college-level coaching jobs, the money was so disappointing that he actually earned more by leaving his head coaching position at Davis & Elkins in '52 to coach at Baldwin High in Pitts-burgh, a tough inner-city school. From Baldwin it was on to Aliquippa High — again for increased wages. Aliquippa was offering $6,500 for teaching and coaching. That salary, combined with a summer job at the steel mill, was as good as Press had done since he began coaching.

But in 1956, after two seasons at Aliquippa High, Press caught a break. At Clemson College in South Carolina, where football was king and the basketball program a mere afterthought, the school's athletic di-rector/football coach, Frank Howard, decided he wanted to have Banks McFadden, a football assistant of his *and* the Tigers' basketball coach for the past decade, devote himself to football exclusively.

When Howard offered the basketball job to Neenie Campbell, who coached football and basketball at McKeesport High School in western Pennsylvania, Campbell turned him down but recommended he hire Press Maravich. Campbell had sent many a big-shouldered football prospect Clemson's way, so Howard, who was from Barlow Bend, Al-abama, trusted his judgment. He agreed to interview this ol' Yankee boy, Maravich, and see if he would do.

The story goes that when Press showed up at the Clemson, South Carolina, campus, Howard showed him a long list of candidates for the job and wondered aloud, "Why should I hire you, Yank?"

Press was eloquent enough to convince the legendary football coach he was the right man. But it was only after accepting the Clemson job that Press discovered he was taking a pay cut of $2,000 from what he had been making in Aliquippa. Not only that. He was coming to a pro-gram that had built-in problems that his Atlantic Coast Conference rivals did not have—a dinky, poorly lit gym seating 4,500 (about which Press would quip: "The gym was so dark that one kid practiced wearing a miner's lamp") and a limited number of scholarships to offer. The school—once a military college—now mandated two years of ROTC, certainly a drawback to an athlete used to privileged treatment. Just the same, Press felt that coaching at Division I Clemson—even for the meager $5,000 offered—was a ripe opportunity.

The town of Clemson, population 2,000 in '56, sat in the northwest corner of the state, 30 miles from Greenville. It was a place of small-town charm—a main street that had no traffic light until the locals fought for one to slow the cars barreling along that stretch of Highway 123 that ran through downtown.

On days when the ROTC cadets would assemble at Bowman Field, the town common, and the band would strike up "The Star-Spangled Banner," traffic along the bordering streets, Clemson Boulevard and Pendleton Road, would come to a standstill, and men would get out of their cars and, hats to their hearts, sing the anthem.

It was Norman Rockwell's Main Street America—a place where nobody locked the doors to his or her house or car, and folks smiled their greetings to one another. On Saturdays, when a wizened black man known to townspeople as "Uncle Bill" drove his relic of a horse-drawn wagon into town, boys and dogs ran after the crate, the youngsters jumping aboard to hear Uncle Bill tell stories from slave times that he'd known first hand.

As Pete's boyhood friend, Sam Hunter, recalled: "Uncle Bill was freed after the Civil War. Lived to be more than 100 years. He'd tell you stories about ole [Thomas G.] Clemson and [John C.] Calhoun and how things were in the days of kerosene lamps and chopping wood."

Into this quaint rural setting came the Maravich brood, a family that quickly stood out for a certain quirkiness—the decibel level at which they conducted their daily affairs. Amidst their soft-spoken southern neighbors, the Maraviches' matter-of-fact, brusque way of communicating with one another—routine communications were delivered with raised voices—startled neighbors like Louise and

Bob Bradley, Bob being the sports information director at Clemson.

As Louise recalled: "They yelled and screamed at each other all the time. A lot of screaming and hollering. Not that they were mad at each other. It was just their manner of speaking. Helen couldn't do enough for them. She was in the kitchen most of the time, cooking. Making sure all their meals were prepared right. Press would shout, 'HELEN, GET SUPPER READY.' And Helen: 'IT'S READY. SIDDOWN.' They laughed at us, at how calm we were and that we never raised our voices."

Press' eccentricities—his tobacco chewing, his amusingly profane use of the King's English, his extreme competitiveness—were duly noted by the locals but readily accepted. Coach Maravich, outgoing and communicative—always ready with a quip, joke, or anecdote, apocryphal or factual—was just so darned much fun to be around that they could forgive his foibles.

Howard Bagwell, who coached football, track, and basketball and was athletic director at Daniel High School in Clemson, lived just down the street from the Maraviches and experienced the competitive compulsiveness of his coaching frater.

"We'd play croquet in my backyard at night," said Bagwell, "and if Press didn't win, he was liable to take the mallet and throw it against the tree. If he'd lose, he'd say, 'Let's play again.' I'd try to beg off: 'I'm tired.' He: 'Nope. Again.' He just wouldn't take no for an answer. Some nights we'd be out there, under the lights, til two in the morning, til he won."

Like father, like son. When the Bradleys played Monopoly with the Maraviches and caught Pete cheating, the boy up and quit. When Bagwell would play Ping-Pong with Pete on the table in the coach's carport, and whup him, the boy would stomp off, tears in his eyes, declaring: "You cheated me."

"I'm saying that he cried," said Bagwell, "but it wasn't like he was a crybaby. He was just so competitive."

By 1956, Pete Maravich was a gym rat whose daily routine was geared to making time to practice. Where other boys might flop onto a sofa after dinner, eyes glued to the TV screen—*I Love Lucy* was an ongoing hit, *Gunsmoke* was the hot new show—Pete was tunneled into the game.

Once he had his homework and chores finished, he would bicycle to an outdoor court or to the YMCA, depending on the time of year and what the weather was like.

Pete worked diligently on his game. For him there were never enough hours for basketball. When boys his age, or older, came around to the local courts, he would join them in choose-up games. Though small for his age, he was already a clever ball handler and possessed an accurate outside shot. What's more, he had a born feel for the game, recognizing in a blink where an edge could be gained, a matchup exploited. Basketball men called it "seeing the court." Even as a boy, Pete saw the court, a trait that in later years led a coach of his to call him "Kodak," after the camera—Kodak for his ability to register the ever-shifting flow on a basketball floor and then to take advantage. In the summer of '56, it didn't take long for other boys to sense the Maravich kid's grasp of the game. Small though he was, the boy was a player, a welcome addition to any skins-and-shirts competition.

But Pete was just as happy to find himself alone in the YMCA gym on, say, a sticky summer night—the still air discouraging the other boys and leaving the place all to him. Up and down the floor he'd go, picturing defenders in his way and responding to the imagined obstacles they posed with spinning pirouettes or behind-the-back dribbles or change-of-pace moves to which he might add a crossover dribble.

Toward closing time, some nights his father would appear and watch from a corner of the gym until Pete spotted him. Then Press would step out from the shadows and critique what he had seen. Nothing gave Press more pleasure than to watch the boy build into his games moves more sophisticated than even some of his own varsity players had.

They were moves Press had shown Pete, anticipating a time when the game would be more go-go than it was when he had played. In the decade since he had been a guard for the Pittsburgh Ironmen, basketball had taken a quantum leap toward the accelerated and more athletic affair he had envisioned.

Sooner than most, Press had recognized that the game was speeding up and going increasingly airborne. The 24-second clock that was legislated into the game for the 1954–55 NBA season produced a more up-tempo game and put a premium on players who could create their own shots.

That coincided with the advent of bigger, stronger athletes, many of whom were capable of generating their shots off the dribble or by simply jumping over their defenders. What's more, no longer was the big man the oafish stereotype that he had often been earlier in the game's history.

In that very year, 1956–57, Bill Russell was a Boston Celtic rookie. He was revolutionary in his defensive skills—6-foot-10 and mongoose quick in swatting away opponents' shots or merely leaping skyward to intimidate. And as Russell was winning praise, and ball games, with his defensive prowess, at Kansas University Wilt Chamberlain was belying the "goon" label often attached to 7-footers, doing it with an offensive arsenal that had teams double- and triple-teaming him.

Great as the Minneapolis Lakers' George Mikan—the Associated Press' player of the first half century—had been, Press knew that the Russells and Chamberlains were far better. Mikan, 6-foot-10 and wide as a bread van, had been an immovable object in the pivot in the late '40s and early '50s.

By the time Russell came into the league, Mikan had retired. But what Russell did to Neil Johnston, a three-time NBA scoring leader with the Philadelphia Warriors (1952–53, '53–54, '54–55), gave folks a pretty clear idea of the advanced species that Russell was. Like Mikan, Johnston was a deadly accurate hook shooter. Now understand this: a hook shot, like most shots, is rooted in rhythm—a series of interlocking steps. The key for the shooter is to be sure the defender is in an indefensible posture before firing away. Well, against Russell, Johnston discovered that the physics of hook-shot angles and distance was thoroughly scrambled. Russell would lurk at a distance—a seemingly "safe" distance—and then insinuate himself in Johnston's rhythm and materialize from so-called nowhere to block the hook. Block it often and with such an emphatic, demoralizing swat that the lantern-jawed Johnston turned passive when Russell was in the game.

Russell and Chamberlain, as Press saw it, were the advance guard of the fast-paced, muscular-yet-balletic game that he had foreseen. While in Elkins, he had watched a high school kid down there play and had marked him not only as a future star but also as an example of the superior athlete who would change the game. The kid—Zeke from Cabin Creek, they called him; real name Jerry West—was now a star at West Virginia University and one of several college players with the quickness and explosive moves to dominate in the pro game.

Press Maravich understood that for a guard to thrive in the game of the future he would have to be nimble on his feet and most especially with the basketball. He had watched his son Pete in schoolyard games and was pleased with the boy's ease with the ball, not to mention his improvisational wit. His son had a flair for making plays, for targeting the less-than-obvious possibility. He was not afraid to thread a pass through a thicket of arms. There was a boldness to his game and a creative spark that was heartening to the father.

In part, Pete's derring-do was fueled by the unconventional moves Press had shown him: the behind-the-back dribble, the knack of spinning the ball on his fingers—flourishes that many coaches of that time were wont to disparage as "hot dogging." But Press thought otherwise. Pete was a small, frail boy, a liability that could be overcome, thought Press, only by making sure he was at total ease with the basketball. If the boy could master extreme and/or unorthodox maneuvers he would be able to play the game instinctively—with a license to wheel and deal.

That spark was already evident in Pete's game, but Press felt obliged not to let it die out. There were many variables that would determine how far his son would go as a player—variables that he could not control: Pete's eventual height and his quickness and strength. But from his own career as a professional player, Press knew that a passion for the game could go a long way toward compensating for whatever physical shortfall a man might have.

By 1956, Pete had a lively interest in the game, but ahead of him lay the temptations of adolescence. Press' objective was to keep him on track. He had thought deeply about how to accomplish that and to come up with an approach that he believed would sustain his son's excitement about basketball while sharpening the skills he already had.

As Press walked across the YMCA floor toward his son, Press was waving for the basketball.

"Come here, son," he said. "I wanna show you something."

Pete threw the ball to Press, who told him: "Watch this." With the ball in his right hand, Press slowly swung his arm behind his head, laying the ball into his left hand. Then the left hand rotated forward, moving the ball past Press' face and into his right hand. Press repeated the maneuver twice before turning to Pete: "Easy, right?"

Pete considered the question and nodded. When Press handed him the ball, Pete did the maneuver, then gave the ball back to his father.

"Too easy," said Press.

This time when Press swung his arm behind his head, he did so with a more rapid movement and, rather than just slap the ball into the waiting left hand, he tossed it. When the left hand gathered the ball and rotated forward, the ball shot past Press' face into his right hand. The ball went around and around, behind Press' neck and then by his nose in a blur.

"Behind the neck," Press said, as he intensified the speed of the drill. "Don't go above the head. That's cheating. Do it right. The left hand is like an electric eye, the right hand passes it behind the neck. Keep your head stationary. . . . A piece of cake, right?"

Pete looked dubious.

"Okay, son. We're going 'round the world with this. Part two."

Now Press was whirling the ball around his waist, the leather ball slapping rhythmically against his hands as it circuited, right to left to right.

"If you're in condition, you can do 60 to 75 repetitions around the waist in 30 seconds," said Press. "Just like this. You do that, son, you can handle the doggone basketball. . . . Okay. 'Round the world, part 3."

Now Press bent at the knees and leaned forward and began passing the ball at blurring speed around his legs.

"Toes together," he said. "Around the calves."

Without a break, Press executed a variation. Dropping his right foot back, he put the ball through the space between his legs before squaring his feet. As the ball swung around, now his left foot dropped back, and the ball was propelled through—again moving at rapid and rhythmic pace.

When Press finished, he handed the ball to Pete and said, "Around the world. It'll make your hands quicker. . . . I'm gonna get a Coke."

He walked out of the gym. Looking back through the windowed portion of the door, he watched his son work up his speed, snaking the ball around his body, north to south. The kid was good. He had the makings of a player. Whether his hunger for the game would remain constant, well, that was another of those variables. All that Press as his father could do was to keep his interest piqued. There was plenty more he could (and would) show the kid, enticing drills to refine his skills and, with any luck, keep the boy pushing, pushing, pushing to be better.

BY NOW little Pete had become, in his term, "a basketball android."

As he would later recall: "I played basketball something like forty-seven weeks of the year. During the summer I was out on the court at eight in the morning and played until it got dark. When we moved to Clemson, I used to open the YMCA and play till they kicked me out."

As Clemson's head coach, Press would take the boy into the team's locker room whenever his squads played. The sights and sounds of the game became ingrained in Pete. He watched the players dress, heard their talk, and was privy to both the good and bad times.

"Sometimes, before our practice sessions," said Press, "he'd challenge them to games of 'horse' or one-on-one, and they were all nice to him and very patient."

Evenings, back at home, Press would challenge him to games of "horse" on their backyard hoop. They were quite a sight—the crew-cut, leathery-faced father and the thin, wide-eyed youngster, throwing shots, grinning, teasing, hollering.

"I'd always encourage him to take different kinds of shots," Press said, "and really make a fuss when he made one. A lot of the times I'd throw the game—let him win—and then make it look as if I was really angry, that I didn't like to lose.

"I also knew that he'd have to learn the fundamentals. But practicing those things over and over can be dull, so I'd always watch his face. When I'd see he was getting bored, I'd change to something else—for instance, go from practicing a two-hand chest pass to maybe a one-hand pass, and then just to keep it interesting, a behind-the-back pass. These kinds of things got Pete excited and kept his interest."

Press continued to devise drills, which sometimes came to him in his sleep. "When that happened, I'd just write the idea down, show it to Pete the next day, and we'd give it a name," said Press.

The "pretzel" was a hand-reaction drill. Pete set his left hand behind his left leg and his right hand in front of and between his legs, leaning forward as he did. He'd hold the ball with his right hand, and then his hands would flash in a figure-eight fashion around his legs, patting the ball with alternate right-hand left-hand touches and yet managing to keep the ball stationary, in front of his body and between his legs. Back and forth the hands would fly, a blur of virtuoso dexterity.

For the "ricochet" Pete stood with his feet shoulder-width apart. He would hold the ball with both hands and then casually toss it between his legs at a 45-degree angle, reaching behind his back for the catch. To complete the ricochet, he would pass the ball from back to front at the same acute angle and repeat that back-and-forth pattern in a steady, rhythmic flow.

A variation—called the "bullet ricochet"—was far more dramatic and carried an element of risk if misplayed. On this maneuver Maravich would raise the ball far above his head and then fire it through his legs as hard as he could, reaching behind him to catch it. "You really can't see my hands move on this one," he said, "they're going so fast. People have sat there and said, honestly, truthfully, that they had no vision of my hands moving. They were a blur. It is that terrific WHAM when I bring the ball down that makes the whole thing so fast. This is a very danger-ous drill, actually. I don't think I have to elaborate on how much it hurts if you catch yourself in the crotch off the bounce. I knew one kid who did the bullet ricochet once and ended up in the hospital."

In another drill, Pete would throw the ball up into the air and catch it behind his back, risking jammed fingers if he miscalculated. But he got so expert at this that he would steadily increase his toss, up as high as 25 to 30 feet into the air. In later years he'd see how many times he could slap his knees before getting his hands in back to catch the ball. The object was to whip his hands behind his body only after the ball had disappeared behind his head.

"This may not sound hard," Pete said, "but when you're slapping your knees 25 times in a matter of a few seconds, then throwing your hands behind you to catch the impact of the ball, your arms feel like 25-pound lead weights."

Maravich had seen professional boxers beat a rat-a-tat on the speed bag and created a basketball variation. Working from his knees, and switching from right hand to left hand, he would make the ball resonate with that machine-gun clatter while keeping it as tight to the floor as he could—a low dribble that might be a mere eighth of an inch from the hardwood.

These—and other drills—built Pete's skill with the ball and imbued him with the confidence to be as wild and woolly as he could on the court. His life was basketball, basketball. He'd go to sleep with the basketball, lying on his back and releasing the ball upward while repeating these words: "fingertip control, backspin, and follow-through." By morning, he would take his ball and dribble it blindfolded about the house before his parents or brother Ronnie awakened. He'd dribble the ball while walking two and a half miles to the YMCA in downtown Clemson; he'd dribble the ball while riding his bicycle and, sometimes, dribble it from the passenger seat of the family car while Press drove at varying speeds.

Press devised these drills to sustain his son's interest in the game *and* to make fundamentals diverting. Pete took the drills and extended them, creatively. "He became completely dedicated, completely," said Press.

Many a night, at late hours, Bagwell, the high school coach who lived down the street, would hear the thump-thump of the ball as Pete—in cold weather bundled up in an overcoat—would dribble it or throw passes off the side of the house. He'd hear the ball resounding and think: "The Maravich kid is at it again."

On weekends, when the YMCA gym was closed or being used by

older boys, Pete and a basketball buddy, Jim Sutherland, would sneak into the Clemson gym, scaling a ledge on a back wall that led to an open tilt window. Through that window they'd go, onto a catwalk that brought them, eventually, into the gym. They'd throw the switch to the lights and be in their idea of paradise.

As a boy, Pete had an approach to the game that was unusual. Virtually all grade-schoolers—and for that matter players of all ages—were shot-happy. Give any hoopster a ball, and he would shoot it without prompting. Again and again. And never get tired or bored. A smaller percentage would work on ballhandling, maybe dribble up and back, or even around chairs strategically placed as obstacles. But practice a behind-the-back pass?

Pete, by contrast, was determined to build his game piece by piece. Press had given him the drills, and the fundamentals, and the boy worked them hour after hour, endlessly, obsessively. Ballhandling, passing, shooting. Every aspect of the game got his attention. It was not enough to be able to throw a behind-the-back pass with his "good" hand, the right hand. Pete worked the left hand, too. He would make behind-the-back passes with either hand, extending the distance little by little, and in time fine-tuning it by putting a piece of tape onto the wall as a bull's-eye.

When he wasn't playing with boys his own age, he was hanging out at Clemson, challenging varsity players to games of "horse" and "around the world" for movie money.

To Pete, the movie house was just another place to practice. He'd dribble his ball to the show, find an aisle seat, and continue bouncing the ball as he watched the film.

"The theaters," he said, "had thick carpeting in all the aisles and I bounced the ball real low, so it wouldn't bother anyone. There were mostly old men and women, and a lot of kids there. The old men and women were watching the film for the tenth time and the kids were all busy talking, so no one ever complained about me."

Winning money from varsity players was no easy feat, especially for a boy who, by the seventh grade, was a mere 5-foot-2, 90-pound peanut and needed a major effort to get his shot to the hoop. As Bobby Roberts, who was an assistant to Press at Clemson, recalled: "He was so skinny and weak-looking that he had to start the ball from the floor on his long shots. It looked like a major struggle on every shot. But damned if the kid didn't make 'em more often than not."

The kid was single-minded about the game, knowing that at the living wage his coach/father earned, he would need a scholarship to get to college. That was a given. Coaching was no get-rich-quick scheme in the late 1950s, certainly not at Clemson. During summers Press was obliged to supplement his income by coaching in Puerto Rico, in a league where an 8-foot fence encircled the court so that players and coaches were protected from overly zealous fans. Press also would work summer basketball camps, his strongest attachment being to the one at Campbell College in Buie's Creek, North Carolina.

That was where Press met the great John Wooden, whose UCLA teams in the '60s and '70s would become a collegiate dynasty—as fundamentally sound and smoothly functioning as any NCAA team that had preceded them. Although the two men had strikingly different personalities—Wooden was refined and straitlaced in deed and speech, and Maravich was a tobacco-chewing, rapid-fire *shpritzer*—they shared a love of basketball that made them fast friends.

Yet Wooden was forever decrying Press' abundant use of profanities. Press' staccato patter was rife with blue words, but, because of the engaging spirit in which he used them, nobody really got offended. Not the players he called "ya little bastard" or the secretaries who sat within earshot of his profanity-filled phone conversations. For them, it was just Press' way.

Certainly, Wooden was not about to ostracize his friend Press for his abuse of the mother tongue. Over the years, they would room together at Campbell, staying up late into the night, talking Xs and Os. But though Wooden accepted Press for who he was—a good-hearted rough-and-tumble sort—his own code of behavior was perpetually challenged by this flaw in Press Maravich.

As a coaching colleague of both men, Les Robinson, recalled: "Coach Wooden would say to me, 'Press is a wonderful person. But oh, you know

his language.' And he'd cover his face with his hands. Well, one summer, he got all twenty coaches at Campbell to agree to put money in a
jar, and every day Press didn't cuss he'd get the jar. . . . Well, I can tell
you this: Press never got one dollar."

By 1959, Pete was a seventh-grader at Clemson Middle School. But
the rules at the time permitted him to play for the junior varsity and/or
the varsity basketball team at Daniel High, even though the high school
had only grades 9 through 12.

"That was my last year at Daniel," said Howard Bagwell. "Pete was
on the junior varsity team and I was coaching the varsity, but he'd still
practice with us. He was just so much better than anybody on the junior varsity team. It was like a pro playing with Sunday school kids at
the time."

In fact, Bagwell, who'd played backcourt for Furman from 1945 to
1948, recognized that Pete was good enough as a 5-foot-2 seventh-
grader to start for the varsity and acknowledged that on a very good
Daniel High team Pete and his brother, 6-foot-4 Ronnie, were the two
best players. But though Bagwell allowed young Maravich to suit up
with the big boys on occasion, he wouldn't let him off the bench. "He
was so frail, I was afraid the kid would get hurt," said Bagwell. "And
Pete—he was dying to play. He'd tell me: 'Coach, I can outshoot anybody.' He could, too. But the kid was like a midget, and so frail."

Fate intervened to give Pete his chance to crack the varsity lineup
that year when late in the season Bagwell was hospitalized with a kidney
stone, and the coach's doctor, Billy Hunter, agreed to take over the
team. This was not as big a stretch as it might sound because Hunter—a
former star lineman for Clemson—loved basketball so much that during
the season he would close his office at three o'clock every day and work
as Bagwell's unpaid assistant and as the team physician. If a medical
emergency arose while Doc Hunter was busy with the Daniel team, the
patient would be brought over to the high school's training room for
Hunter to examine.

When Bagwell asked Hunter to fill in for him, the good doctor told him: "So long as I can run it the way I want to."

That was his way of signaling that he meant to start Pete: "See, during the season, I'd been needling Howard: 'You should be playing Pete.' Well, now we were going into the post-season tournaments and I sat down the regular starter, a senior, and put Pete in his place."

The seventh-grade upstart was not daunted by the challenge. According to Hunter: "He was fabulous. He may have looked funny—with the baggy socks and toothpick legs, but that first game he went out and shot about 16 points, hitting them from way downtown. That boy could shoot the basketball. He'd hit the shot and give you the little smile. Pete was so scrawny that he had to put the ball a way back behind his right shoulder to get it up as high as the hoop. Awkward looking it was, but the ball would go swish."

By Hunter's account, he presided over the team in Daniel's last regular-season game of '59–60, an 80–74 victory over Chapman High, and continued for two games of the conference tournament that followed.

Pete remained in the lineup as Daniel beat Fairforest in the opening round, 63–52, and then played a crucial role in the school's next tournament game, against Palmetto.

"I didn't then and still don't know anything much about the game," said Hunter. "The closest I ever came to doing any coaching is when I called time out that night. We had 54 seconds to play and were four points behind. I told the team, 'Ok, fellows. We've got 'em right where we want them. Go out there and score,' and grabbing Pete by the arm I said in his ear, 'Shoot the ball, Pete.' He stole the ball twice, scored four of our quick six points and we won."

Final: Daniel 44, Palmetto 42.

By now Bagwell had recovered from the removal of his kidney stone and been discharged from Anderson Memorial Hospital, just in time to take over the reins from Hunter for the semifinals against Chapman.

Throughout the season, Daniel, with a record now of 18–3, had relied on Ronnie Maravich and F. M. Julian at forward and Walter Cox at center for board strength. Ronnie in particular was a force. He was rangy and aggressive—an all-state linebacker and end for Bagwell during football season. "Ronnie," said Bagwell, "was mean. He'd fight you in a minute."

Against Chapman, Ronnie and his Daniel teammates would have to go it without Cox. Cox, who would become a federal judge in later years, was to be honored as an outstanding student on the night of the big game against Chapman.

"The honors he was to receive conflicted with the game, and he told me he was going to be recognized, " recalled Hunter. "I couldn't understand it, his leaving the team. His father was a dean at Clemson. We really got into it, the dean and I. All these years later, it's still . . . a sore point."

Without Cox, Daniel lost to Chapman 69–68, ending the season with a touch of heartbreak.

Another ex-Furman player, Pete Carlisle, would succeed Bagwell as Daniel coach for the '60–61 season, and under his regime little Pete would receive regular playing time, toiling in the shadow of his big brother. Not that he minded. Ronnie, now a senior and the Lions' captain, was a hero to his kid brother—a hero and a protector.

With his ballhandling ability, the smallish Pete often made older, bigger defenders look foolish, and many of them resorted to roughhouse tactics. But when they abused Pete, Ronnie would come flying to his defense, and if it led to confrontations Ronnie was not inclined to back off. Although he often incurred technicals in defense of Pete, he was undeterred in his role as his brother's keeper.

To Carlisle, Ronnie—averaging better than 20 points a game while dominating the backboards—was a first-rate high school player, with a feathery shooting touch and an innate feel for the game. He had skills that, Carlisle felt, would travel well to the college game if —a big "if"— he didn't undermine himself.

Because as talented as Ronnie was, there was, as Carlisle put it, "a lot of rebel in him."

"Ronnie," said Carlisle, "was the best high school basketball player you'd ever seen. But he was his own person. He didn't march to the tunes a coach would have liked. He was just . . . well, he was probably the only guy on the team that smoked . . . and the only person on the team that I was aware of who might drink from time to time. And he was much of a party-goer."

As Pete would later note in his autobiography, *Heir to a Dream*:

> His life was the pool hall and as many girls as he could find. He once skipped so many school days that it took the football coach's pleading and some fancy bookwork to keep him on the team roster. He hated school with a passion, but he loved sports and the glory of winning.
>
> Ronnie kept this dark side from me, leading me to believe he was cool and responsible, when in essence, he was creating mischief everywhere he went—such as the time he bombed the girl's restroom or the time he stole an Edsel. I guess my innocence and Ronnie's cleverness prevented me from seeing the real person he was. I was so naive I never knew Ronnie and some of the players drank bourbon before each game. I just knew Ronnie was the greatest athlete around, and I admired him for it. That was all that mattered to me then. Now, I realize his lack of discipline and rebelliousness kept him from reaching his full potential as an athlete.

On graduating from Daniel, Ronnie would land at Georgia Southern as a scholarship athlete, until a conflict there with a coach would short-circuit his college career and lead to a stint in the Marines. While Ronnie began his basic training at Parris Island, South Carolina, Pete was stepping out from his big brother's shadow.

As a 5-foot-8 ninth grader wearing his brother's jersey number 23, he was now a prime-time player for the Daniel Lions under still another coach, Don Carver. As the Anderson, South Carolina, *Independent* reported early in the '60–61 season:

> To look at the boxscore on the Daniel High basketball games you would hardly realize that Ronnie Maravich has graduated. Ronnie was the leading scorer for the Lions last year. Friday night, Pistol Pete Maravich, brother of Ronnie and son of Clemson Coach Press, popped in 33 points against Pendleton.

Pistol Pete—a nickname that romanticized the young stick-thin player and owed to his off-the-hip style in firing up his one-hand push shot. For a 13-year-old it was pretty heady stuff and fed Pete's growing ease on the court—confidence that sometimes struck others as verging on cockiness.

Part of it may have been the privileged status he felt as the coach's son. For instance, when Pete would drop in at the Clemson gym and join in choose-up games of three-on-three with Press' varsity players, he was not shy about shooting the basketball. Jim Brennan, a starting point guard for Clemson, in recalling his earliest encounter with the precocious schoolboy, said, "At 13, 14, he could shoot the ball, and would every chance he got. The older guys told me, 'Don't say anything. Press doesn't like you to yell at him.' But one time I said something and little Pete was cantankerous about it. He knew what he could get away with. He was a cocky little kid. I remember grabbing him and giving him this little noogie. He had a real short hair cut and, fooling around, I got him into a headlock and gave him that noogie."

But though his confidence was growing, Pete continued his near-obsessive practice routine, hell-bent on upgrading his talent. Under Carlisle and now Carver, he would dribble the ball to school and back home and for hours work on the drills Press had devised for him, only once questioning whether his rigorous workouts were worth it.

"It was a Saturday afternoon and I was in the gym, by myself, as usual," Pete said. "I would spend six to ten hours a day there. I remember stopping after several hours and starting to cry. I went over to a corner and started asking myself questions. 'Other kids are out swimming and playing. Why am I here? Why do I have this desire? Why am I killing myself?'"

The question was rhetorical. Pete Maravich's need to succeed was extreme, as evidenced by the lengths he went to, whether in the rigorous daily workouts or in impulsive acts meant to refine him as a player. Years later, he would recall sneaking out of his bedroom window at night during a thunderstorm so that he might dribble the ball under the most trying of circumstances.

"We had a little goal on a pine tree in the back because our house was in the woods," he said. "And it was a very shallow light. And there was a big muddy grid area that was hard. And the rain would pound down on the mud and I would be in my pajamas, put my tennis shoes on, sneak out the window, and go dribble in that muddied area and shoot. Taking my ball and lifting it up to the heavens, letting the rain wash the mud off. Sneak back into the house and go to sleep."

While Pete played under coaches like Bagwell, Carlisle, and Carver, Press remained the last word on basketball for him. Press did not interfere with or second-guess his son's coaches, but he continued to be involved in Pete's evolving game, critiquing him and creating new and challenging drills—more than 40 of them in all. To those who watched them communicate with one another, often in brusque or confrontational interaction, the relationship struck them as more business-like than what one would ordinarily think of as "typically father-son."

Yet beneath the sometimes-barbed surface—beyond the clashes that a strong-willed father and an ever-more-confident son were bound to have—they remained attached to one another in ways that defied appearances. Each had for the other love and admiration that simply weren't often overtly expressed in these years. Though their bond was basketball and though it provoked noisy disagreements at times, in the decades that followed they would never fail to rally to one another when either was under siege. Yet in these years of Pete's development as a basketball player, there were enough of these scenes of sniping at one another that one basketball man who knew both Maraviches would liken the relationship to the complex father-son pairing at the heart of Pat Conroy's novel—later made into a film—*The Great Santini*, saying, "They loved each other but they were at each other. It was not a normal father/son relationship."

What they shared with far less ambiguity was love of the game. Each was entirely immersed in hoops, and in Pete's case his father's involvement as a coach gave him access to the inner workings and the strategic nuances that other boys his age would not have had. At Clemson, back at a time when the game still had a cozy feeling that sneaker endorsements and big-time money would soon enough kill, that might mean sitting in on the postgame fraternizing that went on. Press and rival coaches like Wake Forest's Bones McKinney, Davidson's Lefty Driesell, and Florida State's Bud Kennedy would adjourn to the home of Bob and Louise Bradley after ball games and, over a pot of coffee, talk Xs and Os into the wee hours of the morning. More often than not, the men who had officiated that night's game would join them.

Louise: "Press had a great personality. Everybody loved him. They'd sit in the den and talk, and Press would do most of the talking—80 percent of the time it was about basketball."

Bob: "Back then the ACC had eight teams and there wasn't any flying back home. They'd just drive the next morning. So these guys weren't ready to go to the motel. They'd come over here and shoot the bull."

Louise: "Sometimes 'til 2, 3 in the morning. Or if it was Bones McKinney 'til 4, 5 in the morning. Bones was an ordained Baptist preacher and sometimes he'd do some preaching. Along with everything else."

In January '62, Maravich's ninth-grade year, when Daniel played in the eight-team Florence Invitational Tournament, the Anderson *Independent* noted:

Coach Don Carver's Daniel High Lions have perhaps the best little man in the meet in mighty mite Pete Maravich, who stands only 5-8 but is scoring at the tune of 20 points per contest.

Not only did his scoring increase, but also he was adding the kind of flourishes to his passes that brought crowds to their feet. There was the night he came down the court on a three-on-one fast break. The defender was overplaying him to the left to force him to throw the ball to the teammate on the right. But that was too easy for Pete. As the defender retreated, Maravich noticed the other man's legs moving like the shuttles on a weaving loom, in and out, in and out. So Pete timed the pass and put it right through his opponent's legs to the teammate on the left, leading to an easy basket. The crowd exploded, and, Maravich would say later, showmanship was born in him.

"At first Pete was hesitant to try any of his fancy stuff in a game," said Press. "He thought his teammates would think he was showboating. But I told him to utilize all of his ability. After a game, when he and I would talk, I'd try to show him where he could have used a behind-the-back or over-the-shoulder pass. I told him the fans would come out just to see him do that. So as he got better in high school, he slowly began working these things into his game."

Over the next two years, under the easygoing Carver, Pete and a future Clemson star, Jim Sutherland, provided the firepower for Daniel, though they did so in a sometimes shaky coexistence. The noogie-inflicting Brennan, who would attend the occasional game, recalled seeing the two players argue openly on the court about each getting his fair share of shots. (Sutherland claimed not to remember any such dispute and asserted that he and Pete were good friends in their years at Daniel.)

By February 7, 1963—Pete's tenth-grade year—the *Independent* was comparing Maravich and Sutherland to Duke University's high-scoring tandem of Art Heyman and Jeff Mullins.

> Duke has a 15–2 record, Daniel High has a 16–3 record. The Blue Devils lead the Atlantic Coast Conference and the Lions are tied for the lead in the Western AA league.
>
> Heyman and Mullins are averaging 46 points between them per game, Sutherland and Maravich are averaging 48.2 points per game between them. . . .
>
> Sutherland, 6-5 senior at Daniel, has scored 500 points in 18 games for a 27.7 average per contest. Maravich has popped in 369 points for a 20.5 average.
>
> Sutherland and Maravich have accounted for 869 points of Daniel's 1,192 so far this season. . . .
>
> Anderson Coach Gilly Simmons says, "I don't see how anybody is going to stop them."

But only two weeks later, and just days after Sutherland scored 28 and Maravich 26 in Daniel's 61–53 victory over Pickens in the Western AA

Conference basketball tournament, the team was eliminated by Greer High, 66–60, even as Maravich scored 24 and Sutherland 20.

By now, though, Pete's game had made an impression well beyond schoolboy circles because whatever basketball camps Press worked at during summers, Pete was sure to be there, too.

"We were at the basketball camp at Campbell College back when Pete was in the tenth grade," said Charlie Bryant, then an assistant to Bones McKinney at Wake Forest. "Every night there was a counselors game with the college kids who were on staff. College kids and sometimes they'd let a high school kid or two play. Pete was in there on a night when Bob Cousy was playing. Cousy was a good friend of Bones McKinney, who was working the camp. Anyway, on this night Pete comes across half-court and throws this amazing half-court pass with spin on it and Cousy stops the game. Stops the game and says, 'Time out. Who in hell is that kid?'

"That same summer, Pete would bet other players on free throws. This one night, he bet Len Chappell, who was an All-American at Wake. Pete bet he'd make 24 of 25 free throws and at least twenty would be nothing-but-net. Well, he hit 25 straight and only two hit the rim. He collected his Pepsi from big Len, who was shaking his head. Everybody did. Pete was a magician with the ball."

Through his high school years he was a regular at the summer basketball camps of Lefty Driesell, coach of Davidson, who recalled how dedicated Pete was.

"We had this concrete wall at one end of the gym and Pete used to go off by himself and practice throwing passes off that wall," Driesell said. "Hundreds of them. Between his legs, behind his back, off his head. You name it.

"Then he would go to the center court circle and work on dribbling. Every possible dribble you could imagine. I used to try to get my guards to do those kinds of drills, but they couldn't. They got too tired. He would be out there doing it in 100-degree heat. One time I said to him, 'Pete, all these years I have never once seen Oscar Robertson throw a pass behind his back or between his legs. All he ever throws are two-handed passes and chest passes.' He just looked at me and said, 'Coach, I want to be a millionaire some day and they don't pay you a million dollars for two-hand chest passes.'"

By now, Press had changed jobs, moving on to North Carolina State as an assistant to the veteran Wolfpack coach, Everett Case, who'd come to the Raleigh campus following his discharge from the Navy in 1946.

"Some people thought I was nuts," Press said. "Here I was, a head coach at an Atlantic Coast Conference school, and the basketball program was just getting to the point where I always wanted it."

Indeed, in his last season at Clemson, in 1961–62, Press became the only coach to guide the Tigers to the championship game of the ACC tournament. The team upset North Carolina State 67–46 in the opening round and Duke 77–72 in the semifinals before succumbing in the championship game to Wake Forest 77–72. And although Press never had a winning team in his six seasons at Clemson, the fact that he generated Tiger squads that were competitive was of itself an achievement, given the limited talent pool with which he was working. The job he did made an impression on NC State's Case. When Case hired Press to be his assistant, the understanding was that Maravich would succeed him when the old coach reached the mandatory retirement age at the end of the 1964–65 season.

"Besides, I was earning in the neighborhood of $5,000 at Clemson," said Press, "and it wasn't enough. When North Carolina State offered me $8,500 to be an assistant to Everett Case, I couldn't pass it up."

While Pete finished his tenth-grade year at Daniel, Press was living at the YMCA in Raleigh in his first season at NC State and eating his meals with the players on campus. But by the summer preceding the '63–64 season, Helen and Pete had joined him, and the family was soon ensconced in a ranch-style brick-and-wood, three-bedroom home at 508 Northglen Drive in North Raleigh, 10 minutes from campus.

Gym rat that Pete was, he was soon a regular at the YMCA on Hillsborough Street in Raleigh, where he struck up a friendship with another rabid hoopster, Jimmy Broadway. Broadway's older brother, Olin, was the basketball coach at Broughton High, and pretty soon the 6-foot-5

Jimmy—projected as a starting forward at Broughton—was telling Olin about this new kid Maravich, who, though all skin and bones at 6-foot, 145 pounds, could do things with the ball that would make the great Cousy envious.

Not only that, he reported to his coach/brother, but also the kid was a demon workaholic. Maravich and Jimmy Broadway would show up at the Y at eight in the morning, and, if there were other players there, they would work up skins-and-shirts games. If, as was often the case, they were the only ones there, they'd practice shooting a while before Pete would commence his drills. Jimmy was mesmerized by his new friend's legerdemain—the figure eights through his legs, the dribbling, the behind-the-back passes, the trick shots that the Pistol did to entertain.

"He had the ability," said Jimmy, "to go 'round his back with the ball, through his legs, spin it off his finger, bump it off his head and into the basket. He'd do all these gyrations and score."

Pete's work ethic impressed the younger Broadway. He had only to look at Pete's pipe-stem physique to know, as surely as he knew anything, that the new kid in town was self-made, a basketball boy-genius who'd driven himself to succeed.

At lunch, the two of them would gobble up hamburgers at Broadway's house or at the Y cafeteria, then back to the gym they'd go.

Evenings, there was an open-age Y house league on whose rosters high school players teamed with past and present North Carolina State stars like Bob MacGillvary, Ken Rohloff, and Bob DiStefano, not to mention Olin Broadway, who'd played varsity ball at Wake Forest. It was in the Y summer league that the Broughton coach got his first up-close look at Maravich.

"It was obvious," said Broadway, "that Pete had a lot of skill and savvy. My concern was his size. Was he large enough and would he have the endurance to go all game long? In the summer league games, I could see him pacing himself and, though he did it pretty intelligently, it still remained a concern of mine.

"When we started varsity practice, he'd work hard and get tired. But over the course of the season, he improved his endurance. He just did a lot of running. We had a little weight room upstairs from the gym, and I had the team do some lifting. Pete was not inclined to do much—did just enough to humor me."

The Broughton team—8–13 the season before—had a strong core of returning seniors for '63–64: Jimmy Broadway (who'd go on to play at Wake Forest), 6-foot-4 Doug Bridges (who'd play at the Citadel), 6-foot-2 Steve Horney, 6-foot guard Billy Trott, and 6-foot-1 guard Ed Parker. Parker, Bridges, and Broadway had been starters the previous season. A 6-foot-3, 190-pound junior, Dickie Smith, was penciled in as the starting center.

In newspaper articles previewing the '63–64 campaign, Maravich was viewed as merely one of four potential backcourt starters—Parker, Trott, and a 5-foot-10 junior, David Smith, were the others. But once the season opened, Maravich was the clear-cut leader of the team. Paul Phillips, reporting Broughton's opening-game 57–48 victory over Burlington in the *Raleigh Times*, wrote:

> The final Broughton story was just too much Jimmy Broadway and Pete Maravich. Broadway poured in 24 points from his forward slot and Maravich threaded the cords for 18 markers, but it was the slender guard's steals and ball handling that sparked his play.
>
> "Broadway did a tremendous job," Burlington coach Twig Wiggins said. "He's a real fine one and that Maravich did a great job of setting him up. Maravich is a real cool operator."

With that game, Maravich had put his imprimatur on the team. Not only was he good enough to start, but also he could dominate a game when he had to. He showed that in the Caps' next few contests, scoring 20 against Grimsley, 30 against High Point, 28 against Burlington. But what impressed Olin Broadway was the Pistol's willingness to sacrifice personal stats to accommodate the game plan. Against New Hanover High School of Wilmington, North Carolina, when Broadway designed a play to force the opposition's big man out from the basket to guard his brother Jimmy, Maravich repeatedly hit Broadway with perfectly timed passes as Jimmy came off a screen. Then he watched as Jimmy Broadway drove to the hoop, forcing the Burlington big man to foul—the very objective of Olin Broadway's scheme.

"It kept their big guy on the bench with fouls most of the game and he fouled out at the beginning of the fourth quarter," said Olin Broadway. "At that point, we had the lead, so Wilmington pressed. Pete put on a dribbling show that was unreal. No one could get the ball away from him. He was dribbling through double-teams."

But Pete's forceful presence on a team top-heavy with seniors was not without its unsettling effect.

"Bridges," said Olin Broadway, "had carved out a spot where he thought he'd be the leading scorer. There were several cases where he was supposed to pass off to Pete and didn't. . . . It wasn't a problem for long. Bridges recognized that he'd sit on the bench til he cured the problem. I sat him and talked to him and left him on the bench long enough for him to figure things out. Bridges was a very talented basketball player."

The team adjusted to Maravich. By mid-February, Broughton had a 13–3 record, and Maravich (19.8 ppg) was the Caps' leading scorer, ahead of Bridges (14.8) and Broadway (14.2). Broughton, a powerhouse in the seven-team Eastern 4-A Conference, bolted into first place in regular-season play when it defeated Durham 75–62 on February 14 and then clinched the conference with victories over Wilson and Fayetteville.

That earned the 17–3 Caps a bye in the Eastern 4-A Conference tournament and the right to host the semifinals and finals. The opposition in the semifinals was Wilmington, a team twice beaten by Broughton earlier in the season. But on this night, Broughton had a time of it with the Wildcats from Wilmington. Reason? The Pistol, who had gone into the game averaging 19.3 ppg, on this night was firing blanks.

As Paul Phillips of the *Raleigh Times* recalled: "Pete couldn't hit. It might have been his worst shooting night ever. By the end of regulation time he was something like oh for nineteen from the floor. Then the game went into overtime."

In that overtime, Maravich hit a shot with 1:36 remaining to give

Broughton a 51–49 lead. Then, when Wilmington countered with a basket that tied the game and sent it into a second overtime, Maravich hit successive field goals that gave Broughton a 55–53 lead with 1:44 left and down the stretch hit four straight foul shots to ice the game, 59–55.

In that second overtime, Maravich had scored all eight Broughton points, remarkable for what it showed about his mental toughness.

"Most kids would have been so uptight after missing 19 shots they wouldn't have even tried a layup," said Phillips.

In the finals of the Eastern 4-A Conference tournament, Maravich was back in form: he scored 29 points against a Fayetteville team led by 6-foot-10 center Rusty Clark—a future star at the University of North Carolina—as Broughton won 63–60.

With the victory, the *Raleigh News and Observer* called the Broughton team "the best-ever" in the school's history and made the team a co-favorite with Greensboro Grimsley to win the State 4-A tournament.

But on the way to that projected championship matchup, Broughton came up against a determined opening-round opponent in Winston-Salem Reynolds High. The Caps blew a 60–54 lead with 3:38 remaining and were forced, again, into overtime. But it appeared that the night would be salvaged when Jimmy Broadway nailed a 20-foot shot at the overtime buzzer—a shot that would have given Broughton a 64–62 victory.

But, no. While one official signaled that the basket was good, the other official overruled him, insisting the shot came just after the buzzer. That meant the game was headed into a second overtime. In that second overtime, Broughton would succumb, 64–63, in a game in which Maravich scored 21 points but whose outcome haunted him for months to come.

That summer, he would average 30 points a game in the Raleigh YMCA summer league and would attend basketball clinics with Press. Even as Press had worked long hours at North Carolina State, he remained as watchful as ever of Pete's basketball progress, in a relationship that still struck others as curiously unlike a typical father-son interaction. At times they cursed and fussed at one another, often but not exclusively about basketball matters. Press had an old-fashioned sense of how an athlete should conduct himself and wasn't shy about imposing his views on Pete.

"One time," recalls North Carolina State player Hal Blondeau, "Pete came to practice at Christmas vacation with a black eye. Seems like he'd come home with beer on his breath. Press got mad and popped him one."

During those years, the relationship remained tumultuous, the result of Press and Pete being two strong, distinct personalities.

"Press was a high-strung individual when he was here," said Frank Weedon, sports information director at North Carolina State. "Very excitable, never could sit still. I remember him always chewing tobacco. He had a spittoon right in his office and it didn't matter who was there. He'd chew. As a matter of fact, he was always making noise, no matter what he was doing. I remember him playing poker. He's got to be the worst player in the world. He can raise you, all right, but when someone else raises, it's sacrilege. He'll yell and scream and cuss. But he never cusses AT you and I've never seen anyone get insulted when he swears. If someone else said the same thing, there might be a fight, but with Press it's just words, just vocabulary.

"Press stayed away from Pete's high school coaches. He never butted in or offered advice, but when he got Pete alone, he was much more critical than the average father. He was always telling Pete that he wasn't such a hot shot. Maybe Pete made four really great passes in a game, but Press would pick out the one bad one and dwell on that. He was always out to make Pete improve his game.

"I can't really say I observed a father-son relationship in those days. It was always more like player-coach. Both were dedicated to basketball and that was the prime concern."

During that junior year at Broughton, Pete would routinely go from the practice court at the high school to the practice court at North Carolina State. There he would challenge Wolfpack players to games of one-on-one, more often than not whupping them. But Les Robinson, a future Wolfpack coach who was a varsity player then, recalled the rare instance when he beat Pete.

"Afterward, he went storming through Press' office, slamming the door and cussing," said Robinson. "Press said to him, 'What? You got your ass kicked?' Pete said yeah. Press told him, 'It won't be the last time.' Pete took off, still steamed about getting beat, and not any happier for his father's rubbing it in. Well, when Pete left, Press turned to me and said, 'He's gonna be a great one.'

"It was not a normal father-son relationship. They'd go at each other like brothers. But if you talked to each by himself, the one couldn't say enough about the other. Pete would tell you his dad was a basketball genius. And Press, he worshipped Pete. But together they were like salt and pepper. I thought sometimes it was for effect and sometimes for real.

"You spent any time with Press, it didn't take you long to realize basketball was truly his life. Anyone you talk about—whether it's John Wooden or anybody, any coaches of that era—no one was more devoted to basketball than Press Maravich. He loved basketball to a fault. He lived, slept, ate basketball. As far as he and Pete, Press was like a musician whose son would become Mozart."

FOR 17 YEARS, Everett Case had been a dominant figure at North Carolina State, winning six championships in the Southern Conference and, when seven teams broke away to form the Atlantic Coast Conference in 1953, winning four more championships there.

By the '60s, though, when Press joined the Wolfpack staff, the old coach no longer seemed to be as plugged in to the game as he once was.

"Coach Case," said the Wolfpack's Blondeau, "was living in the past. Press was on the cutting edge with motion offenses and shuffles and double picks for the guards coming around. Case thought that that'd never work. Coach Case's offense was built around a double low post. One of those low posts would move across the lane and set a pick for the guy on the weak side, who'd break to the ball. If he didn't get the pass, then the center who'd picked would come back. Not a lot of motion there for the other men. Absolutely predictable it was. I think Case was a wonderful old gent, but the game had changed.

"When we were sophs [1963–64] and Press was Case's assistant, we had two sets of plays. We'd practice coach Case's at one end of the court and Press' on the other end. As our sophomore year went on, more and more we were using Press'."

Two games into the '64–65 season, Everett Case was diagnosed with cancer and announced his retirement. A year ahead of schedule, Press was named head coach, and Charlie Bryant—who had been frosh coach—would become his assistant. Les Robinson, a senior not expected to play much, was offered and accepted Bryant's position as coach of the freshman team.

The team that Press inherited was, according to sports information director Weedon, a mature squad, with 8 of the 12 players married and 10 of them on the Dean's List. Compared to, say, ACC rival Duke, which had several future pros on its roster—Jack Marin, Bob Verga, Steve Vacendak, Mike Lewis—the Wolfpack had nowhere near the natural talent. But it was a squad that was willing to work hard and one that, virtually to a man, relished playing for Press Maravich.

Hal Blondeau: "The players loved him. He could be all over you in practice, but it was never malicious. Never in-your-face kind of stuff. And he knew the game. When he had you come off a pick, he'd say, 'HIT the goddamn pick. Goddammit, you can't foul your own man.' When we went off picks, you couldn't get a piece of paper through. Press wouldn't tolerate it. . . . He was the first guy I ever heard say, 'Don't step up to the foul line early. Wait til the ref hands you the ball.' And he had these great expressions to drive home the point. Like he'd say, 'If you get on the foul line early, your asshole'll get so tight you can't drive a flax seed up it with a sledgehammer.' Just amazing. He'd say things like that and you'd remember. He was so funny."

Eddie Biedenbach, guard: "Everything he related to basketball. No matter what you were talking about. You could be sitting at a table with him. All of a sudden, the pepper and salt shakers would be guards, the ketchup bottle a center. No matter what you were doing, it always came back to basketball with him. He had such enthusiasm, and was friendly. Cool looking. Athletic looking. Stayed in shape. And he was one of the best teachers. For offensive plays, he could tell you what board on that floor you should be standing on. It could get confusing. He'd say, 'You're supposed to go there.' And I: 'But I thought . . .' And he'd go, 'You little bastard.' Just all the time. I began to think Little Bastard was my name. But Press was like a father. Nobody on our club was ever upset by the way he talked."

Blondeau: "Press was brilliant. Truly brilliant. Tactically incredible on the court. You'd be out there, running plays. And he'd say, 'Okay, playground it.' You'd freelance, then he'd blow his whistle and: 'Go back to where you were three seconds ago.' And he'd analyze it. 'You did this 'cause he did that.' He could see it all."

Biedenbach: "Or he'd say, 'Stop. Do that again' And he'd make up a play off what we just did. One time against Furman, we were beating them badly. And at halftime, Press says, 'Okay, I want to see how you guys adjust. I'm gonna make up some plays and we'll put 'em up on the blackboard. On play #1, Biedenbach, you pass the ball to [Tommy] Mattocks and run a . . . Wait a second. You just go talk to Sam Gealy . . .' Sam was a reserve senior who sat at the end of the bench. Press was going to take me out of the play. He didn't think I could remember. I was not one of the smartest guys, but I worked hard. Anyway, we run that play later in the game. Mattocks throws the ball to a player. Guy shoots it. They go to the other end and defend. I stayed and talked to Gealy. Press sees a guy open at the other end. Says, 'Who's got so-and-so?' Then he sees me, and says, 'You lil bastard.'"

Blondeau: "Everybody gives Dean Smith credit for the four corners. But it was Press who came up with it. The first guy to dribble the four corners was [Wolfpack guard] Kenny Rohloff in '62–63 and '63–64. It was Press' concept of how to cope when your team was outmanned. He did it to keep games close. By '64–65, we used it only once in a while—Press felt we could play.

"Press always concentrated on what people's tendencies were. It's what he passed on to Pete. 'You'll be able to do this 'cause he'll allow you to do it.' It was almost like martial arts—use people's strengths against themselves. Pete was not a great athlete, but Pete understood the game.

People would say, 'How can he throw passes like that?' 'Cause he practiced AND he understood where you would not be."

Biedenbach: "One day I was shooting. And Press said, 'Close your left eye and shoot.' I shot and missed by a lot. Press said, 'What happened?' Told him, 'I lost sight of the basket for a second as I released.' He: 'You're a one-eyed shooter. Your arm is in front of your face. Shoot the ball to the side. The eyes give you depth perception.' I worked on that. It was no major adjustment but it was phenomenal the difference it made. Press knew techniques. If he told you something, it might be awkward at first. But it became natural."

Blondeau: "I remember Wilt Chamberlain and the 76ers came to Raleigh for an exhibition, back when they were coached by Dolph Schayes. Schayes was a friend of Press' and we all looked at Schayes like a god. Dolph and Press got to talking. Press was feeling him out. We always thought Press would be a good pro coach. There was no recruiting in the pros—Press hated recruiting. He asked Dolph what it was like to coach in the pros. And Schayes: 'All I do is carry the balls.' Press told him, 'If I had 'em, I'd have 'em.' Here's Press, he's gonna tell Wilt. But Press didn't care. Either his way or no way. It wasn't in a malicious sense. He just believed what he knew was right, and it was."

AS PRESS was taking the reins at North Carolina State, Pete—now 6-foot-3 1/2, 160 pounds—was stage center in his senior year at Broughton.

With Dickie Smith the only other returnee from the 19–4 Broughton squad of a season before, and a dearth of talent to replace those who had graduated, Pete was greenlighted by new coach Ed McLean to be the show.

In 23 games that year, and even as Broughton was losing more often than it won, the Pistol would emerge as a marquee attraction—a player whose pizzazz and explosive scoring were enough to make a night on the hardwood a must-see event.

As the *Charlotte News* reported just before Christmas 1964:

Young Maravich, a virtual beanpole capped by the well-known Maravich brush cut, scored 81 points in a two-night visit to Charlotte this week for contests against East Mecklenburg and Garinger.

He hit 38 points the first evening and sank two free throws which handed East Mecklenburg its first loss of the season.

Last night he hit a season single-game high of 43 points although the Caps lost to upset-minded Garinger 89–77. . . .

Maravich's best shots are a jumper near the key and a driving, delayed shot from 10 feet on either side of the basket. He is tall enough to play forward in high school, but his ball handling and outside shooting are so valuable he's used at guard.

Though Maravich as a senior would be without a supporting cast, he managed just the same to make the game exciting.

"We played Enloe at Broughton early in the season," McLean said. "Enloe had Randy Denton, who later went to Duke, then the Carolina Cougars. He and Pete were sort of going head to head. The game goes into the final seconds and Denton cans a free throw to win it. Pete really burned up. He just waited for the return at Enloe. Sure enough, there was a packed house. All Pete did that night was score 47 points, steal the ball five or six times, and we win by two. He was so great that night. They just couldn't stop him. I don't think anyone could have."

When Maravich was on his game, he scored points in bunches, even on nights when he might temporarily misfire. Against Rocky Mount High School that February in '65, he was held to two points in the first half as Broughton trailed 30–16. In the second half, the Pistol scored 31 points to give him 33 in all, but that output was still not enough as Broughton lost 73–61.

That was typical of the season. Maravich put up big numbers but couldn't overcome the inexperience of his teammates. Yet he never stopped trying. "Every game was important to Pete," said McLean. "He wanted to win very badly. It hurt Pete when he lost."

The hurt was often more than psychological. Being Broughton's one-man team made Pete a bull's-eye for every cheapshot artist on opposition rosters. Though often roughed up, Maravich played through the bumps and bruises and did so with a stoic's reserve. The best example of his refusal to give in to pain occurred in the conference playoffs when he suffered a foot injury—a torn transverse arch—in a 59–56 victory over Wilmington.

The injury was serious enough to force McLean to sit Maravich that night. With Broughton's next playoff game against Fayetteville and 6-foot-10 Rusty Clark, Maravich's status—would he play or not?—was crucial to the Caps' chances.

"At first Pete was advised not to play," said McLean. "But he kept insisting. Finally the doctor said that there was little chance of him doing further damage, so we taped the arch quite heavily and sent him out there."

Pete was gimpy, no question. Though dragging that injured foot, he managed to make adjustments in his offensive arsenal. He worked off screens, he posted up. He used his guile to compensate for the problems the foot caused. And when the smoke had settled, the Pistol had gone for 45 points. Though Fayetteville won the game, Maravich won the crowd with his gutty performance, in what would be his last game for 10–13 Broughton.

In 23 games, the Pistol would average 32 ppg, scoring 40 points on six occasions. He'd become a hoops phenomenon. More than a decade before, Pete Maravich had had to be baited to take a basketball in hand, but not now. Come crunch time, Maravich not only wanted the basketball, but also he knew what to do with it. The long years of intricate drills, performed with slavish dedication, had given him a command of the basketball that, 30-odd years later as the millennium drew near, some experts still insisted could not and had not been matched.

Rod Hundley, a showman himself on the court at Furman and later in the NBA, came upon Maravich back then at Lefty Driesell's basketball camp at Davidson College. "Pete was down there as a counselor, not getting paid," said Hundley. "I was working with Converse, the sneaker company, making the rounds of basketball camps as a lecturer. That summer I worked out with Pete a little bit and was amazed by what he could do. He was by far the best ball handler I'd ever seen at that age. I still feel that way. The best I've ever seen, period. He could handle the ball, he could make the ball talk."

Press had given the boy a blueprint for excellence, and Pete, investing his time and having a passion for the game, had followed his father-the-maestro's scheme. All of that diligence had brought forth a player brimming with hoopster tricks and unfailing confidence—the confidence, indeed, to continue challenging his father's own athletes at North Carolina State. Challenge them not as some acolyte of Dr. Naismith's game but as a cocksure, more technically advanced player. Schoolboy though he was, Maravich felt sure enough of his ability to relish one-on-one games with Wolfpack players, talking trash to them long before it was fashionable to do so.

Les Robinson: "He'd come around the court, and go, 'Come on, I'll kick your butt.' Oh yeah, he'd be running his mouth. He was young, cocky and could back his stuff up. He beat everybody one on one. He was great with the ball. He'd tease you with the high dribble, bait you and then put it between his legs, behind his back."

Hal Blondeau: "Rather than cross over or spin like Earl the Pearl [Monroe], Pete would look you in the eye and change direction by dribbling through his legs. He could have played ACC as a high school junior, although physically he might have had a little problem—he was so skinny."

Tommy Mattocks: "I played a lot of one-on-one with Pete, sometimes because he wouldn't take no for an answer. Sometimes he played in his socks, sometimes in shoes, but we about split the games we played. Yet I had a feeling about him, that he had what it takes. I never blocked a shot of his and I didn't see speed as a problem. He just had some more maturing to do.

"But the thing that really impressed me about him was his confidence. Here was this high school kid playing against a starting college ballplayer and he's shooting hook shots. I never had the nerve to take a hook in my life, and he's popping them from both sides . . . and hitting them. Then I watched him shooting by himself one day. He was taking all kinds of crazy shots, behind his back, over his head, hooks from all over. I guess he practiced them so much that he knew he could make them when it counted."

Eddie Biedenbach: "When I played him, he didn't seem that quick. But he was a little taller than I was [Biedenbach is 6-foot] and he took me inside where he could use his height and longer reach. I guess we about split even in one-on-one games. But I'll say one thing. I never blocked one of his shots. Never. He would stuff me from time to time, but he just seemed to have the knack of getting that shot of his."

Out of the one-on-one challenges, friendships developed. Pete began spending time with North Carolina State players away from the court.

"One time," said Biedenbach, "the state fair came to town at the Fairgrounds. The fair would have these basketball booths. You know how those go. The baskets are a little off—the rims too high, too small, or bent. The ball would be smooth or have lumps in it. The guy running it would be this sharp little fella in a straw hat. You'd be shooting for teddy bears. Twenty-five cents for a little bear maybe nine, ten inches high, 50 cents for the big bear which was two feet high. You got two shots. You had to make 'em both. It was Pete, myself and a guy already out of school, former player and great shooter named Don Greiner. Anyway, we killed 'em—we'd win the teddy bears and sell 'em to guys that had their kids with them or guys with girl friends. Two-dollars-fifty-cents for the little bear, five bucks for the big bear. Between us we made $99 for the night.

"The guy running the booth eventually cut us off. So we'd change jackets, or try another basketball booth—there were, like, three or four of them at the fair. But come the third or fourth day, those guys would see us and: '. . . oh no, not you boys again.'

"Pete wasn't a social type in high school. He never followed the crowd or did the 'in' things. He went his own way for the most part. Like his father, he dressed conservatively, never wearing sharp clothes or doing anything else that might attract attention to himself.

"Pete was really shy with girls in those days. I remember one time we took him to a party with us. Well, we figured we'd fix him up with this girl. Pete wouldn't even talk to her. He just sort of stood there in that shy way of his and finally couldn't take it any more. He just ran away.

"It was funny—someone meeting Pete, say, at a party, wouldn't really be impressed. Wouldn't be anything for that matter. But on the basketball court he always came off as a great guy. He was always having fun, talking, laughing, enjoying himself . . . and winning. But don't get me wrong, while basketball gave him confidence, he was the same on and off the court in that he wasn't phony. He never put on airs of any kind. Even though he was a hard loser and wouldn't talk sometimes, the one thing Pete Maravich always remained was *real*."

As PETE was making friends and influencing basketball people, so was Press.

From early on, he charmed the Raleigh-area media and Wolfpack fans as well as his players. Intense though he was, he had a way of disarming folks with his directness and the raconteur's gift. Press had a knack for telling stories and jokes and had a lounge comic's wit for giving the other guy the needle. But as with his use of rough language, a Press Maravich insult came with a wink. Friends of his were wont to say: he insults only those he likes.

To the citizens of Raleigh, he was unusual—not a standard-brand buttoned-tight coach. When Wolfpack sports information director Weedon wrote Press' biographical sketch in the '64–65 North Carolina State media guide, it was not the dry-as-dust resume that most were:

> Press Maravich is what is known as a character.
>
> He takes scouting notes in Serbian shorthand, chews towels and tobacco (not at the same time), talks a better golf game than he plays, is a lousy football prognosticator, and is Pete Maravich's father. But in spite of, or because of, all these idiosyncrasies, Press Maravich is also a sound basketball coach.

Press would prove just how sound he was in his first year as head coach of the Wolfpack. Through a '64–65 season in which he did chew towels while on the bench, out of nervous tension, he proved to be a shrewd and capable successor to Everett Case.

On three successive nights early in March 1965, his underdog Wolf-pack team would shock basketball experts by beating Virginia (106–69), Maryland (76–67), and nationally ranked Duke (91–85) to win the ACC championship.

After the championship victory, Blondeau recalled, most of the student body lingered in Reynolds Coliseum: "They were waiting for us. Well, Press sat out there with those kids til the wee hours. Telling stories. Sure he elaborated. It was the kind of guy he was. He LOVED to have the fans and the kids around him."

Although the 21–5 Wolfpack would then lose to Bill Bradley's Princeton team in the opening round of the NCAA Eastern Regionals at College Park, Maryland, the job that Press had done in taking a team that had gone 8–11 the season before was more than a little impressive.

Press' squad hadn't the marquee names other ACC schools did—none of the Wolfpack would go on to play NBA ball—but it was a savvy team whose sum was greater than its parts. That owed in good measure to Press' ingenuity as a coach. Although he gave his players more latitude than Case had allowed them on offense, he did not go overboard. As Les Robinson put it, "Shooters shot the ball. Those that couldn't, didn't. In the clutch, he'd stress, get HIM the ball, depending on matchups.

"And Press was amazing at working out continuity type offenses. We had many offenses—you couldn't be a dummy to play for Press. If you screwed up, he'd tell you, 'You ain't got a basketball gene in you.' Then he'd point to one of the other, smarter guys and say, 'When he shits, you ought to grab some of his genes.'"

On defense, the Wolfpack played Press' "junto" defense, *junto* being Spanish for "together." Junto in action was, said Robinson, a full-court press that appeared to be man to man but actually incorporated zone principles.

Press' team-oriented system, very "junto" in spirit, worked.

"It was," said Les Robinson, "one of the top two or three coaching jobs I've ever seen—taking the talent level we had against what we as a team accomplished."

WHILE PETE and Press were making headlines on the sports pages, at home Helen Maravich had begun to flounder.

Press may have been idiosyncratic, and a "character" to those who traveled in Wolfpack basketball circles, but to Helen he was too often simply an absentee husband, a man consumed by his sport.

It was not uncommon for Press to return from a road game and, arriving in Raleigh at two in the morning, go directly to his office to analyze game films through the night. As coaches tend to be, Press was driven. Maybe more so than most. He had already stipulated in his will that when he died he wanted to be buried with a basketball.

For Helen, who had forbidden Press to become an airline pilot for fear of the deadly consequences of flying and the risk that again she could be abandoned, her thoughtful Plan B had backfired. With Ronnie married and in the Marines, with Pete and Press caught up in their basketball obsession, more and more she felt alone, and was alone. Alone and troubled.

The public image was, of course, another story.

"N.C. State's Head Coach Has Basketball Family" was the headline in a women's section feature about Helen in the December 19, 1964, *Charlotte Observer*:

> . . .Ulcers and two seasons at State as assistant coach halted Coach Maravich's towel and tobacco chewing during the game's frantic moments.
>
> But during his six seasons as head coach at Clemson University, he gave the towel—and the tobacco—quite a workout.
>
> "During his first four of five years at Clemson he chewed the towel until it was shredded," his wife recalls.
>
> "But when he had ulcers, he had to learn to control himself in the last few years and calm down. He's not allowed to chew tobacco anymore because of ulcers."
>
> Despite the increased tension of the job, pretty Helen Maravich is happy that her husband is head of the Wolfpack cagers.
>
> "Press is going to be the happiest man in the world here at State. He loves it here. When you start out in coaching, you start at the bottom and it takes years to work your way up. This is what Press has always wanted, a fine school like State where everybody likes basketball. . . .

"Basketball has just been our life in this family," the blue-eyed brunette said with a smile. "I guess that's why we are all nervous wrecks. My daughter-in-law is visiting here, and she's the calmest person. But just a few more trips home, and she'll probably be like us.

"Basketball has been Press' life, and he wouldn't change it. I think he's definitely out of place in anything else."

On February 28, 1965, days before the ACC tournament, the *Raleigh News and Observer* ran a full-page feature: "Introducing Mrs. Press Maravich/The Woman Behind the Wolfpack Coach."

It was their background—both of them had grandparents from Yugoslavia—that was the subject of their first conversation. But she confided that she wasn't impressed with him that day even though he was a kind of town hero. He had bandages on from his most recent game and "he looked terrible," she recalled. "Professional basketball is rough."

It didn't take her long to change her mind. Two months later Helen Gravor had become Mrs. Press Maravich, a decision she's never regretted.

"Everybody said it would never last," she said with a twinkle in her eye. "But we were just meant for each other." She still has a girl's smooth complexion, slim figure and unwrinkled face. . . .

"Our life is just basketball," she said with pride. She's a fan from way back in high school days when she was a cheerleader. And she's more enthusiastic about it now than then. She has to be. The game's most important with the men in her life, and her whole schedule is geared around them.

Press can't eat anything except eggs before a game and he doesn't eat after the games now since he found out a couple of months ago that he has an ulcer. But Helen tries to wait up until he comes home if the game is in town.

"He's always under pressure and tension," she explained. "And sometimes he can't sleep."

The years have made the strain on her less. "I couldn't cope with it before," she said. "Sometimes I think I'm not even gonna take a bus, but I'm gonna take my bags and walk," she teased.

But she wouldn't leave. She loves basketball, she's glad her family does and "we love it here."

The reality was far from the idyllic family life depicted in newsprint. Helen, who'd always been a fragile personality, was becoming increasingly withdrawn and troubled. Troubled enough to begin drinking heavily on the sly, a habit she was able to conceal from Pete and Press but that she confessed to Louise Bradley, the wife of Clemson sports information director Bob Bradley and a woman to whom she'd remained close even after moving to Raleigh.

"The Helen Maravich I knew in Clemson was a devoted housewife, who couldn't do enough for her husband and boys," recalled Louise Bradley. "Mornings, she'd take Pete and Ronnie to school and then come by our house. Their dog Princess, a black terrier with brown trim, would arrive first, then Helen would come, walking through the woods near our home. She'd have her overcoat over her nightgown and be in a scarf and loafers. And absolutely she looked like a movie star, her hair pulled up in a bun, looking beautiful. She'd come and have a cup of coffee and play with our nine-month-old daughter, Dorma. She was in love with Dorma.

"Her home and family meant more to her than anything else. She always made sure she had those meals cooked for them. She spent a big part of the afternoon making meals. And the house — a spotless house. A lot of washing and ironing. A very particular person."

In Raleigh, not only had Helen begun drinking heavily, but also she confessed to Louise Bradley that she had hallucinatory visions of the deceased aunt who'd raised her and of other people she knew.

"She'd be out on the deck of her home and talk to her aunt like she really was there," said Bradley. "That's when she realized she was out of control and did not know what to do."

Mrs. Bradley's first instinct was to tell Press so that he could get her help, but Helen swore her not to disclose her alcoholism to anybody.

"She told me," said Bradley, "she couldn't bring herself to tell Press — she didn't want him to know. She said, 'The only reason I'm telling you is because I had to tell someone.'"

"I was worried to death. I called a friend of mine, a reformed alcoholic who hadn't had a drink in 15 or so years. I thought she could advise me what to do. She said, 'No, you can't tell Press. You can't tell anybody. It's something she'll have to do on her own.' My friend sent me four or five pamphlets. I was afraid Press might see them but I did send them."

Back in Raleigh, those who were close to Press glimpsed enough of the Maraviches' home life to sense that all was not well—that Helen was troubled. Frank Weedon, the Wolfpack sports information director, on occasion would drive Press home after a game and observe that, more than a year after moving to Raleigh, furniture was still in boxes and that Helen, although not unkempt, would never bother to fix herself up.

In Raleigh, she'd become more reclusive.

"On the college level, there's so much demand for wives to become involved socially and she just didn't want it," said Charlie Bryant, Press' assistant coach. "She didn't want to be around people. She would never go out. At social events, at banquets, Press would be by himself. She just never left the house. She didn't like to be around people. Which was surprising because when she was around people she was outstanding. It was always the thing that buffaloed me, 'cause she was a personable and lovely lady."

The situation grew even more complicated when Ronnie's wife, Romona, turned up with the couple's daughter, Diana, who was five and a half months old as Press' Wolfpack squad was winning the ACC championship. When Romona made it known that she and Ronnie meant to put the child up for adoption, Press and Helen wouldn't hear of it. They took Diana and raised her as their own. And though earlier newspaper stories would show photos of "grandmother" Helen with the infant Diana, the child would grow up being told by Helen and Press that they were her biological parents.

"When they took Diana," said Bryant, "Helen became very very possessive of the girl and very protective and wouldn't let anybody in the house. I was one of the few she let in the house and, if you touched something, she was wiping up behind you. Everything had to be spotless. She'd follow you outdoors and wipe up behind you. It was sad. A woman with all those good qualities, yet . . ."

Although Press was unaware that his wife had become an alcoholic, from early on in the marriage he'd recognized that she was a woman of delicate constitution. His Youngstown Bears teammate, Peter Lalich, recalled that soon after Press retired from the pro game, Press went to see Lalich's brother-in-law, Nick Radlick, a Cleveland councilman, hoping Radlick could steer him to somebody who could help Helen with her problems.

In Clemson, although the Maraviches appeared to be a normal family, and Helen the picture of domestic bliss, Dr. Billy Hunter, the family's physician, knew a darker side. "Helen was my patient," he said. "I kinda hesitate to talk about it. But there were problems there."

Although those problems were kept on the QT in Clemson, and later in Raleigh, they would make for an increasingly complicated Maravich family life.

THAT AUGUST of 1965, Pete Maravich was the star of the 17th annual North Carolina high school all-star game. Playing for the East team, he scored a record-breaking 42 points in leading his squad to a 110–79 victory.

St. Joseph College coach Jack Ramsay was at the game and afterward told newsmen that Maravich was ready to play college ball.

"Like, tomorrow, maybe," Ramsay said with a grin. "The boy is a very outstanding shooter. He has some things to learn, however. . . . Pete has to learn to play more with his team and to play defense."

There was one other problem. Pete was 6-foot-4 now, but still quite thin, hardly the build for college ball. Press decided to send him to Edwards Military Academy in Salemburg, North Carolina, for a year of prep school.

"I spoke to Press about it at the time," said Eddie Biedenbach. "He felt Pete was not strong enough to take the pounding he'd get in college. And he figured another year would give him the strength he needed. Besides, the way Pete practiced, another year would make him all the better."

While Pete chafed at the spit-and-polish atmosphere of a military set-ting, he thrived on the fast-break style of the Edwards basketball team, in one game scoring 50 points and then grinning as he read the headline in a local paper the next day: "50? Maravich."

His most satisfying games came against the North Carolina State freshman team. In Salemburg, Pete scored 26 points to lead his team to a 90–73 victory over the Wolfpack frosh. The second contest was held in Raleigh. Although Press coached the varsity and not the frosh, the local papers nevertheless billed the game as a father-son confrontation. Many of the varsity players who knew Pete were there, needling him as he took his warmups.

That night Maravich hit 15 of 28 shots from the floor and added five more points from the foul line for a game-high 33 points. It was no con-test. At halftime, Edwards led 50–33. The final was 91–57. In the sec-ond half, Pete entertained the crowd with behind-the-back and no-look passes.

Although Press had to be pleased with Pete's evolving game, he was not as happy with his son's academic progress. Press' burning desire was to coach Pete at North Carolina State. But the school required an SAT score of 800 from incoming freshmen, and Pistol—obsessed with basket-ball and neglectful of his studies—had fallen way short of that at Broughton.

After a year at Edwards, he still tested well below the 800 standard. Even though Press was happy at North Carolina State—he had taken the 18–8 Wolfpack to the ACC finals again, where this time Duke had won—he still wanted to coach the player he had helped create, his son Pete.

An opportunity arose when Jim Corbett, the athletic director at Louisiana State University, sought to hire Press to coach basketball in the bayou.

"It seemed," said Press, "we were always in debt in those days, some-times starving. At that time I asked the North Carolina State people to pay the bills I had—you know, rent, food, clothing, electricity, that stuff, besides a salary. They turned me down."

That gave Press the impetus to enter into negotiations with Corbett with a what-the-hell attitude. In a face-to-face meeting, Maravich demanded a salary of $15,000 and a five-year contract, never expecting LSU to agree to his terms. But Corbett said "done deal."

Soon after, Les Robinson was sitting with the Maraviches at their home in Raleigh when Bucky Walters, basketball coach at the University of West Virginia, phoned for Pete.

"Pete takes the phone in the other room, and is on the line for five, ten minutes," recalled Robinson. "He comes back. Press says, 'What was that about?' Pete says, 'He wants me to visit.' Press says, 'Visit my ass. You ain't going to West Virginia. Forget that.' And Pete: 'The only way I go to LSU is if I get a car.' Press turns to me and says, 'Listen to the son of a bitch. Car, my ass.'

"Fast forward now—a few months later, Press has moved on to LSU. We're on the phone talking, and Press is claiming to be broke. I say, 'Fifteen thousand a year and you're broke?' He says, 'I got house payments and two car payments and—' 'Two car payments?' I interrupt. He goes: 'Well, yeah. I got that damn Pete a Volks.' But he said it with affection. And you know what? There was never any doubt in my mind that Pete would play for Press. LSU just had to happen."

4

THE PRIORITIES in Baton Rouge, Louisiana, were well established by the time Press Maravich settled into his new job on the LSU campus.

In his office, Press covered the walls with photos of basketball players and coaches, and over his wastebasket he placed a miniature hoop and backboard. But though basketball would be his office motif, the fact was that he and Pete had come to football country.

Autumn Saturday afternoons, when LSU's purple-and-gold-clad football team played, were a grand civic tradition in this industrial city of 165,000, located on the east bank of the Mississippi River, 84 miles northwest of New Orleans. Tiger Stadium—capacity 68,000—regularly sold out for football, its seats jammed with Tiger partisans waving pennants and pom-poms and shouting themselves hoarse for their boys.

Those who hadn't tickets to see the games tuned in on their radios. From small diners on highways where Burma Shave signs teased passing motorists to upscale cocktail lounges downtown, the game was the thing. Local sportswriters liked to say, "There are two sport seasons here—football and spring football."

Although ordinary folks turned out in droves for those bright and noisy autumn Saturdays, they were not the only ones stirred by college football. As far back as the 1930s, when Huey P. Long sat in the governor's mansion, football had cut across class lines. The famed "Kingfish," as the governor was called, was crazy for football, impassioned enough to trot onto the field with LSU teams and even compose a fight song in collaboration with the school's bandmaster.

Once, at halftime of a game against arch rival Tulane, Long was jogging to the LSU locker room when an aide of his reminded him he was obliged to pose for a shot by Paramount News. Snapped Huey: "To hell with 'em. I'm running my team."

During games he would assist the team's trainer and mop the grimy faces of "his boys." For injured LSU players, he suggested his down-home remedies, once concocting a brew whose base was Epsom salt. The ailing player drank it and promptly vomited.

Gubernatorial concern in those years, and for many years to follow, rarely strayed to Dr. Naismith's fine old game. Basketball was seen as a dandyish pursuit not worthy of attention. And indeed, the way it was played at LSU, it was hard to fault the people's choice. Basketball could not approximate football's glories.

Over the years, there had been rare exceptions. The Sparky Wade-led LSU teams of the '30s had been special, but basketball back then was a "waltzing Matilda" compared to the run-and-gun version it would become. Even when Bob Pettit played at LSU, before turning pro, it was not enough to fire up a football-mad populace. Through the years when "Big Blue," as Pettit was known, was at LSU, and even beyond, Tiger football remained center stage. It was no accident. A truly great player like Pettit was rare to LSU basketball, while blue-chip athletes were common enough to LSU football. The school regularly turned out players who went on to star in the pro leagues—men like Steve Van Buren, Jim Taylor, Billy Cannon, Johnny Robinson, Mel Branch, Dennis Gaubatz, Bill Truax, and Jerry Stovall, among others.

Even nondescript talent was raised to mythical proportions in bayou land. One third-string unit in the late 1950s was used defensively to spell the regulars and proceeded with such vigor that it won the name "the Chinese Bandits," plus enormous publicity.

When Corbett hired Press Maravich, he had the radical notion of changing basketball's image at LSU. So taken was he by his notion that he whimsically said after a season in which he'd suffered a heart attack, a gunshot wound, and the Tigers' 6–20 record: "I don't want to be hanged, or shot, or die a natural death. I want to be trampled to death by the crowd trying to get in to see an LSU basketball game."

It seemed a hallucinatory idea at the time because the basketball team was not only a chronic loser at LSU but also was accorded second-class treatment, as the new coach soon enough would discover. Not long after Press Maravich's arrival in Baton Rouge, his assistant coach, Jay McCreary—a holdover from the previous basketball regime—gave him a tour of the campus.

"Jay was taking me all over, showing me this and that," said Press. "But when we went by the John M. Parker Agricultural Center [home court of LSU] he stepped on the accelerator and shut up. It wasn't until later that I found out that we'd have to practice in a high school gym with a short floor because a walking-horse show had rights to our gym until two weeks before the first game. To make matters worse, we'd also be forced to close on the road each year because of a rodeo."

Throughout the Maraviches' tenure at LSU, the team would remain shut out from its home court by these events. But even when the 8,800-seat Parker Center, also known as the "Cow Palace," became available— the wooden basketball court laid over its dirt floor—the arena was no bargain. The scent of horse manure lingered in a facility that for years had gone unheated, obliging the players to practice in sweat clothes and the few fans who showed up to make some hard fashion decisions.

As Bud Johnson, the sports information director at LSU, recalled: "When I first got there in 1958, fans would wear topcoats while in their seats. I wore one once on press row when we played Alabama and it was 22 degrees outside. In those days, the roof leaked frequently and games had to be postponed or the site changed to University High School gym, which was part of a lab school on campus that gave education majors a chance to practice-teach. And *that* gym was not a top-of-the-line high school gym. What got them to heat the place, finally, was our failure to recruit Cotton Nash, who instead went on to become a star at Kentucky. Only the critiquing by Cotton's father motivated the administration to heat the building."

But even with heat flowing through the pipes, the Cow Palace, as well as LSU's basketball program, remained decidedly second rate. "When I went over to LSU as an assistant s-i-d assigned to baseball and basketball, after being at a smalltime school, Southeast Louisiana College in Hammond, I assumed I was going to the big time," said Johnson. "Well, I turn up at basketball practice and what do I see? The head coach at the time, Jay McCreary, is wrapping ankles. No way that's a bigtime program. At Southeast Louisiana, we had a trainer who not only wrapped ankles but taped them."

In the years just preceding the Maraviches' arrival in Baton Rouge, the local papers, the *Morning Advocate* and *State-Times*, thought so little of LSU basketball that they rarely covered road games. On those occasions when athletic director Corbett, a former executive with NBC-TV Sports, persuaded his old employer to televise LSU versus Kentucky at the Cow Palace, fan support was so thin that Corbett and his minions would stack the meager crowd on the side of the arena facing the TV camera so as not to expose the endless empty seats—and the apathy they expressed—to a national audience.

PRESS MARAVICH—ever the realist—saw the indifference he faced as a basketball man and set out to change it. He brought in a pep band and pom-pom girls, gave clinics throughout the Baton Rouge area, and wrote daily newspaper columns on the game. Anything to get people thinking hoops.

Inheriting a team that went 6–20 the previous season, he sought to rebuild Tiger basketball. In past coaching stints, he had expressed a strong distaste for recruiting, abhorring the hypocrisy involved. And that hadn't changed.

"He was not a good recruiter," said Charlie Bryant. "He'd say, 'It's the cancer that kills your spirit. You kiss ass and tell everybody how wonderful they are. Then you bring 'em in and break 'em like wild horses.'"

"As great a coach as he was," said Les Robinson, "he was that bad as a recruiter. He was too honest. He'd bring a recruit through the cafeteria line and go: 'Man, this food is rotten.' He was honest to a fault. He never put on airs. What you saw was what you got."

With LSU's varsity a squad of transparently limited potential—"There are no lofty expectations of the 1966–67 Tiger basketball team," the team's media guide stated—Press recruited with an eye to the future. The future was Peter Press Maravich, his son. By NCAA rules in force then, the Pistol, as a freshman, was not allowed to play varsity ball. But Press believed that once Pete Maravich became eligible, LSU basketball would become a hot ticket. His job while Pete was playing for frosh coach Greg Bernbrock was to surround him with talent that would complement him.

In that quest, he was prepared to become the first SEC basketball coach to recruit black athletes. But the LSU administration was not as liberal. As Bud Johnson recalled: "Press arrived in Baton Rouge in April 1966, and at a press conference he laid out his plan for LSU. One, he wanted to play nationally-ranked teams like UCLA, which eventually we did. Two, he wanted to recruit black athletes, which, while Pete was there, we didn't. Because soon after Press expressed that intention, the president of LSU, Dr. John A. Hunter, said, 'My coach was misquoted.'"

Instead, that year a 6-foot-5 forward, Perry Wallace of Vanderbilt, would become the first black to sign a Southeastern Conference grant-in-aid in basketball.

If Pete was going to dominate the offense, as Press imagined he would, then the players who constituted his supporting cast would have to be comfortable as white-complected role players—a job description that fit two recruits who would come in with the Pistol as freshmen and remain as key components through Maravich's varsity years.

One of them was Jeff Tribbett, a 6-foot, 178-pound guard from Lebanon, Indiana, who was already accustomed to playing second banana. At Lebanon High, Tribbett's role had been to set up teammate Rick Mount, a future college (Purdue) and pro (ABA Indiana Pacers) player with a shooter's perpetual need for the basketball.

Like Tribbett, Rich Hickman, 6-foot, 165 pounds, had a supporting player's mentality. "To be honest," he said, "I was maybe a little better than average at Aliquippa High School. I didn't start until the sixth game of my senior year. But Press was looking for someone who could handle the ball and complement Pete. He wanted to make sure they were guys that would hustle and would stay in school. I was in National Honor Society in high school. An 'A' student. I was probably classified as a gym rat. I'd be out there shoveling snow off the playground to shoot baskets in winters. At the time Press took the job at LSU a lot of the superstars wouldn't have considered LSU. So Press was looking for fundamentally-solid, hustling types. For one skinny kid from Aliquippa, LSU was a pretty big deal."

A willing supporting cast would allow Press his objective of showcasing the unique player his son had become. For Baton Rouge and for those times, Pete Maravich was unlike what folks were used to.

Bud Johnson: "That summer [1966] Press was teaching a basketball theory course here for teachers working on their Masters degree. Pete came down for his first look at Baton Rouge. Press had him put on ball-handling drills for these graduate students, most of them high school football coaches. Well, you could tell he was very gifted, a player with skills well beyond his peer group. You knew he'd be a star. But for these coaches, it didn't register. They thought of him as a Globetrotter. They couldn't project what they saw—how he could fit into an offensive scheme . . . the impact he would have. You'd have thought there would have been an excitement. But to these guys he was just a curiosity."

Ralph Jukkola, 6-foot-3, 190-pound sophomore forward on the LSU varsity: "Late that summer, several of us returning varsity players—Rusty Bergman, Chuck Legler, Dave Ramsden and I—went up to the gym. We walk in—the frosh were in early for orientation and were playing. We're trying to figure out which one is Pete. He made a couple of moves—we knew. Once you played with him, you found out pretty quick he had moves none of us had seen. I was from a high school program—no fancy stuff. You sat on the bench if you threw a behind-the-back pass. My coach senior year would say, 'If you want to be fancy, play church league.' To go from that to Pete was like night and day. He was so fluid in his movement. He'd come down and throw the behind-the-back pass, dribble through the legs. Seemed like a hot dog until you played with him. Then you realized it was just the way he played. He did things on the court I hadn't seen anybody do that easy, that smooth."

Rusty Bergman, 6-foot-2, 170-pound sophomore on the LSU varsity: "I was totally amazed. He'd come down on a three-on-two fast break and would be in the middle, a teammate on each wing. Without premeditating, he'd react to what the defense would do. Sometimes he'd act like he was going to hit the ball off the dribble to the wing with one hand and instead fake it and slap it with the other hand. Other times he'd go through his legs, behind his back, or make the no-look pass for the easy layup. He had ten different ways to make the play. Another thing: he could take the ball to one side of the court, with defenders on him, and anticipate where teammates would be and throw blind to the open man. It takes skills and unbelievable know-how to do that."

Bear in mind that this was an era when the coach was king, a time when his was the last word on how the game was played. Like Jukkola's coach, most of these men preferred a straitlaced approach, viewing any curlicues in a player's game as risky business. Coaches then—and now, for that matter—viewed any turnover as a personal affront, more so if it was brought on by an attempt to be "fancy." Coaches were constitutionally wired to control, as best they could, what transpired on the hardwood. Players indulging the trickster's maneuver would find that any misfire on such a move was cause for being summarily benched. That was enough to repress the freewheeler in most players.

Pete Maravich—another story. He had had caution weaned out of him. The drills that his father had created had been meant to give a frail boy the confidence to conquer bigger and better bodies. In his willingness to work long, long hours to be more dexterous than his peers with the dribble and every sort of pass, Pete had developed into a player with a showman's impulse. What else to do with all the flourishes he had mastered?

It was his good fortune that in a basketball era when caution ruled, he would be coached by his father, the very man who had encouraged the heretic notion that a player might entertain even as he whupped his defender regularly as clockwork over the course of a game.

The advent of a free-spirited Maravich at LSU would occur on the cusp of a cultural revolution that encouraged more permissive behavior—the drugs, sex, and rock and roll of the Pistol's generation. Against that emphasis on self-expression, in 1966 a coach stood as a sentinel of an older, more conservative order. In a society growing more divisive over the Vietnam conflict, a coach's greatest issue was whether or not to allow his players to have mustaches or wear their hair long.

As for the game itself, it remained largely untouched by the socio-political spasms occurring outside the arena. For a coach, less continued to be more—and go stick that between-the-legs dribble where the sun doesn't shine. Basketball remained a game played with safety belt secured.

Indeed, it was in these late '60s that the NCAA, in its all-knowing wisdom, clamped down on the slam dunk, legislating it into a violation. The rule was widely construed as being aimed at UCLA's Lew Alcindor—the future Kareem Abdul-Jabbar—and other black athletes possessed of inordinate jumping ability. But it fed into the chaos of a period of cultural divisiveness.

All of which made Pete Maravich a player far in advance of his time, though as an LSU freshman—and in an era before the electronic highway brought us nightly highlights of every rising star—he would remain pretty much a bayou secret at first. But basketball insiders were hip to Pistol Pete quickly enough, as word of his exploits spread. His scoring binges against opposition frosh surprised even those who had worked out with him regularly in the Gym Armory—the on-campus high school court—in preseason sessions that on Saturdays after LSU football games would find Pete and pals like Hickman and Tribbett playing until two in the morning.

Even Tribbett, who had never seen a passer as spectacular as Maravich, would admit he hadn't imagined that Pete would dominate the way he did once the freshman season got under way. But from his first game, when he scored 50 points against Southeastern with 14 rebounds and 11 assists, Maravich, now weighing 162 pounds, was a marquee attraction, his flair for the game entrancing fans who had never given hoops attention in the past.

When the Pistol suited up—here scoring 43 against Ole Miss, 44 against Auburn, 50 against Loyola, 57 against Auburn, and doing it with more pizzazz than anybody since Bob Cousy—the locals couldn't resist. In fact, a curious situation developed during that '66–67 season at the Cow Palace. The stands would fill up to near capacity for the 5:30 P.M. preliminary game, featuring Pete's freshman team, all of them with their hair growing back on heads that had been shaved for ROTC. Sometimes even Louisiana Governor John J. McKeithen would be in attendance. Then, when the final buzzer sounded, the crowd of, say, 8,000 would shrink radically so that the varsity would trot onto the court and perform layup drills before a ghost assemblage of 3,000 to 4,000 diehards.

Not a shock, really. As Pete's freshman team won game after game, Press' varsity was suffering through a nightmarish 3–23 season. Losing was not easy for the coach. As highly intense about the game as ever, Press saw his wrinkles grow deeper, his crew-cut hair turn gray. He reverted to chewing Five Brothers pipe tobacco during practice, depositing the by-product into a paper cup. On game nights he was back to his bland diet of skimmed milk and cereal. And during that long season he took to twisting and gnawing on a rolled-up towel, gulping tranquilizers at halftime or maybe a few shots of antacid to ease that recurring ulcer.

As Jukkola put it, "The longer the season went, the worse it became."

Not for Pete. By January 1967, as *Sports Illustrated* planned a spread on the nation's top freshman players, a stringer fired off this memo to the magazine's editors:

Pete Maravich of LSU most definitely should be included among top freshmen. Not only for his ability but also because of the colorful story behind him. A six-foot-five guard who can shoot from all-over, the skinny, 165-pounder, is averaging 38.5 points per game and has LSU fans as excited about basketball as Jimmy [sic] Cannon had them about football. The LSU freshmen are undefeated in ten games. . . . The boy shoots from outside extremely well and is an outstanding ballhandler.

The boy was also a joy to watch as he sped along the court with his long, limber strides, the basketball moving like a yo-yo off his fingertips. As the defender crouched, trying to guess what next, Pete would stare him in the eye, baiting him with the high dribble before swinging the ball behind his back to elude the man overplaying him, or pushing it out in front of him and just beyond the reach of a foe trying to double up. Then down the lane he'd go, springing into the air as the big men peeled off to block his way.

Airborne, he was capable of improvising his way through traffic to get the ball to the basket, twisting his body to avoid the leaping defenders and even shifting the ball from one hand to the other while up there. Or, with no hint of his intent, he might look straight ahead and send the ball careening east or west through a thicket of arms to a teammate standing free and clear under the basket, or out on the perimeter for an open jump shot.

"As the season went on," said Tribbett, "we slowly learned what he was going to do. It got so you could anticipate his moves by watching for a head fake here, a dip of the shoulder there. Just by watching for these movements, you knew whether to expect a behind-the-back or over-the-shoulder pass. Of course, every now and then he'd do something different and still surprise you."

Added Hickman: "There was no way you could relax on the court when Pete Maravich had the ball. You had to expect anything at any time. He was constantly working to improve his weaknesses and trying to learn different things. He was never satisfied."

Nor was Press. He was growing increasingly frustrated as the varsity's losses piled up. The only solace he could find was the excellence that Pete and his frosh teammates were showing. A portent, he hoped, of LSU teams to come. In practices, he often had the varsity scrimmage the freshmen, taking these occasions to talk up the first-year squad. "The frosh are doing better," Press would announce as the players went up and down the floor, a tack that generally raised the fever of these games.

As Hickman recalled: "There were plenty of busted-up lips, puffed-up eyes from those scrimmages. The frosh team took it upon ourselves that we were going to start people talking about something other than football."

MEANWHILE, the varsity season wound down like the Bataan Death March—a passage in time to be endured but never to be forgotten. Rusty Bergman said, "Press demanded a lot. And we were not able to do everything he wanted us to do. He'd get mad at the players and the players got mad at him. Anytime there's that many losses, it's difficult for everybody. I can remember one player talking back—Wayne Tipton, a starting forward and a senior. It was a situation where Wayne had sprained his ankle against Vanderbilt. The next game—and our last of the season—was against Tennessee, which was Wayne's hometown. A sign in the arena read, 'Go Vols [nickname of Tennessee]! Go Tipton!' He got to play very sparingly because of his sprained ankle. It did not set well with Wayne. A lot of people had been there to see him. So . . . Wayne went off on the coach and told him how wrong he was. Coach Maravich ignored it. He would not get into a verbal confrontation. It shocked me because rarely did you ever talk back to the coach. Especially Coach Maravich. 'Cause when he got mad, his facial expressions scared hell out of you. He looked mean enough to rip your head off."

For Pete, Tennessee was no happy experience, either. The LSU frosh, undefeated in 17 contests, lost the final game of the season to the Tennessee frosh, 75–74, when Pete blew the second of two free throws in the final seconds.

"After the game," Press recalled, "I became worried. I couldn't find

Pete. Then someone told me that he had left the gym on his own and had walked two miles back to the hotel. . . . Guess I should have known. When I was playing for Aliquippa High and we got our butts kicked by Rochester, I walked about 12 miles back to town."

Teammate Hickman said, "We were worried too. Pete had never disappeared like that before. Later, we learned that it was just part of his personality. When we lost, you just left him alone. He'd just go to his room, lock the door, and get into bed. And that was it."

That was it for the Pistol's freshman year. In spite of a Tennessee game that had marred an otherwise unblemished season, Maravich had emerged as an offensive force unlike any in LSU history. In 17 games— he had missed one because of illness—Pete had averaged 43.6 ppg, 10.4 rebounds, and 6.9 assists a game. In one game, against Mississippi Southern, he had left the game in the first half so that nine stitches could be applied to a cut above his eye. Yet he had returned to score 42 points. In a football-mad setting, the Pistol's flair with the basketball was so radically different from what folks there were used to that it altered their consciousness. Suddenly, basketball mattered, too.

Even as Maravich was drawing capacity crowds to the Cow Palace, sporting goods stores in Baton Rouge and surrounding burgs had a run on backyard hoops and basketballs. Drive within a radius of 50 miles of the LSU campus, and now you saw schoolboys trying the behind-the-back dribble in their driveways, just as young Pete had when he was growing up. And by now his reputation had spread beyond the mostly white LSU community and the subdivisions in which it lived. After Carl Stewart, coach of all-black McKinley High School, caught a glimpse of the Pistol's freewheeling game, he said: "My God, he's one of us."

Still, what reputation Maravich had was mostly limited to the Baton Rouge area. There was no ESPN SportsCenter, no Fox Sports Net, no Internet back then to spread word of this unconventional player. The media world was a far smaller place, enabling the freshman Maravich to walk among his fellow beings largely unrecognized outside of the Baton Rouge area. That anonymity worked to his advantage when Tribbett and he took their '67 spring break in Fort Lauderdale, Florida.

"My aunt and uncle lived there," said Tribbett, "so we stayed with them. Neither one of us had two nickels to rub together. And because Pete's reputation hadn't spread yet, we were able to go down to the outdoor basketball courts by the Yankee Clipper Hotel, down on the beach and not be recognized. We'd go down there and make a few dollars playing ball for beer money. Two on two. Bait somebody. Sometimes we'd keep it close. Other times we'd just want to beat 'em. We'd win $10, $20 and go somewhere to drink."

That summer Pete climbed into his tan Volks—the one Press had reluctantly bought him—and traveled to basketball clinics around the country, a postseason tradition that would last his lifetime. For Pete it was more than a job—it was part of his upbringing, a chance to be among basketball men, a chance to walk and talk the game. Even at the camps and clinics, he relished the opportunity to show what he could do with the basketball. Where once he had been happy to do it for free, now as Pistol Pete, college hot shot, he commanded a price. As Dave Cowens—a future Boston Celtic great—recalled: "The first time I met him was at Lefty Driesell's camp [at Davidson College]. We were the same age, working. Charlie Scott was there. Mike Maloy. We all were working in the 110-degree heat in North Carolina for maybe $35 a week that Lefty was paying us through his benevolence. Everyone . . . except for Pete. Every night he was giving a lecture. He was doing all these tricks with the ball. Spinning it on a finger, along his arm, across his back. Catching it different ways. He was getting $100 a lecture, about $1,800 for the camp.

"I remember I left that camp and went home and started working on all those tricks. Worked the rest of the summer. I figured that if he was getting that kind of money for spinning the ball, I'd spin the ball, too. Never got one of those speaking deals, but whatever success I had as a ballhandler I probably owe to that summer."

Back on campus that fall, Maravich was now hyped as the man who could rescue LSU's basketball program. In its preseason survey of the SEC, *Sports Illustrated* noted: "LSU should get out of the cellar this year, chiefly because Press Maravich will have his son on the varsity. Pete hit 44 points a game as a freshman guard."

Attention would be paid. Whereas the varsity in the past couldn't excite the locals, that changed now that Pete was on hand. Before Maravich, Tiger basketball rarely had even 100 season-ticket holders. But as the Pistol's sophomore year approached, LSU now could boast 4,000 season-ticket patrons, a figure that would have gone higher except for the need to allot the rest to students whose fees provided for their attending games for free.

All of those spectators, and even Maravich's teammates, wondered whether the Pistol could dominate against seasoned opposition as he had against frosh defenders. One man who had no doubts was Doug Moe, one of the American Basketball Association's high scorers with the New Orleans Buccaneers. Moe had caught Maravich in action at a basketball camp over the summer and later told a reporter: "He's as good as any basketball player I've ever seen. I think sometimes he might handle the ball too much, but he's a fantastic passer with an uncanny knack of being able to get off a shot in any position.

"Some people say he shoots too much, but you've got to take into consideration the men he's playing with. I would definitely have to put him in a class with Oscar Robertson when Oscar was a sophomore.

"I bet a teammate of mine on the Bucs [Leland Mitchell of Mississippi State] that Pete will average 35 points in the SEC. He says, 'No chance.' He says the defense in the SEC will toughen up on him. I know Leland talks from experience from his playing days at Mississippi State. But I played against Maravich—and I'll take my chances."

Press tried to counter unreasonable expectations, telling newsmen: "Naturally, we're excited about playing to capacity crowds. That always brings out the best in good athletes. But I hope our fans won't expect too much of the team this year. We're the youngest team in the Southeastern Conference and have the least depth. There is a big difference between freshman basketball and major-college basketball."

With that caveat served up, Press announced that he would team Pete with three sophomores—Hickman, Tribbett, and 6-foot-8, 220-pound center Randy Lamont—and a smallish junior forward, Jukkola. The Tigers' three-guard offense would feature a go-go pace and Pistol Pete firing at will.

Firing and hitting. From the season's opener, against Tampa, Maravich was the show. He hit 48 points on 20 of 50 field goal attempts and eight of nine free throws as the Tigers beat Tampa 97–81 before 7,500 spectators in the Cow Palace. That was a pretty fair transition to varsity ball, and Maravich proved able to sustain that kind of offensive output through the season.

"It's a funny thing," said Tribbett, "but even when Pete was averaging 43 as a freshman, I didn't realize he was going to be that good. I just didn't think anyone could score like that in the big time."

Pistol scored: 42 in the next game against Texas, 51 against Loyola, 42 against Wisconsin, and 42 again against Florida State. He did more than score, though. He threw passes calculated to excite crowds. Whether the pass was behind the back, over the shoulder, bounced between a defender's legs, or simply thrown through a maze of arms, it was worth seeing. Nothing like this had ever happened at LSU, or anywhere else, for that matter.

LSU team manager David Tate recalled a move that the Pistol executed against a powerful Kentucky team. When a Wildcat defender tried to foil Maravich's between-the-legs, no-look pass to a teammate on his left by jumping into the passing lane, Pete improvised.

"As the Kentucky player stepped over," said Tate, "Pete caught the ball with his left hand and shovel-passed it to a guy on the right for the layup. The crowd went crazy."

Very quickly opponents abandoned straight-up defenses and began playing Maravich with variations of the box-and-one defense. Press and his assistant, Jay McCreary, would size up the particulars of the defense — be it box-and-one, diamond-and-one, or triangle-and-two — call time out and diagram how to attack the latest get-Maravich strategy.

"All the plays we had were not set up for these defenses," said Jukkola. "So most of the offenses would be drawn up after the first time-out and after the coaches had seen what kind of gimmick defense the other team was playing."

Few had expected Maravich to perform at this level. Nine games into the season, he was averaging better than 46 points a game and threatening to break the Division I single-season scoring average of 41.6 ppg set by Frank Selvy of Furman in 1953–54.

Even Tiger sports information director Bud Johnson had not anticipated that Maravich would be able to transform a perpetual loser into an
SEC upstart so quickly. In the preseason forecast in the team's media
guide, Johnson had written: "Although the Tigers are expected to lose
more than they win in 1967–68, the presence of fabulous sophomore
Pete Maravich should not only increase home attendance but add an
exciting explosive element to LSU basketball."

Well, it turned out that Maravich's fireworks and LSU victories were
not mutually exclusive. Even though the Pistol was hoisting up 40, 50
shots a game, the team was winning. And although that equation defied
conventional notions about teams dominated by one man, the results
were plain enough — seven victories in LSU's first nine games.

All of that was enough to prompt the local papers — the *Morning Advocate* and the *State-Times* — to revise policy and begin sending their
basketball-beat men on the road with the team, providing one of them,
Sam King, with an up-close look at the longstanding volatile relationship between Pete and Press.

"The first SEC game I went on the road for was LSU-Florida," said
King. "By this time, most teams were playing Pete with the box-and-one
defense. That night, as the team called time-out to discuss how to handle what Florida was doing, I walked down to the court to shoot a picture for the paper. Just in time to hear Pete tell Press, 'Let's try this . . .'
and for Press to slap him in the face and say, 'Shut up. I'm running this
fucking team. . . .' Press was always big on 'fuck.'

"The next night, the team was practicing in Athens, Georgia. Press
was running the team through a play that had four, five picks and Pete
wasn't throwing the ball to the right guy. Press tells him on one run-
through, 'Throw the fucking ball, will ya?' Pete got angry and threw the
ball . . . to the top row of the arena.

"Some time later, there was a game in which Pete got hit with a technical at the end of the game. A technical that cost the team the game.
We fly back to Baton Rouge in one of those old DC-7s. On this plane
was a little wall, separating the front from the back of the plane. Up
front sat Jay McCreary, myself, Pete and Press. And during the whole

flight not one word was spoken. Both Pete and Press had the red-ass about the game. Not a word. As we approach New Orleans, Pete finally says, 'Listen, about that technical . . .' Press tells him, 'Keep your fuckin' mouth shut.' They begin shoving each other until Jay stepped in between them."

For father and son it was nothing new. Theirs was a relationship that, from the time Pete was a junior high school phenom, could turn combative in the blink of an eye. At bottom, they shared a deep and abiding love for each other, but in their quest for basketball excellence each's headstrong nature made temper outbursts inevitable. Eventually LSU players grew used to the sometimes fractious moments between their star and their coach.

"I was brought up—no backtalk to the coach," said Jukkola. "Being as it was his dad, Pete got away with a little more. After a while, we realized: 'This is the way it is.' At first it probably shocked me a little bit. I was never in a program where you could yell or talk back to the coach."

Those tumults aside, Press couldn't have been more pleased with his son's play. Pete, a mere sophomore, was dominating ballgames. LSU fans saw him break Pettit's single-game SEC scoring record of 57 points when he netted 58 points against Mississippi State on December 22, 1967. Maravich proved just as effective before hostile crowds. Two weeks later, on January 8, in front of 14,000 Georgia fans, Maravich scored 17 of LSU's final 24 points, including two foul shots he sank in the last four seconds to ice a 79–76 Tiger victory.

He managed this in spite of having to work against still another box-and-one. Georgia assigned burly forward Ray Jeffords to hound the Pistol's every step. And when Jeffords drew four personal fouls, the Bulldogs shifted Dick McIntosh, a scrappy 5-foot-8 guard, to Maravich.

Maravich eventually fouled out both men, and abused each in the process, posting up the smaller McIntosh and against Jeffords firing up long-range jumpers or driving past him, finishing with 42 points.

Although Maravich's scoring would have been enough to create a stir, he provided far more for the spectator than points per game. In an era of buttoned-up basketball, the Pistol played with a flair that crowds found irresistible. Maravich knew that his "blind" passes and trick moves turned on the fans, and he relished their delighted reactions. He had a showman's love of provoking.

Even the team's warmup drills played to that penchant for stylish excitement. Rather than assay staid layup lines, LSU embellished the format by having Pistol stand at the foul line and, as the LSU band played "Sweet Georgia Brown," funnel the ball to cutting teammates with passes improvised on the spur of the moment, bounced through his legs, punched with a fist, or even headbutted, soccer style.

"Man, when that music starts I go *crazy!*" Maravich told a writer. "I move that ball around my body so fast that sometimes even I don't know where it is. I mean I *move!* . . . And the crowd *loves* it."

As a ballplayer the Pistol was different, and it added to his intrigue. To begin with, he was not built like your classic sinewy star. He remained, at 6-foot-5, thin enough to bring out the comedic wit in every sports columnist.

Wrote the *Atlanta Journal's* Jim Minter after seeing Maravich: "From the neck up, Pete looks like first clarinet in the school band. From the neck down, he's thin as one of those new extra long filter cigarettes."

Another columnist, Bob Collins, noted: "Put him in front of a crowd and I'll give odds that more people would lead him to an oxygen tent than would throw him a basketball. His shoulders slope almost to his hips—which is a bad thing because it calls attention to his hips. This is a bad thing mainly because he doesn't have any hips."

Nor did Maravich possess the classic square-jawed crew-cut look of that era's star athletes. He was no Gil Thorpe clone but rather a more waifish figure with his Beatles-style hair and large saucer eyes that gave him the look of one of those soulful figures in the paintings of the artist Walter Keane, so popular at the time.

Then there were the trademark floppy socks. Whereas his teammates wore tight-fitting purple-and-white hose that stayed up over the calf, Maravich's "lucky" gray socks drooped around his ankles. He'd heisted them from the North Carolina State athletic department when Press was coaching there and worn them in high school games. After each game, he would wash and dry them in his room. Later, when asked if they had special significance, he'd wink and just say they were comfortable, that was all.

Maravich was at ease being, as newsmen said of New York Jets quarterback Joe Namath, show business. Namath—"Broadway Joe" to the tabloids—was a man after Maravich's heart. "Namath—this is a guy that goes his own way," said Maravich. "Maybe he is a little different. But didn't the Beatles look different to us when they first showed up? Just because he showed up with the hair and the Fu Manchu mustache is no reason to knock him. We're all different, aren't we?"

Even the basic jump shot was different when Pistol executed it. Often he looked off balance or even ungainly in the air. His legs drifted in opposite directions or hung limply. They didn't stay tucked together, and there was no kick of the heels upon release. The ball would spin sideways because he shot off the side of his left hand.

"I've always shot that way," he said. "I know the ball doesn't spin right, but the most important thing for me is to be a two-eyed shooter. You've got to have two eyes on the basket for depth perception. My release isn't as high as Oscar's [Robertson] or Jerry's [West], so I put my left hand to the side to get it out of the way."

The difference in Maravich's case proved appealing to the media. By January, *Time* magazine was breathless in its praise of Maravich:

Some players are best close in, with driving lay-ups, looping hook shots and little tap-ins; others are long-distance gunners. Maravich has the feathery touch and fluid coordination to do it all. Davidson Coach Lefty Driesell remembers one practice session when Pete demonstrated one-handed push shots. "He got out about two feet past the top of the circle—21 feet from the basket—and drilled in 40 straight. I never saw anything like it."

That was often the reaction of SEC fans to Maravich. Though they baited him from the sidelines in pregame warmups, by the time they left the arena, they were as likely to be shaking their heads in wonder at what Maravich had wrought. Once when opposition fans heckled him during pregame warmups, Maravich seduced them by throwing behind-the-back passes into the stands to one heckler after another, all the while smiling his boyish smile.

It was pure showtime—a celebration of his dazzle and the sheer joy of improvising that the hardy pioneers of the game had never dreamed of. It took considerable nerve at that point in the game's evolution to throw fancy passes or use a slick dribble. Mess up, and you looked the fool. But Maravich didn't care. When he was on the court, the night belonged to him.

Pat Williams, presently the general manager of the NBA's Orlando Magic, was a front office executive with the Philadelphia Phillies' Spartanburg, South Carolina, team in the Western Carolinas League that year.

"I was," said Williams, "27 years old. LSU came to Georgia. A couple of sportswriters who were going to cover the game invited me to drive along. Most nights in sports run together. This one was memorable. A packed rock 'n' rolling crowd. Pete with his floppy hair. Total domination. It was a happening. I drove home that night, electrified by the scene. It was like the Beatles. People shrieking and gasping. What it became for those three years when Pete came to town, it was like the circus or Garth Brooks or Michael [Jordan]. So from Starksville, Mississippi, to Lexington, Kentucky, the night Pete comes to town was an event."

In Baton Rouge—that football-mad city—it was that way, too. Maravich brought the nouveau basketball crowd out. Attendance in excess of 8,000 was routine now, and on January 29, 1968, when Vanderbilt came to the Cow Palace, the fire marshals allowed 9,000 fans to be shoehorned into the arena, the biggest crowd of the year.

Governor McKeithen continued to show up, as did ex-Governor Jimmie Davis, jazz trumpeter Al Hirt, actor James Drury, heart-transplant specialist Dr. Denton Cooley, Kansas City Chiefs coach Hank Stram, and Richard Katz's friend the Iceman. Katz, a student at LSU who got to know Maravich years later while a New Orleans Jazz season-ticket holder, had a pal who was desperate to see the Pistol play at the Cow Palace but lacked a ticket.

"So what he did," said Katz, "was he went and bought a big block of ice, and walked up to the gate with it on his shoulder, saying, 'The Iceman cometh, the Iceman cometh.' The student ticket-taker, thinking he was part of the concession, let him pass by. The guy then dropped the ice and ran, disappearing into the crowd."

On teams dominated by one player—and Maravich certainly was such a figure—the potential for dissension was ever present. At LSU, though, the griping was minimal, the result of a willingness by the Pistol's teammates to accept their subservient roles and acknowledge that the likeliest chance for victory required Peter Maravich to shoot 40 to 50 times a game.

Maravich's teammates bought into the notion, and, though the Pistol had license to shoot that few players were granted, it did not sour the others on the game. They regarded Maravich as worthy of his on-court privileges—Pete even had *his* ball during pregame warmups—and they liked his outgoing manner away from the court, too.

Rich Hickman: "If you saw one of us, you saw four or five of us. We went everywhere together."

Jeff Tribbett: "Pete tried to be one of the guys."

Rusty Bergman: "He went out of his way to be one of the guys. He wanted to be liked. Off the court, he hung out with everybody else."

Ralph Jukkola: "We were like a big family. We hung out at the dorms together—sit around and chit chat, do practical jokes—shaving-cream fights or messing up guys' beds before bedcheck . . ."

Hickman: "One time we put some dead shrimps in the hubcaps of a buddy's car. Boy, did that ever smell."

Bergman: "Pete'd tease guys like everybody else. If you couldn't take teasing, you were in trouble. Because everybody was teased to the hilt."

Sam King: "When LSU played Florida, we'd fly to Jacksonville and rent three cars to get to Gainesville. Press, Jay McCreary and I would drive. On the way to Gainesville this one time, Pete says to me, 'Pull up to Jay's car. I got something to tell him.' So I pulled up and . . . wouldn't you know it . . . Pete mooned him."

Jukkola: "If you were going anywhere, you all went out and partied at the same place, or over people's apartments, at bars."

Bergman: "LSU was a party school. Pete and all of us had a tendency to want to be a hero on the field and James Bond off it."

Pete Maravich to writer Furman Bisher: "During the season it's strictly basketball, but once the season's over . . . I let it roll. Fun and games all the way! Believe that. I'd like Pete Maravich to have a good image, but I'm not going to be in a dorm 12 months a year playing Pete Maravich. Everyone on this team likes to party, put that in there."

Jukkola: "In looking back, part of it was—if Pete was with us and something happened we were all safe. . . . I remember that one time some of the varsity guys missed curfew and Press was so mad he was going to kick 'em off the team. Until the associate coach told him: 'Hey, Pete was with 'em.' Instead, Press ended up running their tails off in practice."

Hickman: "We had recruits—high school all-stars—come in. We'd talk about Pete and how it was. And lots of them couldn't take that one person was getting the majority of press. It didn't bother me. It didn't bother most of us. It was an opportunity to get a college education. To travel."

Bergman: "We were just a bunch of average or below-average players playing with a great all-American. Rightfully so, any coach would have tried to run the offense for him."

Tribbett: "There wasn't a lot of bitching. You didn't hear, 'He's getting too many points.'"

In fact, he was scoring more points than any other Division I player in the nation. At Alabama on February 17, in the final seconds of the game, Jukkola stole the ball under the LSU basket and, whipping his outlet pass to Maravich at midcourt, he hollered, "Shoot, shoot."

Pete stumbled forward and shot a long two-hander that went in as the final buzzer sounded. The basket gave the Pistol 59 points, his highest-scoring game of the season, a total that upped his earlier mark of 58 as the most points scored in a single SEC game. No surprise that in Baton Rouge novelty shops a wooden figure of a basketball player wearing jersey number 23—the Pistol's number—had begun to outsell those figures representing LSU football players.

As the season wound down, Maravich continued on his record-breaking pace: 34 points against Mississippi State, 55 against Tulane, 40 against Ole Miss. In 26 games, he ended up averaging 43.8 ppg while shooting .422 from the field and .810 from the foul line. That made him the nation's leading scorer, well ahead of another sophomore, Calvin Murphy, a future NBA star who, playing for Niagara, averaged 38.2 ppg. The Pistol's 43.8 ppg also smashed Selvy's per-game scoring record.

It was a dream season. Because not only had Maravich gained individual recognition, but also he had delivered LSU a winner: The team finished with a 14–12 record, its first winning season since 1961–62. The Pistol was named to various wire service All-American teams and was the only sophomore to be selected by the United States Basketball Coaches Association to its All-America squad of Wes Unseld, Elvin Hayes, Don May, and Lew Alcindor (Kareem Abdul-Jabbar).

In the postseason, more honors followed when Maravich—playing in spite of a painful groin muscle pull—was given the Star of Stars award in the nationally televised East-West college all-star game before 14,500 fans in Indianapolis' Hinkle Fieldhouse. The Pistol hit 8 of 14 shots for 16 points and thrilled the crowd with his sensational passing in a losing effort. Yet in a curious reaction to his award selection, the coach of Maravich's West team, John Bach of Penn State, seemed to question the wisdom of the voters, suggesting that the East's Rick Mount—who had scored 24 points—deserved the award more than Maravich: "I think they took the balloting a little too early. Pete did a great job, in fact both of them did, but it was Mount who killed us."

Regardless, the season was over, leaving Maravich more time for the party life. It was an opportunity he grasped with a gusto that sometimes exceeded reasonable limits, as this stringer's report to a national sports magazine shows:

Although basketball is a far way off, All-America Pete Maravich provided some July 4 fireworks in Baton Rouge. Home between summer clinics, Maravich was out celebrating with brother Ronnie, who received his army discharge after a year's duty in Vietnam. Police chief E. O. Bauer

said Pete posted bond on counts of driving while intoxicated and failure
to maintain control of his car after running into the stalled automobile of
a Baton Rouge teenager. Shortly afterward, Maravich was hauled back to
police headquarters. Bauer said an automatic contempt of court citation
had been issued against him for failure to appear at a court hearing on a
charge of running a stop sign. This offense took place during the basketball season.

Unmentioned was the fact that the wrecked car was not Pete's own
Volks but rather the new navy-blue two-door Plymouth GTX that he
had borrowed—special for the occasion—from Press. Press went ballis-
tic when he saw the mangled car the next morning but calmed somewhat when Pete told him that he was the victim of "an innocent
accident that could have happened to anyone."

Of course, that was whitewashing the truth—and by plenty. Pete had
been drunk, and not for the first or last time. Earlier that year, he had
been part of a rowdy, boozed-up group of LSU athletes who had de-
stroyed the wall of a local tavern on a whim. Though the incident was
hushed after Press assured the proprietor that the boys would resurrect
his wall—which they did—it did not spell the end of Pete's misadven-
tures in night life. He had developed a taste for alcohol that would not
be allayed by Press' stern lectures on a role model's responsibilities.

That summer, Pete would ignore another warning of Press'—that his
chance of making the 1968 U.S. Olympic basketball team would likely
run afoul of the team's head coach, Henry Iba, who was a proponent of a
conservatively grounded approach to basketball. Hoops in a straitjacket.

The Pistol—buoyed by a season of heroics—saw himself as invincible
and headed for Albuquerque, New Mexico, where the tryouts were to be
held. There, the 88 players were divided into 8 teams of 11 and would play
a round-robin series of games. Pete ended up on a squad coached by an Iba
assistant, John Bach, the same man who had questioned Maravich's Star
of Stars award at the East-West all-star game earlier in the year.

Bach, it was clear, was no fan of the Pistol's style, and Maravich spent
more time on the bench than he could abide. As another Olympic team

candidate, Bill Hosket of Ohio State, recalled: "Pete didn't start one day, and somehow Bach and he had words. Well, I'm watching from the stands—I'd never seen Pete live. He was just hearsay to me. Back then, there was no ESPN or anything like that.

"Anyway, Pete finally comes off the bench, and into the game. He's upset by the fact he hadn't started and he's going to show people he's a different style of player. Wearing those droopy socks, he comes across half-court and shoots a two-hand set from half-court. It hits off the backboard, Pete gets the rebound and shoots a jumper that circles the rim three times and spins out. Well, everybody mistimed it. The ball landed on the floor. Everybody went for it. Pete comes up with it, he takes two dribbles toward the right corner, as if he's going to re-set the offense. But instead of doing that, with his back to the basket he flips the ball over his head and it goes in. In my first five seconds of seeing him play live, he's one-for-three with two rebounds. Pretty amazing."

Although Hosket would make the team, Maravich would not. Neither did two other sophomore aspirants: Calvin Murphy and Rick Mount. But then again Rick Barry had been cut in 1964, and John Havlicek had suffered the same fate in 1960.

"Henry Iba," said Hosket, "was looking for guys 180 degrees from Pete's style.

Said Bud Johnson: "As far as I'm concerned, it was one of the first times that an athlete, by his dress and attitude, actually flaunted the establishment. In that way, Pete was ahead of his time. John Bach was a meticulous, well-dressed man who couldn't handle him. Pete became temperamental, was late for practice sessions. Press had warned him it was all politics, but he didn't listen."

SUCCESS so early on as a collegian had its price.

As Maravich began his junior year at LSU, he was now a target for every physically inclined defender, not to mention the cheap-shot artists who elbowed, pushed, and prodded him.

As if the box-and-one, and its variations, were not challenge enough for the 192-pound Pistol, he now had to contend with the endless rough stuff, calculated in many instances to make him lose his focus.

The pressure was compounded by the premeditated antics of the crowds he faced on the road. At Ole Miss, the courtside students chanted: "Maravich, Maravich, you're a son of a bitch." At Mississippi State, the fans rang cowbells and fired the flashbulbs on their cameras when Maravich shot free throws.

Yet for all the provocations, Maravich was Maravich, scoring points in bunches— 52 points in the season's opener against Loyola, 38 against Clemson, 55 against Tulane in double overtime, 45 against Florida in overtime. Once again, he flourished in the spotlight, even as his growing fame stiffened the resolve of SEC opponents like John Mengelt of Auburn, Neal Walk of Florida, Dan Issel, Mike Pratt, and Larry Steele of Kentucky, and Herb White of Georgia—all future pros.

When the 4–1 Tigers turned up in Oklahoma City for the All-College Tournament during the Christmas holidays, Wyoming guard Harry Hall—regarded as a defensive whiz—boasted he would "jam the Pistol" and hold him to no more than seven points. No man or beast had kept Maravich under double figures as a collegian.

But as a snowstorm raged through the streets of Oklahoma City, Hall looked as though he might be equal to his boast. Over the first five minutes of the game, Maravich did not score. But just when Hall seemed about to make his reputation, the Pistol busted him, going on a first-half tear in which he hit 10 of 16 shots from the floor and nine free throws for 29 points.

Midway through the second half, Maravich fouled out Hall and left him for the idle boaster he was. Then, when Wyoming drew to within a point of LSU at 70–69 with five minutes remaining, he hit crucial basket after basket, many of them acrobatic drives that left the locals raised on Henry Iba's stodgy game wide-eyed. Maravich finished with 45 points in an 84–78 LSU victory that exposed brother Hall as a false prophet.

"He jammed me, all right," Maravich said afterward, grinning. "I went for 45 and fouled him out just after the half. Now that was just stupid of him, saying something like that. If I've got to stick the ball in my pants and jump through the hoop myself to win, I'll do it."

In the Tigers' next tournament game, against Oklahoma City, Maravich hit 19 of 36 from the floor and scored 40 points in a 101–85 victory that sent LSU into the championship game against an unbeaten Duquesne squad featuring 6-foot-10 twins Garry and Barry Nelson and guard Moe Barr. Once again, Maravich saved his best for last.

With five minutes left, Duquesne had an 81–74 lead and the look of a winner. All that LSU had on this night was Pistol Pete Maravich, who proved fearless as he rallied the Tigers, taking the ball right at the altitudinous Nelson brothers. Time and again, he gave them the slip and, when he couldn't, he relied on uncanny "English" to bank shots from impossible angles off the glass board and into the hoop.

Then, with a minute left, Pete pounded down the lane again. "I thought it was open," he said later. "But all of a sudden here comes one of those Nelsons. They're twins, both big and tough. Anyway, I gave him a pump fake and he took it. But just when I thought I had the hoop, the other one comes flying at me all set for the stuff. I was a pigeon, a goner. Well, I didn't quite holler, 'It's Showtime,' but I pumped a couple more times, brought the ball tight to my chest, and flipped it up as I was falling. It hit the side of the board and banked in. I couldn't believe it."

In all, Maravich hit 18 of 36 shots and 17 free throws for 53 points as LSU rallied to win 94–91. Maravich was voted the tournament's most valuable player and drew the praise of *Daily Oklahoman* columnist Bob Dellinger, who wrote: "The All-College Tournament truly has never seen one like him. It may be a long time before it does again."

That 7–1 start raised hopes in Baton Rouge that at long last LSU might have a team good enough to qualify for the postseason NCAA Tournament or, failing that, for the still-highly regarded National Invitational Tournament at Madison Square Garden.

But just when Tiger boosters were most optimistic, the team experienced a letdown, losing SEC games to Alabama, Vanderbilt, Auburn, Kentucky, and Tennessee—five successive defeats that jarred the team's psyche and exposed the Maraviches' raw nerve.

The losses exacerbated the Maraviches' longstanding grievance about the roughhouse tactics that SEC teams used to blunt the Pistol. When the team was winning, it was easier to overlook the borderline physicality. Not now, though. The volatile tempers of father and son were exposed. After 13 games, Pete and Press had been hit with eight technical fouls, assessed when one or the other railed too vociferously or with language too crude for official ears.

Later in the season, against Vanderbilt, Pete became so incensed at a no-call when a defender bumped him out of bounds that he cocked his fist while confronting the official. And although he never let the punch fly, he drew a technical and was ejected from the game.

Incidents like that led one SEC official to say, "Pete's got to learn to settle down. He has great talent, all right, but there are times when he's a crybaby. He doesn't think it's possible for someone to block his shot or knock the ball out of his hands without a foul being called. I'd suggest he mature before trying it in the pros."

Tribbett, however, didn't buy the criticism, saying: "As far as I'm concerned, Pete kept his composure remarkably well. He was getting worked over pretty good every time we played. After most games there were scratches up and down his arms and all over his body. He was always double- and triple-teamed, and they were always testing him with jabs and elbows. I think the thing that saved him from constantly blowing off was his concentration. Pete was always so intent on the game itself and concentrated so hard on what he was doing out there, that he didn't even realize that some of those things were happening to him. That's how fierce a competitor he was."

Indeed, when the Pistol injured his right knee in the team's very next game, against Pittsburgh—a 120–79 victory in which Maravich scored 40 points—it underscored just how fierce his competitive nature was. As Bud Johnson recalled, the injury occurred while Maravich was attempting to make a trick pass. When the student trainer covering the game— the regular trainer was otherwise occupied—recommended he retire to the bench, Pete declined to do so.

"Pete could be pretty bullheaded," said Johnson.

Johnson asserts that Maravich suffered cartilage damage to the knee and that the long-term welfare of that knee would have been better served by his resting. Maravich wouldn't hear of it. Instead, the knee was heavily wrapped through the next few games, as Maravich soldiered on, scoring 31 points against Ole Miss, then 33 against Mississippi State.

"Mississippi State," said Johnson, "used a four-corners offense. They gave the ball to this little point guard, and there was no one else on the team with the quickness to guard him but Pete. Pete was taped from the middle of his thigh to the middle of his calf. Yet he stayed with that little guy and, in spite of that knee, wore him down and LSU won [95–71]. You don't hear many stories about Pete's defense, but that one's always stuck with me. Particularly because of the trying circumstances."

The taping of the knee would diminish in extent, but Maravich would need to wear an elastic brace for the rest of the season. It did not deter him, though. Four games after incurring the injury, he went on his biggest scoring binge of the year, hitting 25 of 51 shots from the floor and 16 of 20 free throws for 66 points against Tulane. He followed that with 50 points against Florida and was still on fire against Auburn when his knee buckled as he took the ball to the hoop, causing him to collapse onto the floor. That brought Press and the team doctor hurrying onto the court, both of whom urged him to leave the game. Pete refused. He had 28 points when he fell to the floor, just before halftime, and would score 26 more in the second half—54 points in all as LSU beat Auburn 93–81.

"My knee has been bothering me quite a bit," Maravich conceded afterward. "They tell me I have torn cartilage, but no one knows whether an operation will be necessary. In the meantime . . . I have to go to the right most of the time and our opponents know it. That doesn't leave me with much of an alternative, so I simply try to beat them to the right. But I'd have to say that right now I'm playing at 75 percent effectiveness . . . no more, no less."

Even so, Maravich was breaking records. With his 54 points against Auburn, he topped Oscar Robertson's mark of 1,962 points for combined sophomore and junior years and became LSU's all-time lead-ing scorer, moving ahead of Bob Pettit, who had tallied 1,972 points during his career.

As records fell, his fame spread through profiles in mass-circulation magazines like *Sport Magazine*, *Sports Illustrated*, and *Life*. But with fame came the pressures of living under constant scrutiny and the inevitable questions about the purity of the Maraviches' motives. Were father and son just "using" LSU to advance their objective of a fat pro basketball contract down the road? Was that what was behind an offensive system tailor-made for the coach's son? Was that the meaning of the dollar bill that hung on the wall of Press' office—a bill whose picture of George Washington had been replaced by one of Peter Press Maravich?

Question begat question. Life in the spotlight was as much a chal-lenge as any box-and-one. For Pete, the party life had become an anti-dote to the pressures of an encroaching world. But as Furman Bisher would note in *Sport Magazine*:

> Pete's love for good times has occasionally gotten him into trouble. This past fall ['68] he suffered campus confinement and was banned from the athletes' training table for some misdemeanors.

For Press, there was far less maneuvering room against pressures. Away from the court, local newsmen found him still the fun-loving raconteur who was a joy to be around, whether in the confines of his office or on the golf course, where he was not above bending the rules to his advan-tage. But once he was involved with LSU basketball, he was not the same man. His players saw him as a gruff, distant coach, a far cry from the father figure he'd been to his North Carolina State boys. Gone were the humor, the compassion that had made him beloved in their eyes.

"I always thought a good coach is one who can kick ass and pat ass," said Tribbett. "Press was not as good at pat-ass. Some guys can handle that, some guys couldn't."

No doubt the fact that Pete was playing for him made Press even more intense about his Xs and Os and less inclined to treat his players as anything more than chess pieces. Press Maravich was obsessed about his son the basketball prodigy. Later that year, when he bumped into his old Wolfpack assistant, Charlie Bryant, and several other coaches at the ACC tournament in Charlotte, North Carolina, he began talking up Pete.

"There were six of us coaches in the hospitality room," said Bryant. "And Press is going: 'You should see Pete do this, you should see Pete do that.' Going on and on about Pete Pete Pete. After a while, I interrupted him, said, 'Press, Pete-who?' Well, I tell you the other coaches erupted. And Press—he looked like somebody stole his wallet . . . Say this about him: Press worshipped that boy."

For Press, the years at LSU would be the culmination of his master plan for Pete. It was no shock, then, that he would be tightly wound with his players, or volatile with officials who blew a call. In defense of Pete, everything became very personal for Press. But the raw nerve that he exposed owed to more than just his allegiance to his son. His life was complicated terribly by his wife's rapidly declining emotional state.

Rusty Bergman: "When Pete first played at LSU, Helen came to the first couple of games. She was a typical parent, all for her son. But a little too vocal. Either hollering too much at Pete or at the refs."

Rich Hickman: "She'd be wearing sunglasses. 'Cause her eyes were bloodshot. And she'd get really loud when the place was quiet. Screaming, 'Petey Petey Petey—that's my Petey.'"

Ralph Jukkola: "She'd get wild. Nothing was said. We knew she was sick."

Bud Montet, sports editor of the *Baton Rouge Morning Advocate*: "She was a nuisance, sitting behind the scorer's table, yelling. She was loud and contemptuous of the other team's kids. She was in bad shape. People felt embarrassed."

Bergman: "After two games, she never came again."

Hickman: "I can only remember one or two times that she was at social events. Press made it a point NOT to have Helen out . . . for her own benefit . . . Pete? He never talked about it."

Bud Johnson: "Pete kind of wanted to ignore the problem for a while.

So he'd immerse himself in campus activities. To avoid having regular contact with Helen. I think he was somehow ashamed that his mother was not normal."

Bergman: "A couple of times I was invited to Coach's house for dinner. At dinner, Helen could be the nicest person in the world. But when she was drinking—a totally different person. She became louder, not really stable. Overexcited. Overly nervous. She became extremely talkative. She wasn't the calm, down-to-earth woman that was sweet and kind-hearted. I'd never been around people that were alcoholic. I didn't know if all alcoholics were like that. When she wasn't drinking, it was easy to be around her at the house. When she was drinking, she made me uneasy. You felt really uncomfortable being there. Coach Maravich had a difficult life at home. As a coach, you need a supportive stable wife. [Bergman later coached in college and in the Continental Basketball Association.] My wife pays the bills, raises the kids. Coach Maravich did not have that luxury. Which made it very difficult for him to be a success."

Johnson: "Press' days at LSU were ruined by his wife's alcoholism. I would hear stories from Press and Pete . . . a lot of episodes where Helen had to go into a psychiatric hospital, where they deal with alcoholism and depression, both of which she was treated for. It was hard. He'd say, 'I don't know what to do about Helen.' I felt a lot of sympathy for him."

Bergman: "When you live with an alcoholic and are trying to do your job and at the same time be a father and husband, it's not easy. When the Maraviches came to LSU, they had Diana. And it was Press, not Helen, who was raising her."

Montet: "He had to get her ready for school. Her mother was incapable."

Johnson: "Press prepared the meals, washed clothes, dishes. He was responsible for keeping the house clean and preparing the food. At certain points, he had domestic help but they never lasted long because of Helen."

Bergman: "Diana was daddy's girl. Press was a good father . . . to Diana and to Pete. He did as much as any father for his child. He bent over backwards to give them what they needed and wanted. And was a good disciplinarian. He did not put up with malarkey on or off the court."

Johnson: "I don't think people knew how little a personal life Press had. You try operating on three, four hours sleep. Press was torn between basketball and rearing Diana. And often doing the laundry. He'd try to do everything. And never had enough time for himself personally. His temper began to fray. He was less patient with Pete and with referees. Problems with Helen would spill over to the rest of his life. If Helen had a problem, he had to solve the problem. If it meant not going to practice, or not reviewing a scouting report, we got on without him. Did it happen? Yes, and it should have happened more. Basketball was the only fun in his life. It was sad to see him trying to manage a problem like Helen while taking care of Diana and looking after a team in the national spotlight."

Bergman: "I can remember us being at Vanderbilt. Typically we would fly back the next morning. But Press had talked to Diana after the game and she told him Helen was having problems. Press said, 'Let's go home tonight.' We left that night."

Johnson: "On the road, he'd get calls from Diana about Helen. Many times he was in total war with Helen: 'No, you don't need to do that.' Helen was always excited about something. She'd go to the shopping mall and imagine someone stole her purse when nothing had happened."

Hickman: "Pete never talked about it. But at the back of his mind was: something's gonna happen with Diana and Helen. He took Diana lots of places with him. Pete did a helluva job. He'd bring her to the dorm. She was the little sister to the rest of the group. It was nothing for five, six guys to go somewhere and Diana to tag along like our little sister. Out to eat. A movie. Or to Broussard Hall, the athletic dorm, where we'd sit and watch TV. At the time she was in lower elementary school."

Johnson: "Diana worshipped Press. You could see it the way her eyes would light up when he walked in. She was an important part of Press' life. He did everything he could to make her happy. He'd read to her. Talk to her. Take her for rides. Everything you'd do to entertain a child."

AMID THE domestic tumults, Pete Maravich continued to dazzle crowds wherever he went with his on-court improvisations.

The *State-Times'* Sam King recalled the night Maravich threw a pass with backspin between a defender's legs. "When the guy turned," said King, "the ball came right back to Pete, who drove around him. Unbelievable."

Rusty Bergman's most vivid memory was of Maravich fielding an outlet pass as a defender jumped in front of him, hopeful of drawing a charge. "Pete screeched to a stop and practically in the same breath threw a three-quarters court windmill pass to a teammate for an easy layup," said Bergman.

Moments like these thrilled fans, even those of rival teams. Although they rooted for their own, they were eager to see what unconventional move or pass the visitor from LSU would execute. And the Pistol rarely disappointed. Even as he was scoring 40 points or better most nights, he would give them a touch of showtime.

As the legend grew, songwriter Woody Jenkins wrote "The Ballad of Pete Maravich," whose lyrics—sung by Bob Tinney—went like this: ". . . Maravich, oh Maravich, / Try to guard you two on one, / There's no way to stop your gun. / The people came to see you score. / Fake one man then fake two, / You turn to shoot and it bumps through; / Listen to people roar. / Maravich, oh Maravich, / Talk of you in years to come, / How you could pass, how you could run, / How you could make the Tigers hum. / Arch it high and sink it deep, / Make the crowd take to its feet; / Listen to the people roar. . . ."

Although the showman in Maravich relished the pleasure that others took in his game, he was not content to rest on his laurels. He continued to practice the boyhood drills that had sharpened his ballhandling and was open to any means of making himself a better player.

"Whenever he discovered a weakness, he pushed to overcome it," said Bud Johnson. "I remember the game with Kentucky that year. They beat the tar out of us as usual. In the locker room, Pete was very low. I started talking to him when he suddenly said, 'Bud, these big guys [Kentucky's Dan Issel and Mike Pratt] pushed me around like a rag doll tonight. I've just got to beef up.'"

For Maravich, the final game of his junior year would burnish his reputation even more. That night, against the Georgia Bulldogs before 10,458 fans in Athens, Georgia, Maravich scored 24 of LSU's last 29 points to overcome a 15-point Georgia lead and send the game into overtime. Then he hit a shot that brought a second overtime. By the final minute of that second overtime, LSU had an 88–80 lead and the basketball.

As Georgia's Herb White recalled: "With 45 seconds to go we had to get the ball back from Pete, who was dribbling the clock out, like Cousy or Marques Haynes. He was putting on a show for the crowd. Pete's Globetrotter act. Behind-the-back, between-the-legs. All that. Guys falling down. Nobody can come close to touching him. As the final seconds tick down, Pete dribbles to halfcourt and launches a hook at the buzzer."

Like Babe Ruth pointing his homer, or Namath guaranteeing a Super Bowl win, Maravich added a touch of pizzazz. As teammate Hickman remembered: "Even while the ball was in the air, Pete just turned his back and started running off the court with hands up in the victory sign. Then the ball went in . . . swish . . . just like that. The fans loved it. They ran out onto the court and actually carried us off. And this was in Georgia."

Later, more than a thousand Bulldog fans lingered outside the LSU dressing room, eager to catch a glimpse of the college game's most colorful player. Said Maravich, who had scored 56 points: "I'll tell you one thing. They didn't take any films of that game, but I don't mind. When I'm 70 years old and telling my grandchildren about the shot, I imagine the distance will match my age."

For Maravich, the season had ended, fittingly, with a bang. Nobody in the history of the college game had captivated fans as he had. Not Cousy playing at Holy Cross, or Oscar Robertson at Cincinnati, or Jerry West at West Virginia. What's more, Maravich took pleasure in the excitement he generated—took pleasure and went to lengths to generate it, even as some critics faulted him for being a "showboat" or "hot dog."

"I can't see anything wrong with showboating," he said. "I think basketball's the most exciting game in the world. It's entertainment, or it should be, for both the players and the fans. It's something you just have to feel. The people are so close to you. You can see their faces and they can see yours, not like some football game where you're 50 miles up in the boondocks, trying to make out some guy's number. It all happens *right there* in basketball. I mean they see you sweat. Look, I don't criticize the way other people play. If they can't or don't want to do any of the fancy stuff I do, then they shouldn't."

Maravich's flair was so unique that it prompted Joe Anzivino, promotion director of the Harlem Globetrotters, to quip: "He's so fantastic we'd integrate to get him."

Once again, Pete Maravich was the nation's leading scorer: In 26 games as a junior he ended with a total of 1,148 points for a 44.2 average, almost 11 points per game better than the next best, Rick Mount of Purdue. He'd upped his field goal percentage to .444 while averaging 6.5 rebounds and 4.9 assists a game. LSU finished the season with a 13–13 record.

Maravich was named to wire service All-America teams and an All-America squad selected by NBA coaches whose players included Spencer Haywood of the University of Detroit, Rick Mount of Purdue, Jo Jo White of Kansas, and Lew Alcindor of UCLA.

As MARAVICH's fame spread and his image recurred in newspapers and on magazine covers, the backlash intensified.

The thrust of the backlash was that the Maraviches had collaborated in creating a Frankenstein monster of a player—an athlete whose only concern was Pete Maravich.

Those who held that view asserted that Press Maravich had cynically provided his son with a stage on which the boy could flash his skills, even at the expense of the team. LSU, this assertion went, was a launching pad for what the Maraviches were really after—a fat contract in the pros. There was something to that. From early on Press had imagined the unimaginable. At a time when NBA players were lucky to make $25,000, $30,000 a year, and even as Pete was merely a grade-schooler, Press saw a more roseate future. Recalled his longtime friend, the legendary UCLA

MINUTES SECONDS

HOME VISITOR

Pistol Pete Maravich, here shooting a foul shot in his senior year at LSU in 1970, was on the verge of becoming the most prolific scorer in college basketball history, a record he still holds. (UPI/Corbis)

Pete's father, Press, was raised in the steel town of Aliquippa, Pennsylvania. The Logstown section in which he lived is seen here, hard by the railroad tracks along which the Pittsburgh & Lake Erie Railroad transported iron ore from the Great Lakes region. (Courtesy of Violet Walsh)

After mustering out of the military during World War II and then playing two years of pro basketball, Press Maravich began coaching the game. Here he is seen diagramming a play as head coach of West Virginia Wesleyan. (Courtesy of Sharon Danovich)

Press Maravich (*second row, third from left*) as the coach of the Davis & Elkins team, his alma mater. (Courtesy of Sharon Danovich)

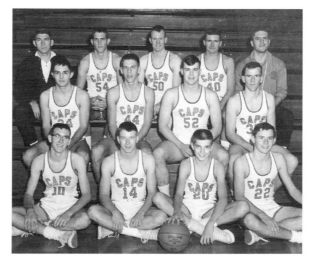

In 1963, a baby-faced Pete Maravich, number 20, became an immediate star at Broughton High School when he moved to Raleigh, North Carolina. The move there was occasioned by his father's acceptance of a position as assistant coach at North Carolina State. (Courtesy of Jimmy Broadway)

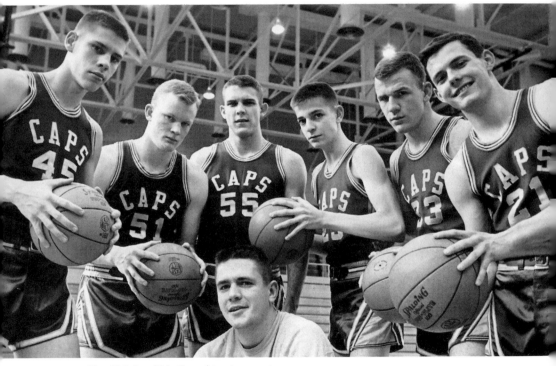

The Pistol and his Broughton teammates, junior year (*left to right*): Jimmy Broadway, Dickie Smith, Doug Bridges, Olin Broadway (*seated*), Pete, Steve Horney, Billy Trott. (Courtesy of Jimmy Broadway)

By his senior year at Broughton, the Pistol, as he became known, averaged 32 points a game and had begun flashing the fancy moves that excited crowds. (Courtesy of Ed McLean)

Pete, wearing jersey number one, ended a sterling schoolboy career in the 17th annual North Carolina high school all-star game when he scored a record-breaking 42 points. (Courtesy of Ed McLean)

Although LSU hadn't much of a
basketball tradition, Maravich had reason
enough to go there: Press was the coach. (LSU)

In 1966, Maravich entered
Louisiana State University
and set about changing the
football orientation of that
institution. (LSU)

ABOVE From his first varsity-eligible year, as a
sophomore in 1967-68, Maravich was the nation's perennial high scorer, averaging in
excess of 40 points a game—on outside shots
and driving moves to the basket like the one
pictured here against Loyola. (Basketball Hall
of Fame, Springfield, MA)

RIGHT Once the Pistol began displaying his
ingenious moves, a basketball boom took hold
in Baton Rouge, home of LSU. Season ticket
sales soared and sporting goods stores suddenly found a healthy market in backyard hoops.
(Basketball Hall of Fame, Springfield, MA)

The Pistol, here spinning the ball, became the symbol of backcourt ingenuity, his improvisations endearing him to many fans but offending some purists. (LSU)

FACING PAGE The Pistol sank a 23-footer against Ole Miss to break Oscar Robertson's all-time NCAA scoring record. (LSU)

From college, it was on to the NBA. Maravich signed
a lucrative contract that would, it turned out,
alienate his Atlanta Hawk teammates. (UPI/Corbis)

By his second season, Maravich overcame the negative reaction of Atlanta teammates and local writers covering the
team. But it was sometimes rough going. Here, with his left
eye gashed, puffy, and purple and his left thigh heavily ban-
daged because of a pulled tendon, the Pistol drives around
Laker Gail Goodrich and scores. (UPI/Corbis)

Maravich in action. Here he flips out an airborne pass as the 76ers' Luke Jackson defends. (UPI/Corbis)

Maravich hovers over Detroit guard Stu Lantz. (Basketball Hall of Fame, Springfield, MA)

By 1974-75, Maravich was playing for the New Orleans Jazz, an expansion franchise. (Basketball Hall of Fame, Springfield, MA)

As a former LSU star, Maravich was the draw for New Orleans fans who prized their memories of him from college days. (Basketball Hall of Fame, Springfield, MA)

Through his years with the Jazz, the Pistol, here launching a jumper against the Hawks, was the team's leading scorer and most exciting performer. (Basketball Hall of Fame, Springfield, MA)

In spite of his incredible success as a ballplayer, Maravich was an unhappy and unfulfilled man. He would tell people it was not until after he retired from the game that he found serenity as a Born Again Christian. In pursuit of his faith, he often preached the gospel, as he is seen doing here at a Billy Graham Crusade. (Courtesy of John Lotz)

In 1987, Maravich, shown here with his wife Jackie and sons Jaeson and Joshua, was inducted into the Basketball Hall of Fame. (Basketball Hall of Fame, Springfield, MA)

By late 1987, LSU unveiled a portrait of Pistol and his deceased father, Press, and Maravich gave a tearful speech. (LSU)

In December 1987, shortly before he died at the age of 40, Maravich had his Broughton jersey number retired. The occasion brought him together with a former Broughton coach of his, Ed McLean (*left*). (Courtesy of Ed McLean)

coach John Wooden: "I remember Press telling me: 'I'm going to turn that boy into the first million-dollar pro basketball player.'"

By giving Pete the green light to shoot as often as he desired, and to show his crowd-pleasing ballhandling whenever he chose to, the coach had created a basketball spectacle so popular with the public, and so intriguing to the media, that ABA or NBA teams would be forced into a bidding frenzy once the boy's college eligibility was used up. That, by now, was a given.

Although the Maraviches denied such ulterior motives, the naysayers were not about to go away. For them, the Maraviches were me-first opportunists, providing a basketball sideshow. Joked ABC-TV publicist Beano Cook: "If Pete Maravich had been at Bunker Hill, we'd have lost the Revolutionary War. No one else would have gotten a shot."

Overlooked by the cynics was what the Maraviches had wrought in Baton Rouge: They had taken a moribund program and raised it from the dead. A loser was transformed—the basketball program was no longer *LSWho*. And if, amid a group of self-confessed ordinary players, Pete had flourished, where was the crime in that?

Remember this: When the Maraviches landed in Baton Rouge, LSU was a dead zone for high school prospects. The school's long years as a loser had made the program unappealing to the best and brightest hoops talents. But by Pete's senior year, the situation was beginning to change. The LSU squad now had the talented big men it had previously lacked, three players good enough to go on to limited pro careers—6-foot-7 Al (Apple) Sanders (four games with the 1972–73 ABA Virginia Squires); 6-foot-9 Bill (Fig) Newton (two seasons with the ABA Indianapolis Pacers—a total of 35 games and a 2.1 ppg average); and 6-foot-8 Danny Hester (one season with ABA teams in Kentucky and Denver—42 games, a 5.9 ppg average).

The Maraviches had brought the LSU basketball program out of the Dark Ages. In the years to come, future pros like Chris Jackson (later known as Mahmoud Abdul-Rauf), Shaquille O'Neal, and Stanley Roberts would wear LSU's purple and gold while playing in a new 15,000-seat arena that the success of Pete Maravich surely had facilitated.

"I don't think the LSU Assembly Center would have been completed when it was [1971] if Pete had not made a basketball fan out of Governor John McKeithen," said Bud Johnson. "McKeithen personally moved the Assembly Center project up on the legislature's priority list. Pete turned on the governor of the state and made a basketball fan out of him."

The air-conditioned structure would house facilities for a wrestling team; varsity, freshman, and visitors dressing rooms; offices for coaches of all LSU varsity sports except football; sports information offices and workroom; building administration offices; theater dressing room; and an "L" Club room with simple kitchen facilities. The building would be used for commencements, theatrical productions, concerts, and major addresses.

The $11.5 million Assembly Center building—already referred to as "the house that Pete built"—was under construction even as the '69–70 Tiger squad returned to the funky ol' Cow Palace for Pete's senior year. Although the Pistol would be the cover subject of *Sports Illustrated*'s college basketball issue, the experts figured his team to do no better than seventh place in the SEC.

In the familiar confines of the Cow Palace, the Maraviches set out to answer the critics the best way they knew how: by winning ball games. Pete—up to 205 pounds after a summer regimen of weight lifting—played with his usual flair, scoring 43 points against Oregon State in the season's opener, 45 against Loyola, 61 against Vanderbilt, and 46 against Tulane—all victories for LSU.

Once again, he faced defenses whose foremost objective was to stop Pete Maravich. That was nothing new to the Pistol, who continued to shoot over and dribble through these stacked configurations, undaunted by whatever latest wrinkle adversaries tried. Opponents continued to push and elbow him while their fans assailed him with insults and jeers that tended to become cheers when Maravich pulled off another unorthodox move.

But not all of the unorthodox moves were his. When Maravich went up against Loyola, he faced a defender who tried to unnerve him by first pinching his butt and then kissing him on the neck. As an angry Pete cocked his fist, ready to retaliate for the kiss, the Loyola player confounded him when he stuck out his hand in friendship.

In a return match against Oregon State, at Corvallis, Oregon, Maravich confronted State's stall game by sitting down on the court and urging the crowd to shout for action. When the fans heeded him and booed the delay tactics, they embarrassed their home team into forsaking that fan-unfriendly game plan. Maravich led the Tigers to a 76–68 victory, scoring 46 points, making an amazing 30 of 31 free throws.

By senior year, Maravich had tired of the fishbowl existence his stardom had brought.

Rusty Bergman: "Up to his senior year, Pete had roomed with Jeff Tribbett in Broussard Hall, the jock dorm, and been one of the guys. But by the time he was a senior, everybody wanted to talk to him, get an autograph for their brother or sister. Pete couldn't get peace 'n' quiet."

Rich Hickman: "By senior year, some distance was developing. More and more Pete was secluding himself because he couldn't go anywhere without people hounding him. I lived next door in Broussard Hall, and the wall with the pay phone separated our rooms. That phone rang all hours day and night for Pete. The media. Girls. If we went out to eat, people came up to him for autographs, or to ask questions, whether we were at McDonald's or out for a pizza. Even when we worked out on our own at the Gym Armory, people would show up to watch. All that kind of wore on him."

Jeff Tribbett: "I really don't know how he took it for so long. Enough people recognized me during my senior year so I know how he felt. There were times when my fiancée and I would rather stay home than go into a public place. Pete likes his privacy. He really stayed cool under pressure."

Hickman: "People could be rude, obnoxious. 'Sign this.' Or, 'You guys should have done this.' Or, 'Why did you do that?' He'd say, 'I don't need somebody telling me how to play.' It wore on him."

Bud Johnson: "He was living with pressure uncommon to any college athlete ever. Right from his freshman to his senior year. There were skeptical sports writers constantly criticizing him. His opponents were always trying to find new ways of stopping him, and finally there were his own personal demands. Pete put a lot of pressure on himself by his own desire to excel. He wanted to please the fans every time out. After a while they came to expect it of him, and when he didn't do it, he got down on himself.

"He was always a hard loser. He found it very difficult to bounce back from a tough loss or a poor performance. He brooded. You know, most of the other kids had other interests. They could forget a bad game. But not Pete. His whole life was basketball. And it got to him.

"During the season, he was always uptight, worried about the next game, worried about the injuries. There is no substitute to fill his shoes. You know, he's a 21-year-old with the legs of a 30-year-old man. His feet and ankles are always in terrible shape—from the years of running and jumping. It might not have been as bad if Pete was willing to settle for 25–30 points per game. But he was always reckless, always going at top speed, playing it to the hilt.

"By his senior year, he was tired of everything . . . the endless interviews, the same questions. One time a reporter was asking him some questions when he suddenly turned to me and said, 'Why didn't you just bring the clips?' The kid was emotionally whipped. After a game, when the rest of the team had showered and dressed, Pete was still in his uniform, trying to answer the questions. That, too, made it more difficult for him to relate to his teammates that last year. He didn't want the attention any more. It was enough getting up for the games. When they were over, he just wanted to melt into the woodwork."

Hickman: "For three years we all hung around together. But senior year, Pete was different. He seemed to feel that everyone was putting him above us, and he started keeping to himself. I guess you could say he became more of a loner. He often seemed down-in-the-mouth and sometimes despondent. He wasn't as lively as before. Even some girls who knew him said he wasn't acting normal . . . It's a funny thing. The only place these low moods weren't reflected was on the court. Even at practice, he seemed more relaxed and had fun again. He was more like his old self. It was as if basketball allowed him to forget about his troubles."

No doubt his mother's fragile emotional state and the consequences that followed were no boon to a cheery disposition. As Helen's well-being deteriorated, Pete concluded—long before Press did—that his mother was an alcoholic. In fact, Helen had become a secret drinker, hiding bottles in closets or filling vinegar bottles with vodka. When Pete accused her of being an alcoholic, she bemoaned her fate as odd woman out in the basketball odyssey of the Maravich men and railed against the loneliness and trying times she had faced.

But no explanations could satisfy her son. He saw only the shell of a once-vibrant woman and was angered enough by the sight of a diminished Helen not only to resist her explanations but also, in response, to slam his fist past her head and into the plaster wall.

As Pete would write in his autobiography:

The pain ate at me, but to the outside world I maintained the image the public wanted to perceive. I put on my plastic smile and carried the hurt into the only refuge I knew, the basketball court.

To compound the complications of his life, agents eager to represent the Pistol after he turned pro had begun showing up in Baton Rouge. Press imposed himself as an obstacle, insisting that all agents go through him. But even *he* wearied of their hyped talk and promises, their snake-oil suasions. He felt he couldn't trust any of them. So he contacted a Pittsburgh attorney, Art Herskovitz, with whom he had grown up in Aliquippa. The Herskovitzes had lived in Plan 11, and Art was an old friend.

But when Press told Herskovitz that he wanted him to represent Pete when the time came for the boy to go pro, Herskovitz protested, "Press, I don't know anything about representing athletes. I've never done that."

"I don't care," said Press. "I can trust you."

An uneasy Herskovitz contacted another Pittsburgh attorney, Les Zittrain, and suggested they partner up in the venture, figuring he could use the help. Zittrain, who did personal injury work in Allegheny County, agreed to collaborate. Because NCAA rules forbade undergraduate athletes from having agents, Herskovitz and Zittrain circumvented the restriction by representing Press instead—a Trojan horse arrangement.

Meanwhile, Pete continued to advance his case for a pro basketball windfall by decimating opposition defenses and doing it with a flash that turned on crowds—and even rival coaches. Take what Maravich did against Lou Carnesecca's St. John's squad in the opening round of the Rainbow Classic in Honolulu during the 1969 Christmas season.

In the game's first half, the Redmen held Maravich to just 13 points and left the court with the lead. But just when Carnesecca thought the game was under control, Maravich turned it on. As Carnesecca would tell newsmen: "In the last 15 minutes he was just too much. The more men we put on him the better he got."

With his floppy hair and gray droopy socks, Pete went on a scoring binge. Baseline, backdoor, up, over, he soared through the air, delaying his shot until the last possible moment and then casually tossing the ball as if he were discarding an old candy wrapper. Hook shot, jump shot, every shot he took fell during those final 15 minutes.

He also dazzled with his passes. On one play, as Maravich took an outlet pass, a St. John's player stepped in front of him, trying to draw a charging foul.

"Pete gets the ball," recalled Bud Johnson, "and sees the player planted. He gets his body under control and comes to a complete stop, facing the defender. He takes the ball behind his back and with two hands throws the ball underhanded through his legs AND through the defender's legs to Newton 30 feet up the court for the layup. I was sitting next to an actor from the 'Hawaii Five-oh' show and he turns to me and says, 'Does he do that all the time?'"

Carnesecca came away just as amazed after Pete, by himself, outscored St. John's in the second half, 40 to 39, as LSU won 80–70 and Maravich finished with 53 points.

"The guy's always entertaining," said Carnesecca. "He's always on. He almost hypnotizes you on the court. Here I am trying to coach my club, watching the action all over the court. And what am I doing? Watching him! He did some unbelievable things. On one play he double-pumped and hits this guy with a pass off his wrist. He does it all going at full speed. That's what's so amazing.

"When I was a kid there was this guy in Far Rockaway who used to be the big rebounder who would get the ball. You would throw it up and yell, 'Get it, Slippery Sam.' This guy [Pete] is three Slippery Sams. They get the ball and give it to him and he gets it up.

"You talk of Jerry West or Oscar Robertson or any of those great ones who scored and passed so well. Maravich is better. He's a show."

It was inevitable that as the college game's dominant player Maravich would invite comparisons to NBA legends. But while those comparisons filled up sports page columns, Maravich contented himself with being Maravich—firing upward of 40 shots a game and entertaining crowds with his passing.

In late January 1970, the Pistol scored 55 in his last appearance on the home court of the perennial SEC champion Kentucky team, a performance greeted warmly by the partisan Wildcat crowd. After three varsity years, Maravich was now accorded affectionate farewells in many of the gyms of long-standing SEC rivals.

"That night," said Bud Johnson, "Coach [Adolph] Rupp had the gout. So they had a little stool by the Kentucky bench that he could put his foot up on. At halftime, they had a ceremony at midcourt, honoring Pete. Rupp motioned for him to come over so he could shake hands. The crowd gave Pete a standing ovation that lasted almost five minutes.

"In the same game, Larry Steele later had Pete cornered in the right-hand corner of the floor. When Pete couldn't get out—and with nobody coming to get the ball—out of frustration Pete leaped backward and shot the ball as he was going out of bounds: nothing but net. Well, that crowd gave him another standing ovation."

With each game, Maravich was zeroing in on the last major scoring record that did not belong to him. Reported the *New York Times* on January 25, 1970:

After last night's loss to the University of Kentucky, he [Maravich] passed Elvin Hayes of Houston and was second in career college scoring, trailing

Oscar Robertson. He needs 69 points to pass Robertson's total of 2973 for Cincinnati University.

Robertson—known then and now as "the Big O"—had set his record a decade earlier and had been a boyhood hero of Maravich at the time.

In LSU's next game, Maravich closed on Robertson, getting a mere 29 points against coach Ray Mears' Tennessee, a ball-control club that historically had limited his scoring. That night, Pete hit 12 of 23 shots from the floor and five of seven free throws as LSU beat the Vols 71–59.

Ole Miss was next on January 31, 1970. With the possibility of Robertson's record being broken, the demand for tickets created a Cow Palace permissiveness that allowed 11,856 fans, not to mention the team's mascot, a 350-pound tiger named Mike III, into the arena, far in excess of its capacity. More than 1,000 LSU students, turned away at the gate, would watch the contest on closed-circuit television in the student union.

By halftime, LSU led 53–40 and the Pistol had 25 points, just 15 shy of the record. With 7:53 left in the game, Maravich hit a 25-foot jumper over Ole Miss' 2-3 zone that gave him 39 points and tied the Big O's record. Now the crowd was revved, shouting: "One more . . . one more . . . one more."

As Peter Finney would report in *The Sporting News*:

> For the pressure-proof kid with the pipe-cleaner arms, they had to be the most pressurized minutes of a lifetime dedicated to one game.
>
> As a battery of 21 photographers lined the baseline to record the moment for posterity, Pete's large Serbian eyes reflected inner turmoil. Five times he shot and five times he missed, once on a twisting drive up the middle. The ball rimmed in and out.

With 4:41 left in the game, Maravich stopped and popped from the top of the key, and this time the ball fell through the hoop. The crowd erupted as teammates Al Sanders and Bob Lang hoisted Maravich onto their shoulders.

Play was suspended so that Maravich could receive the game ball and the photographers could snap their shots. That done, Pete scored 12 more points for a total of 53 as LSU won 109–86. Maravich had hit on 21 of 46 from the floor and 11 of 15 from the foul line while being credited with 12 assists, one below the school record.

The record-shattering performance would trigger this congratulatory telegram:

Dear Pete: You can take great pride in your recent efforts which have established you as the leading scorer in major college basketball history. I just want you to know that the Nixons are among your fans saluting this success. Congratulations!

It was signed by the president of the United States, Richard Nixon.

THE PISTOL's final college season wound down.

On the road, record SEC crowds turned out to see his last appearance there. Elvis was leaving the building, but doing it in his usual crowd-pleasing fashion.

Against Florida in Gainesville, Pete stole a pass, and, as he and Hester raced to the basket, Maravich flipped the ball toward the defender with back spin. As the Florida player reached for it, Pete punched the ball with his fist through the arms of the defender right to Hester for the easy layup.

The Gainesville crowd rose to its feet and gave Maravich a standing ovation for a minute. As local columnist Rick O'Shea later reported:

Good news on campus was the game being a sellout and closed-circuit TV going to two different buildings; bad news was most of the 5,000 Gator fans in the gym wound up pulling for Pete instead of Florida before the game was over and doing it quite loudly.

Every basket Pete made was cheered enthusiastically and more so towards the end as he approached the Alligator Alley record. Fact is, when they announced he had tied the record of 50 in the gym, you'd have thought all of the fans were Tiger diehards as they chanted, "Pete! Pete! Pete!" trying to spur him to the record.

When he hit, there was sheer pandemonium and the Florida Gators must have been wondering just what was going on.

Fans everywhere like the wizard of the court, so much that every road game left on the Bengals' slate is a complete sellout.

For the Maraviches, it was the best of times. Not only was Pete leading the nation again in scoring—he hit 52 against Florida and a season-high 69 (47 in the second half) against Alabama in the team's next game—but also LSU had confounded the critics by having its best season of the Pistol's varsity career.

The Tigers ended their regular-season schedule with a 20–8 record, finishing a surprising second to SEC champion Kentucky. That was good enough to earn Maravich & Co. an invitation to the postseason National Invitational Tournament at New York's Madison Square Garden.

Though the NIT had lost some top-flight teams to the more-prestigious NCAA tournament, it still could boast of a formidable field. Al McGuire's Marquette Warriors had aimed at an at-large berth in the NCAAs, and their 22–3 record was deemed good enough to make it. But McGuire was disenchanted with the NCAA's placing the team in the Midwest regionals in Fort Worth rather than in the easier Mideast bracket at Dayton. McGuire believed the tournament directors had done so with malice aforethought, so he elected to take his team to his old stomping ground in New York. The Warriors immediately became the NIT favorite.

But it was Maravich and LSU that were the attraction for the city's basketball sophisticates. Most of them had not seen the Pistol up close and were eager to gauge whether he merited all the hyperbole that had trailed his career at LSU.

For Maravich—steeped in the history of the game, through Press—playing in Madison Square Garden was special. The building had history. It was in the Garden that a former sportswriter-turned-promoter named Ned Irish had made the college game into a box office attraction in the late 1930s, and it remained so until the point-shaving scandal of the early 1950s soured ticket-buyers.

But in those decades when New York schools like CCNY, LIU, Manhattan College, NYU, and St. John's were perennial powers, the city was crazy for the college game—doubleheaders there routinely sold out. In fact, when the New York Knicks were organized in 1946–47, most fans believed that these new-fangled pros were inferior to their college heroes. To repudiate that notion, the Knicks were obliged to scrimmage the local colleges, relying on press reports to persuade the die-hard college fans that theirs was a superior brand of basketball, one worth seeing.

By 1970, New Yorkers were doting on a Knicks team bound for glory—a club whose sharp passing and team-oriented defense would carry it to its first NBA championship. And although these Knicks of Willis Reed, Walt Frazier, Dave DeBusschere, Bill Bradley, and Dick Barnett were mesmerizing the city with their team-oriented game, New Yorkers were not so provincial that they couldn't appreciate the artistry of visiting performers. Earl the Pearl, Jerry West, the Big O—the crowds at the Garden turned on to their games.

And now it was Maravich they queued up to see. As columnist Larry Merchant wrote in the *New York Post*:

> Pete Maravich has been putting on his act for three phantasmagoric seasons, dribbling through the southland like Peter Fonda's "Captain America." Now, as the seconds tick off the clock of his varsity career, it is time to take the hook shot from 31st St. to 33rd St.
>
> No doubt he will make it, for Pete Maravich and the Garden and the NIT are made for each other. He comes to the Garden in the best tradition of Luisetti, Mikan, Gola, Robertson and Bradley, to show the big town his stuff. He comes to the NIT, which is less a tournament than a Broadway musical these days, to do his number.
>
> And as the Garden and the NIT are exploiting him, using the American boyhood to pay off the mortgage, he will be exploiting them, using their ballgame for a showcase. As Sonny Werblin said of Joe Namath in

his last college game in the Orange Bowl, it can be a terrific pilot film for the real thing. There's a lovely war going on between basketball leagues, with defense-appropriation type money being used as ammunition. Pete Maravich is going to be bombarded. Said one agent to Press Maravich, the father and coach: "I don't want a penny from the first million. . . ."

Meanwhile, Maravich was telling newsmen: "I've always insisted that basketball is an entertainment, and New York is where the fans love basketball."

Even though LSU's opening-round game against Georgetown was shown on network TV, 16,000 fans paid their way in to watch Maravich. Maravich got their immediate attention. The first time he had the ball, he dribbled to his left and whipped a behind-the-back cross-court pass through a crowd of Hoyas to an LSU teammate who blew the easy layup. But just the same a loud "ooooo" resounded from courtside to the cheap seats upstairs. It looked as if showtime was about to begin.

But it was a false promise. Georgetown's defense worked Maravich hard, guard Mike Laska playing him straight-up while getting backup from teammates. The Pistol had faced such gang defenses before and beaten them easily. But by halftime, he had managed to get off only four shots, hitting just one of them. Wrote Leonard Koppett of the *New York Times*:

> There were three reasons for this: his nervousness in a staggeringly over-publicized situation, Georgetown's well-executed defensive plan and, surprisingly, the tendency of his teammates not to make full use of him.

Bud Johnson insisted there was one other reason: "At the NIT, he was in pain and didn't want to show it. His knee was bothering him, but he very much wanted to play in Madison Square Garden."

In the end, Maravich overcame Georgetown. At one point in the second half, he hit three longer jumpers in a row. But he never approached past heroics. He finished with 20 points on 6 of 16 field goal attempts, the second-lowest point output of his 81-game college career.

However, the final two points he scored, on free throws with nine seconds remaining, gave LSU its 83–82 victory.

Even so, Maravich said afterward: "I was terrible, pitiful. I just stunk. It was one of my worst ball games ever."

"He played like he had a tranquilizer," said Press. "He looked about a step slower than usual. I think he was emotionally wiped out and had a case of Garden jitters."

Against Oklahoma in the next round he was better. Better but hardly vintage Maravich. Although he scored 37 points on 14-for-33 shooting and again iced the 97–94 victory with two late free throws, he played like a runaway train, committing 14 of his team's 27 turnovers while twisting his ankle and getting banged up from several collisions.

The poor play of Pete and his LSU teammates brought this postgame fusillade from Press: "Pounding the pavements. Up till 4 a.m. I keep telling them we're in a national tournament now, but those little bastards won't listen to me. They watch TV till all hours and then try to go out and play a fucking ballgame. I can tell when they get up in the morning. They look like they'd been on a three-day drunk. The little bastards. . . .

"I told the little bastards before they came here, 'Look, this is New York, the NIT. A prestigious tournament. It's not a little Podunk tournament with 30 or 40 teams in it. This thing has history behind it. So what do they do? They watch TV all night. I don't have enough detectives to check all those fucking rooms. And they've got 17,000 fucking channels in this town. . . . Hey, if you radio guys are getting all this, you'd better cut out all the bad words."

In truth, it was more than TV that would divert Maravich as LSU's semifinal game against tournament favorite Marquette loomed. On the eve of the big game, Maravich sat up all night in his room at the New Yorker Hotel, drinking and reminiscing with college mates about four years of good times at the Baton Rouge campus. Came game day, and he was a spent bullet as Marquette pounded LSU and him 101–79.

When Maravich hit a jumper with 1:12 remaining in the game, the Marquette fans gave a mocking cheer. The Pistol had gone almost 19 minutes without a field goal, finishing with 20 points in a performance dismal enough to prompt the Warriors' star guard, Dean Meminger, to say: "I see better players on the New York City playground all the time."

Adding insult to injury, Marquette reserve guard Jack Burke needled: "I'll play pro ball for cab fare and a hamburger if they just let me play Maravich every night."

At the time, the drinking binge went unrecorded, Maravich not confessing his poorly timed hangover until many years later. But in retrospect, the drinking already had become Pete Maravich's answer to the fame game, with its unrelenting pressure, its sometimes cockeyed demands. Neither his success nor his struggle to cope with it would cease with the end of his collegiate career.

Yet even as he experienced a letdown at the NIT, the dream of basketball success had been fulfilled at LSU. For the third straight year as a consensus All-American, he'd led the nation in scoring—a 44.5 ppg average and a career total of 3,667 points—figures that 30 years later, on the very cusp of the millennium, had not been surpassed. Nobody had had the impact on the college game that the Pistol had.

What's more, he had achieved his record totals in an era before the three-point shot and a shot clock.

"After he finished at LSU," said Sam King of the *Baton Rouge State-Times*, "I went through the score sheets of all his varsity games and figured out that he would have averaged 7.8 points a game more if there'd been the three point shot. The game he scored his record 69 points would have ended up as 81. With the three point shot, Pete'd have made LSU a national contender. His favorite shot was the pullup at the top of the key."

Although he would have preferred a better showing in the New York spotlight, Maravich knew it would not make him any less desirable at the next level. The game would go on for Pistol Pete. In the pros. For the kind of money that would leave ex-pipe-threader Press breathless.

5

Back when Press Maravich was mustered out of the armed services, a basketball player could make a modest living in either of two pro leagues—the more-established National Basketball League (NBL) or the newly founded Basketball Association of America (BAA).

But by 1948, the BAA had absorbed a number of the NBL's stronger franchises, and soon after the older league was out of business. For nearly two decades the surviving, expanded league—renamed the National Basketball Association (NBA)—was *the* pro basketball entity.

That exclusivity gave NBA team owners enough leverage in contract negotiations to keep a lid on players' salaries. In the mid-50s the average NBA player earned between $15,000 and $20,000, and in the years that followed no breakthrough would occur to radically raise the salary structure.

At least not until a rival league, the American Basketball Association, began doing business in 1967–68. The ABA—with its red-white-

and-blue basketball and innovative three-point field goal—not only provided a Plan B for financially disgruntled NBA players but also aggressively recruited them. Suddenly stars like Rick Barry and Zelmo Beaty found they could play one league against the other and make quantum leaps in their earning power.

The timing couldn't have been better for Peter Press Maravich.

At a secret ABA meeting in January 1970, in the midst of the college basketball season, the Carolina Cougars secured the draft rights to Maravich over the protest of the New Orleans Buccaneers franchise. Signing the Pistol became a high priority for the team's owner, a hard-charger named Jim Gardner.

Although only 37 years old, Gardner had built a fortune on the Hardee's hamburger chain and in 1966 had won a seat in the U.S. House of Representatives. Gardner's Cougars figured to have a realistic shot at Maravich if only for their location: The team played its home games at alternate sites in Greensboro, Raleigh, and Charlotte. For Maravich, who had grown up in the Carolinas and developed an affinity for the South and its people, the chance to play on familiar turf was a plus.

Gardner was aggressive—some say too aggressive—in his pursuit of Maravich. As Pete's senior year wound down, the Cougars' owner besieged Press with phone calls, outlining a package deal that would include Pete's participation in Hardee's franchises. Unbeknownst to Gardner, while at LSU Press had become involved in a fast-food franchise that had gone bust, subverting at least that part of the Cougars' proposed deal.

What's more, Pete's preference—the money being roughly equal—was to play in the NBA, the league in which boyhood heroes like Oscar Robertson and Jerry West had performed, the league universally considered more competitive. His only stipulation was that that NBA city be in a warm-weather climate. For a while, it appeared as though that NBA team of choice would be the San Diego Rockets. Because with first choice in the draft, the Detroit Pistons were expected to take Bob Lanier, the 6-foot-11 center from St. Bonaventure. Left up in the air was whether the Rockets, who had the second pick, could cough up the money to satisfy Maravich's demands.

As one of the Maraviches' attorneys, Les Zittrain, recalled: "San Diego wanted Pete. Then we told them what kind of money we were looking for. Forty eight hours later, the team's owner, Bob Breitbard—a nice guy—called back and said: 'Sorry. It's much too rich for us.' He said the Rockets would draft Rudy Tomjanovich instead."

That should have swung the advantage to the Cougars in the bidding war for Maravich. But suddenly another NBA team, the Atlanta Hawks, stepped forward, having gained possession of the third draft pick through a chain of improbable circumstances. See, that February the San Francisco Warriors had ceded their first-round draft choice to Atlanta in return for the negotiating rights to Zelmo Beaty. Beaty, who had played seven seasons with the Hawks, was sitting out his option year after announcing he intended to play for the ABA Los Angeles Stars. The Warriors' owner, Franklin Mieuli, gambled—a losing gamble ultimately—that he could dissuade Beaty from bolting the NBA.

The Warriors' unexpectedly poor finish in '69–70—at least partly caused by an injury to star center Nate Thurmond—brought the Hawks that third draft pick and gave the team's 38-year-old owner, Tom Cousins, a chance not only to boost interest in a new basketball market through the dashing Maravich but also to gain impetus through the same player for a related civic project.

Cousins was chairman of the board and chief executive officer of Cousins Properties Incorporated—an Atlanta-based real estate operation that started in 1958 with a $3,000 capitalization and now boasted assets in excess of $30 million. So successful had Cousins become that by the late '60s the city's movers and shakers looked to him to revive a slumping downtown area by masterminding the financing and building of a complex that would include a hotel, arena, restaurants, and shops. His construction firm had profited from Atlanta's boom years, and now the political elite let him know it was his civic duty to get the downtown project in gear.

For the arena to be feasible, Cousins knew, major league sports franchises had to be brought to Atlanta. In 1968, he and future Georgia Governor Carl Sanders bought the St. Louis Hawks franchise for $3.5

million, the league approving the transfer on the condition that the plans for the 16,378-seat arena—the Omni, as it would be known—go forward. At the time, the Hawks played their home games in Georgia Tech's Alexander Memorial Coliseum—a 7,192-seat arena regarded as being well below NBA standards.

"Tom Cousins was a civic-minded fella," said *Atlanta Constitution* sports columnist Furman Bisher. "He was not interested in owning a sports franchise any more than I am. He built the Omni without public money. As a way for the Omni to pay for itself, he had to get basketball and hockey teams."

The hockey team, the Atlanta Flames, cost him $6 million when he bought it in 1971.

With the Cougars' Jim Gardner still in hot pursuit of Maravich, Cousins knew he would have to go deep into pocket to secure the Pistol. But he had no choice. Maravich, as the Hawks saw it, was the gate attraction that could rouse Atlanta, a southern city lacking the basketball tradition. Indeed, with ticket prices ranging from $2.50 to $6.50, home attendance the year before had averaged barely more than 5,300 paying customers per game—and this for a team that had won the Western Division title. Cousins lost more than $250,000 that season.

Zittrain and Herskovitz—worried that they had overplayed their hand with San Diego and blown Pete's opportunity to play in the NBA—were thrilled to have this second chance. The lawyers recognized that circumstances peculiar to Atlanta made Maravich a property the Hawks could ill afford to lose. Not only did the team need him as an inducement to push through that Omni complex, but also its predominantly white fan base—rooting for a team that started five blacks—presumably could be broadened through a white player of Maravich's crowd-pleasing appeal.

As negotiations between the Hawks and Maravich heated up, so did Jim Gardner.

"Cousins," he threatened, "will think Quantrill's Raiders were a bunch of rank amateurs if Atlanta lucks out and signs Maravich. If we don't get the kid, we're going to take the money and call Lou Hudson or Walt Hazzard . . . or both of them."

Hudson and Hazzard were backcourt starters with Atlanta.

"Mr. Cousins," Gardner continued, "should be more concerned about them than trying to sign some untested, unproven college player."

In Memphis late that March, Gardner and ABA commissioner Jack Dolph made a final pitch for Maravich, one that would have given the Pistol financial participation in the Cougars and Press a $50,000-a-year job coaching the ABA franchise in Pittsburgh.

But in the end it was the Hawks offer that Maravich accepted—a five-year deal variously reported as being worth $1.5 to $2 million. "Closer to $2 million," said Zittrain. "With fringe benefits."

Those benefits included a 1970 Plymouth GTX with a green alligator roof and a lighter shade of green body, a 452 engine, mag wheels, five-stereo speaker, and a telephone; a country club membership; and a $280-a-month two-bedroom Atlanta townhouse apartment with a pool table, a seven-place bar, and sheets, towels, bedspreads, shower curtains, dishes, glasses, and even soaps bearing the monogram "Pistol"—a touch Pete said he'd dreamed of since acquiring the nickname as a youngster.

Later, Cougars general manager Don Dejardin would claim that his team's offer had been better: $2.5 million for five years with a $20,000 annuity for life starting at age 40 *and* a $250,000 life insurance policy.

Compared to what players would earn by the end of the millennium—minimum NBA salary in 1999 was $275,000 for a rookie, $1 million for a 10-year veteran—Maravich's deal seems small change now. But his contract was as good as it got in 1970. As Pete observed: "For a few days, I was in the Guinness book of world records as having signed the largest contract ever agreed upon in the history of sports."

WHEN THE San Diego Rockets declined to ante up for Maravich, money was a reason—but not the only reason why the Rockets opted to pass on Maravich.

The Rockets' star player, 6-foot-9 Elvin Hayes—known as the "Big E"—was given to tantrums when he didn't get the ball enough. During one game, San Diego writer Bud Maloney kept a chart that showed that

Hayes had shot the ball 28 of 29 times he had it in his hands. Later, when team captain Don Kojis and Hayes bickered about a diary that Kojis kept that enumerated Hayes' quirks, management traded Kojis and kept Hayes, overlooking the Big E's attitude for the productiveness of his shots.

Given that Maravich was a player who needed the ball in his hands, Rockets management feared that teaming him with Hayes would make for a combustible situation. The Rockets' decision not to sign Maravich offered an insight into the dynamics involved in putting a team together and, though no one knew it at the time, foreshadowed the effect that Pistol Pete would have on Hawks chemistry. Because even as Maravich—expelled from LSU for excessive absences from class— moved into a Baton Rouge apartment and began a thrice-weekly weight training routine to beef up for the pros, his big-buck contract had begun to shake up the smooth works that the Hawks team had been before him.

Hardly had the ink dried on Maravich's contract when the team's captain, Bill Bridges, a 6-foot-6 forward who'd been the fourth-best re- bounder in the league in '69–70, sought to renegotiate his four-year, $50,000 per annum deal. When Hawks management made clear it had no intention of returning to the bargaining table, Bridges issued a "pay me or trade me" ultimatum. And though Bridges would retreat from that position and turn up at the team's Jacksonville, Florida, training camp that fall, his was not an isolated instance of discontent on this hitherto closely bonded team.

Joe Caldwell, a tenacious defender and dangerous open-court player, was considered by many to be the heart of the Hawks team. His team- mates admired his competitiveness on the court, and his sunny disposi- tion in the locker room. But as the new season loomed, Caldwell was angry about the disproportion between what he and the other Hawks were earning and what Maravich would earn.

Not only did the 6-foot-5 Caldwell want more than the reported $60,000 he was making, but also he publicly stated he wanted to be paid a dollar more than that untested rookie Maravich. When the Hawks were slow to respond to his demands, Caldwell, known as "Pogo Joe" for his leaping ability, began negotiating with the ABA Carolina Cougars. But Hawks management figured that he, like Bridges, would eventually fall in line. Even after he failed to report to training camp, the Hawks expected that their offer—virtually double what Caldwell had been making—would keep Pogo Joe in an Atlanta uniform.

Bridges and Caldwell overtly reflected the hard feelings that Maravich had stirred up on this prideful team. Although money was at the core of it, it would oversimplify things to say that the discord that Maravich's presence had triggered was only about money. Race was also an issue. Maravich not only got the big money but also was made out to be Atlanta basketball's savior by the front office—in no small part, it seemed, due to the color of his skin. Maravich had, as Muhammad Ali used to say of white opponents, "the complexion to get the connection." In management's rush to capitalize on a great white hope's marquee value, Maravich's black teammates were made to feel like second-class citizens in spite of their past success as a unit. As soon as Maravich signed on, the Atlanta organization built its promotional campaign around him. New green-blue-and-white uniforms were designed. Ads spoke of "the new Hawks," giving pause to the veteran black players, who wondered what in hell was wrong with the old Hawks.

As Noah Sanders would write in the *New York Times* Sunday magazine:

> As the playoffs opened last year, many people picked the Hawks to go all the way, and if scoring leader Lou Hudson had not gone ice cold and playmaker Walt Hazzard had not broken his wrist they might well have. Moreover, the Hawks without Maravich are an especially firmed-up and cohesive team—uniformly strong at every position, five near-but-not-quite-superstars who have grown used to one another and who talk out their problems in open-forum team meetings.
>
> Besides Hazzard and Hudson, the starters last year were Joe (Pogo—as in pogo stick) Caldwell, who . . . once jumped, from a standing start, over a parked car; Bill Bridges . . ., a rebounding and spiritual leader; and Walt Bellamy, who suddenly developed *esprit de corps* after eight and a half

years of maintaining a bad attitude with New York, Baltimore and Detroit. Head coach Richie Guerin, after having "Hawk Team" engraved on
last year's most valuable player trophy, said, "In my heart and soul I've
never seen a more close-knit team."

A year later and even before the regular season had begun, that unity
was coming unglued. With Maravich's arrival, the Hawks had turned
into a motley lot of individuals who felt underpaid and underappreci-
ated. Players became sensitive to every nuance of slight. For instance,
when the Hawks undertook to refurbish their Atlanta office and failed
to contact Caldwell—an off-season carpet salesman—about his mer-
chandise, he took it personally. The oversight compounded the inequity
in salary Caldwell was stewing over. When Pogo Joe decided to accept
the Cougars' offer of $175,000, it was a blow that would undo the deli-
cate chemistry that had bound the team together—a blow from which
the Hawks would not recover. Nobody would fill the defensive void left
by Caldwell, who was unique in his ability to stymie the other team's
biggest threat at either guard or forward.

The blame for Caldwell's departure fell on Maravich, whose seven-
figure deal had thrown the Hawks' budget out of whack. The players'
antagonism toward the high-priced rookie intensified when, in the exhibition season, Maravich's go-go open-court game proved an uneasy fit with
that of the remaining Hawks—a Lou Hudson slowed by a hamstring pull and
big men Bridges, Bellamy, and Jim Davis, who much preferred the
walk-it-up half-court game. As Maravich ran the ball and fired off shots,
sometimes before his front line could get position for rebounds, or threw
passes that caught teammates unaware, he was not making any friends. From
the start, the Hawks looked out of sync, no one more so than Maravich.

After Maravich's first exhibition game, a 121–105 loss to the Celtics,
George Cunningham of the *Atlanta Constitution* would observe:

It was a rude professional introduction for highly regarded guard Pete
Maravich whose only comment on his performance was, "You saw it.
What can I say? I was horrible."

Maravich went seven of 17 from the field for 16 points and had just three assists over the 32 minutes he played. It was the most action seen by any Hawk as Guerin used all 12 players.

If Maravich was lousy, he had plenty of rookie and veteran company among those wearing Hawk uniforms. It was probably the most disorganized game ever played by the Hawks since they came to Atlanta.

It did not get better. The Hawks, and Maravich, continued to flounder, with Maravich looking like odd man out with these teammates. During one exhibition game in Tampa, also against the Celtics, Bellamy—known in the clubhouse as "the Lawyer"—turned to Boston's rookie pivot man, Dave Cowens, and asked, facetiously, "How's the game going?" It was his way of saying he felt no part of the contest because of the rambunctious rookie Maravich's ball-hogging. One man's showtime was another's purgatory.

Maravich soldiered on, struggling through exhibition games against NBA defenses that sought to debunk the Pistol's mystique. Time and again, he turned the ball over, most often when he dribbled into corners of the court and was trapped. On defense—an aspect of the game he'd given casual regard at LSU—he was often beaten. His rookie mistakes were compounded by that uneasy coexistence with his teammates. In his desire to get along with fellow Hawks, he found himself hesitating or, as he put it, "thinking . . . instead of just going out there and doing what came naturally."

The regular season had not begun, yet it was obvious that a year of turmoil lay ahead. Caldwell was gone. Bridges was unhappy about his contract. And Walt Hazzard, who, like Maravich, was used to handling the basketball in the backcourt, feared he was on borrowed time, his skills redundant on an Atlanta team with a white-complected ballhandling whiz like Maravich.

"I remember asking Walt to pose for some publicity shots during the preseason and he got really uptight about it," said Hawks publicity director Tom McCollister. "'Whaddaya got me here for?' he said to me. 'I'm on my way out anyway.' And I understand he made similar statements all around the league. Like in each town he visited he'd look around and say, 'I wonder if I'll be a Hawk the next time I come here.'"

As for Bellamy, he had performed with gusto through the exhibition games, until Caldwell left for the Cougars. Then Bellamy appeared to lose interest. This was not exactly a deviation in his history. In the late '60s, before Bellamy and Howard Komives were traded to Detroit for Dave DeBusschere (December 19, 1968), Knicks teams had been rife with dissension. In his own inscrutable way, Bellamy did as much to sabotage the collective sanity of the Knicks as anybody else. When he chose to, Bellamy could play his position with as much ability as anybody; the nub was consistency. More often than not, particularly against the lesser names of pivot play, he seemed to receive the game on delayed tape.

Good nights or bad, Bellamy went through them with an abstracted expression. That appearance of impenetrability and the unevenness of his performances drove people to distraction. A coach of his once banged at Bellamy's door in a drunken stupor and berated him in outrageously racial terms, offering to transport him back to Africa if an adequate replacement could be found that evening.

"I don't think anybody ever had any antagonisms against Walt Bellamy," said Knicks teammate Phil Jackson. "Walt was the most honest guy on the club. He wasn't fooling anybody. He got paid his seventy, eighty, ninety thousand dollars—whatever he was getting paid—came, played basketball, went home and that was it. It didn't ever enter his mind that he wanted to win a national basketball championship, I don't think. And he was honest about it, you know, he didn't play defense, he wasn't going to play defense and that was it."

Bellamy's "take" on the Hawks' tumults was that "management didn't have the vision to pair an exciting African-American [Caldwell] with an exciting white player [Maravich]."

Said Bellamy: "It was conveyed to the team by management that in order for the Hawks to win, Pete has to shoot the ball . . . Mr. Maravich had confidence in his shot. He thought it'd go in from whatever distance. . . . We got away from the traditional things that made the team a success."

In other words, Maravich was gumming up the works.

That would be the theme played out through dreary exhibition games as the regular season drew near. Maravich was not oblivious to the unhappiness his arrival had caused. In an attempt to overcome it—to be "one of the boys"—he took to picking up teammates' tabs when dining out, only to discover that the gesture was dismissed as grandstanding.

Money combined with race had turned the locker room into a cauldron of discontent. In that environment, racial sensitivity was never far from the surface. Herb White, a 6-foot-2 rookie from the University of Georgia, saw it up close as he battled for the last spot on the Hawks roster.

"It came down to myself and a player from Hillsdale College in Michigan—a nice guy, a black player," said White, who is Caucasian. "Like me, he was a forward in college who was being converted to a guard. This guy and I battled, and I got the spot. Some of it might have had to do with my being local. Anyway, Walt Hazzard comes up to me and says, 'They wanted a white player.' Something along those lines."

White signed with the Hawks for $18,500.

Wherever the Hawks went in their exhibition season, the media focus was always on Maravich. Beat reporters and TV crews acted as though he was the only Atlanta player who merited coverage. No matter if another Hawk might have played better, after every exhibition the media descended on Maravich's locker. Given the VIP treatment that this untested rookie—possessing the lion's share of the payroll—was accorded, it was not hard to understand the wounded egos of his teammates.

Maravich, in turn, was a victim of his success—the celebrity he had garnered playing for his father at LSU. Yet who among his teammates would not have gladly accepted this spotlit hour—and the financial rewards that accompanied it? But as the Hawks' Great White Hope, on a squad that had been committed to team play—one for all and all for one—he had turned life topsy-turvy. Dealing with all of that—the burden of his contract and the disruptive impact of his game—proved tricky, as he later described in *Sport Magazine*:

"The crowd and the newspapermen had come to see me, and I was too eager to please. I was rushing my shots. I was throwing the ball away. After the first five preseason games I was barely hitting 40 percent from the field, averaging seven turnovers and only three assists a game. With little help from me, we won four of 12 exhibition games."

"It isn't surprising, then, that I was totally psyched out by the time of our opening game of the season. All during the exhibitions there had been these television spots saying something like: 'Watch the Milwaukee Bucks play Pete Maravich in his pro debut.' ABC-TV had signed a contract to televise our opener, but only on the guarantee that I would play in the game. There was no mention of the defending [Western Division] champs, only a blurb about 'Pistol Pete.' I didn't get much sleep the night before. When I finally got into the game and ran down the court one time, I wanted to come out immediately. My legs felt like spaghetti, my hands like ping-pong paddles. I couldn't even take the ball and dribble it. I hit three out of 13 shots from the field, we got wiped out and it was all an omen of things to come."

All during the exhibition season, and now into the regular season, the team's coach, Richie Guerin, was faced with the dilemma of how to handle Maravich without opening himself up to charges by his veteran players that he was coddling the rookie.

In his time, a career that spanned 13 seasons, Guerin had been one of the league's premier guards. He was the first backcourt player in NBA history to score 2,000 points in a season, totaling 2,303 for a 29.5 ppg average in 1962. Guerin was an aggressive player who went hard to the basket and never backed off from confrontations. His fiery nature and his determination were well-established. Indeed, during the '69–70 season, two years after he had retired as a player so that he could coach the Hawks full-time, he returned to active status when injuries required another body on the roster. On April 19, 1970, in the playoffs against the Los Angeles Lakers, the 36-year-old Guerin inserted himself into the lineup in the first quarter, with Atlanta trailing 12–2. It would be the last game of his career. That night, when McCollister, the Hawks' publicity director, phoned in the details of the game to the NBA office, he reported, "Guerin played 35 minutes, made 12 of 17 field goal attempts, 7 for 7 free throws, had 5 rebounds, 3 assists and 4 personal fouls. Thirty-one points." He paused for effect. "They are burying him tomorrow morning at 10 o'clock."

A joke, of course. But the subtext was that, at age 36 or younger, Guerin was still a fierce competitor, a trait that remained intact when he worked a game as a coach. There was no pussyfooting with Guerin when he was unhappy with his players. Although he dressed in the "mod" fashions—multicolored sports coats, bell-bottom trousers—that players favored then and made himself available after games at hotel bars, there was never any mistaking who was boss. In team huddles, Guerin was to the point, imparting his displeasure in language that was often profane. But the momentary pique did not carry over. Guerin was not one for grudges, and until Maravich's arrival his players felt he was tough but evenhanded in his dealings with them.

Dealing with Maravich would require the skill of a diplomat as Guerin balanced his history with Hawks veterans against the obvious pressures the front office had imposed by signing the Pistol for all that money and then reasonably expecting to make good on their investment.

As a former NBA backcourt star, Guerin understood how difficult the transition from college to the pros was for a guard. And though he had not known until the night before the draft that the Hawks would select Maravich ("I expected we'd draft Rudy Tomjanovich or Dan Issel."), he was now obliged to deal with the fact that in Maravich he had a wild card that made his job more complicated.

"Obviously, there was resentment about his pay," said Guerin. "Even though they had a small building at Georgia Tech, now all of a sudden they were giving this kid all that money. The players naturally felt: 'Geez, are you telling me this is what you can afford because he's white?' And it was, after all, the south. A lot of people there were racially prejudiced. But you find that in every city you go to. So . . . the players felt:

'What about me?' The money created a problem, but the biggest problem was Pete's performance. He couldn't do some of the things he did in
college because of the level of talent."

Guerin's was a purist view of the game. You played hard and
together—and kept it simple. As a Knick on March 2, 1962, he had
been offended by the tack the Philadelphia Warriors took the night Wilt
Chamberlain set an all-time single-game record by scoring 100 points in
Hershey, Pennsylvania.

"The Warriors," Guerin said, "decided to get Wilt the ball as often as
they could so he could go for the record. Most points in a single game.
Well, to do that they began fouling us in the backcourt to kill the clock
and give Wilt more time to operate. To me it was embarrassing to play
the game that way—a mockery of the sport. I just didn't want any part of
it, so I began intentionally fouling, looking to get my six personal fouls
and leave the court. I'd had enough. But talk of adding insult to injury.
The referee, Willie Smith, wouldn't call the fouls on me. He was telling
me: 'Eh, come on, Richie, play the game.' I was steaming. 'You're calling
fouls on them when they hit us in the backcourt,' I told him. 'Why don't
you call 'em on me?' Well, Willie looked at me and said, 'Cause I know
why you're doing it.'"

For Guerin, the fundamental things applied. There was a right way
and wrong way to play the game. In Maravich's case, the typical rookie
mistakes were compounded, the coach felt, by Pete's impulse for the
crowd-pleasing gesture, particularly when a simpler risk-free maneuver
likelier would have gotten results.

"A three-on-one fast break," said Guerin, "should be an easy layup. If
you go behind your back or through your legs, and it backfires, the fans
boo and your teammates get annoyed. And as a coach, I get mad at you.
There's a time and place for the fancy stuff. Cousy's a good friend—I
play golf with him these days. He was one of the first with a little razzle-
dazzle. But when he went behind his back it was deception. Pete's idea
was to do it for show. He was taught by his dad that showtime puts people in the stands. Truth is that in the pros wins put people in the stands.

"Yet . . . if you try to change his style, his natural response is, 'Why did you draft me?' Fact of the matter was he was a great ball handler. I had a basketball camp in Atlanta. Pete would come and perform at it. I was amazed at his skills. You could see he must have practiced and worked on it for a long time. He was not born with that kind of talent. But when he came to Atlanta, it was a case of . . . like any other rookie . . . there are things you can't do at the next level. Those things take time to teach. Some pick it up quicker than others. Some learn by their mistakes. It took Pete time to do it."

That time was spent on the bench.

"I had known all along," said Maravich, "that I couldn't seriously expect to be a starter immediately—I mean, even Jerry West didn't break into the starting lineup until halfway into his rookie year—so for the first three weeks I sat on the bench and tried to get my bearings. It's a strange feeling, being on the sidelines for the first time in your life, and I hardly knew what to do with myself. I was getting in for about 20 minutes a game, but even then I was contributing little to the team. It went like that for a dozen games—I averaged 13.5 points over that span—and then, after I had missed the 13th game with an injury, Richie called me aside and told me I was going to get my chance to start.

"It's funny, but that's when my real problems began. I don't really know how to explain it. I wasn't doing that badly on the court, in spite of the pressure—in my first six games as a starter I hit for 23, 28, 32, 32, 32 and 40 points—and my ballhandling and defense were improving. I guess it was the timing of everything. At the precise moment the Hawks were stumbling all over themselves and Joe Caldwell was officially jumping to the Carolina Cougars in the ABA, the 'millionaire rookie' was moving into the starting lineup and getting all of the attention from the fans and the press. By the time we had played 30 games—we were 9–21 at that point, exactly the reverse of our record at that time the year before—my morale and everybody else's on the team hit bottom."

As the Hawks sank in the standings, the team's beat writers, Cunningham of the *Atlanta Constitution* and Frank Hyland of the *Atlanta Journal*, were quick to insist that Maravich had to shoulder a good portion of the blame for the team's decline.

"He wasn't well-received by the players," said Hyland. "For instance, Walt Hazzard. Walt didn't like him worth a damn and there was animosity because he was such a hot dog. . . . The Hawks had very good chemistry for the first two years in Atlanta. Then Pete Maravich came here and it disappeared. People may not like to hear it, but it's true.

"Cunningham and I were the original beat writers and, truth be told, we were probably a little resentful too because we had had a good time with the team. There was a lot of camaraderie between the press and the players. We sort of saw Pete Maravich as an intruder. We probably didn't treat him very fairly. We expected him to be perfect. He wasn't. He thought his game was a notch above anybody else's. Not true. We took him to task.

"The fact of the matter was he wasn't at LSU any more. He was not as good as everybody expected. People expected him to set the league on fire. Against the University of Georgia, he'd come in and get his 45 points. But Georgia sucked. Here in the NBA, he wasn't quite as good. And we pointed it out. He became very upset. I'd say to him, 'What's your problem?' He'd say, 'You're crucifying me.' I told him, 'This ain't Baton Rouge.'"

IN PHILADELPHIA, as the Hawks struggled through an early-season game against the 76ers, a large banner was unfurled in the balcony of the Spectrum. It read: "Hey, Pistol Pete, Why Do Hot Dogs Cost Two Million Dollars in Atlanta and Only 35 Cents in Philadelphia?"

The spotlight was on him. He was the one and only Pistol, and that was his lot. Good games, bad games, he was constantly being assessed, his advanced style of play captivating some while turning off others. Few hoops fans were neutral about Pete Maravich.

On the court, he was a target, too, opponents resorting to roughhouse tactics, if necessary, to stop him. In a game against Phoenix, when the Suns' Dick Van Arsdale got overly physical with Maravich and Maravich failed to respond, Guerin called a time-out.

"In the huddle," said Guerin, "I made the point that if one of us is being abused, we have to deal with it."

Said Herb White: "Richie said, 'Okay, Pete. We're going to help you out this time. Next time Van Arsdale gets the ball at the head of the key, take his fake and let him go to the hoop.' Well, the lane opens up like the Red Sea and here goes Van Arsdale. And boom—Jimmy Davis and Bridges nailed him. It was unbelievable. Crushed him. Van Arsdale went down and was very slow in getting up. Next huddle, Richie says, 'Good job.' Then he turns to Pete and says, 'Now you're on your own.'"

Added Guerin: "I told Pete, 'By and large, you take care of your own business.' But Pete by nature was mild-mannered. He did not have that kind of disposition. He was not looking to get into a scuffle. He was the type—it took a while before he decided: 'I can't become a punching bag. I've got to give it back.' And he did. It just took a while. You could see him become more aggressive as the season went on."

But even as he overcame the physicality of stronger men, even as he established himself as an NBA-caliber guard, he remained the bugaboo of his teammates, his every move subject to scrutiny. Early in the year when the team played in Chicago, Maravich and Herb White got off the plane and out of the airport ahead of the others. Arriving at their hotel, they found that the team had been given two single rooms and the rest doubles. They took—what else?—the single rooms and left. When the other Hawks arrived and discovered what their lodgings were, they were not happy. Bridges ranted about the nerve of these rookies.

Soon after, Pete had to leave the team to film a commercial in Jacksonville. In his rookie year, Maravich had endorsement deals with Vitalis, Pro Keds, the United States Hosiery Corporation, and the Seamless Company, which manufactured the Pistol Pete Maravich basketball. The veteran players did not like that their millionaire guard not only was getting outside revenues that they as black players didn't, but also that he could cut out on the team as he pleased.

Another time, a television crew arrived in Atlanta to prepare a documentary on this rookie under siege. The arrangement made beforehand with the team publicity department was that Maravich, Hudson, Hazzard, and Bridges would be made available for on-camera interviews.

"The other Hawks made their position quite obvious," said Al Silverman, then-editor of *Sport Magazine* and the man in charge of the filming. "They were boycotting the interview. The three of them just sat there and wouldn't come out of the office. They'd had enough questions about Pete."

In time, the constant attentions grated on Maravich, too.

"It was," he said, "the same old story everywhere we went. 'See the Bulls play Pete Maravich,' read the ads. Sportswriters were saying all kinds of things about 'dissension' among the Hawks,' putting the blame on me for all of it. They wouldn't leave me alone. One time a guy in Detroit wrote that I was uncooperative with the press. What really happened—as I tried to explain to him—was that I didn't have time for an interview right then because as a rookie I had to rush to the auditorium to get taped before the veterans. Another time, after a bad game in Boston, I stayed in the shower too long to suit a writer there and he blistered me the next morning.

"The best example of the trouble we were having with the press is something that happened early in the season at New York. We had lost to the Knicks, 128–119, but had given them a run for it toward the end. It had been my first regular-season game as a pro at Madison Square Garden, and with Walt Frazier guarding me I'd had a good night: 40 points, 5 assists, some good passing that had turned on the crowd. But the big star that night for us was Bill Bridges, who had gone all 48 minutes and held Dave DeBusschere to 12 points and 5 rebounds, scoring 21 points and pulling down 20 rebounds himself. As soon as the game was over and we were back in the dressing room, the writers began swarming all over us. At least they had enough sense to go to Bridges first, but guess what the first question was. Right. 'What did you think about Maravich tonight?'

"From that night on, I went into hiding. After a game I would stay in the showers for as long as 30 minutes, hoping the writers would just go away. What the hell, I figured, if they're going to draw their own conclusions when we're bad let 'em draw their own conclusions when we're good. When we would get off the plane, with a television crew invariably there waiting for me, I would get in the middle of a crowd of people and look straight ahead and walk as fast as I could. When we would get to the hotel I would go straight to my room and lock the door and shut off all calls and stay there until time to leave for the auditorium."

The Hawks continued to flounder. Team meetings were convened, without success, to air out "the problem"—a euphemism for the uneasy relationship between Maravich and the rest of the team.

"A lot of team meetings," said Herb White. "Meetings where people bared their souls. 'Pete, you gotta do this. You gotta do that.' Usually Bridges or Hazzard talking it up—they were the leaders. . . . Some pretty nasty confrontations. Richie Guerin, an old-school guy, was trying to blend Pete into the team. It was tough. Pete was used to doing things his way. He'd never played defense in college, though he had the ability to—long arms, quickness. He was trying to learn.

"Before Pete, Lou Hudson had been the shooter, the team worked a lot of low post to Bridges and Bellamy, Hazzard would get his 14, 15 points. When Pete came along, he tried to blend in. But the Hawks didn't play his style—they were not a running team 'cause Bridges, Bellamy and Jim Davis—that wasn't their game. They were low post players.

"At these meetings Pete was amicable—he wanted to fit in. But in his four years at LSU he'd been undisciplined—it was going to take him a while. He had no experience playing that type of game.

"During games, Richie would holler at Pete, and Pete would holler back. Or one of the other players would holler at Pete. The front office people would get into it. We were in a fish bowl. It wasn't like the media circus the NBA is today. But in every city the media wanted to talk to him."

In this unhappy atmosphere, Guerin saw his once-unified team grow increasingly quarrelsome. Paranoia reigned. Were those swift and unexpected passes that caromed off of a teammate's head or shoulders really Maravich's way of "showing him up"? And Maravich began to wonder: What was the deal with Hazzard, who often seemed blind to him when he was open for the shot?

"It was," said White, "mostly subtle, covert. But you could feel the tension. Sometimes Pete couldn't understand where all this was coming from. He didn't realize how much his celebrity affected those guys."

Guerin kept trying to overcome the problem, meeting from time to time after games with Maravich at hotel bars. Maravich sometimes would be accompanied by White, his best friend on the Hawks. Guerin and his two players talked as they drank. Once the coach bet he could drink a vodka martini for every beer that Maravich and White slugged down. In the wee hours, Guerin saw his boys stagger off to their rooms while he continued to run up his bar tab, no worse for wear. Amidst the intense pressures—the turmoil on the team, the perpetual media attention, the public coveting a moment of his time—Maravich tried mightily to have a private life. Hawks management helped by secreting him out of Alexander Coliseum after home games through an exit at the back of the building, one with which the public was unacquainted. As the team's business manager, Irv Gack, said, "Most of the players would go out a side door, where the fans waited. Out the side door to where they parked their cars. We had the means of getting Pete in his car and out the back door."

Whether in Atlanta or on the road, Maravich escaped through an active night life. He would have his beers in the dressing room after games, then hang out at the popular bars in whatever NBA city he landed. His readiness to drink was never quite matched by his ability to hold his liquor. At LSU, his alcohol consumption had led to run-ins with the law—some that got covered up, some that didn't—and that summer he had been arrested in Knoxville, Tennessee, for public drunkenness and disorderly conduct (use of profanity), ultimately forfeiting a $60 bond in city court on July 15.

It didn't discourage him in his eagerness to party.

Hal Blondeau, former NC State player and friend of Maravich: "I was living in New York when Pete joined the Hawks. When Atlanta played up here, we'd hang out afterward at an Irish bar. Pete was kind of a willing party-goer. The leader of the pack. Toast of the town. It was funtime and beer. Women groupies everywhere. Pete liked to hoot with the owls and soar with the eagles."

Irv Gack: "He'd take a couple of drinks and get crazy."

Herb White: "He liked to party. And had the money to do it. Women everywhere. In our hotel room, the phone would ring and there'd be a woman on the other end: 'Hello. Is Pete there?' In Chicago, we'd go to Rush Street. In New York, there were several clubs. Boston—a club owned by some football players. Pete never hesitated to pick up the tab. He wasn't tight with the dollar. Once in Chicago, I almost got into a fight with a cabbie at 4 or 5 in the morning. The guy drops us at our hotel, and Pete—drunk as hell—from the backseat throws him his wallet to take out his fare. Well, there were several thousand dollars in the wallet. I grabbed the wallet back from the driver, who didn't want to let go, while Pete's standing on a corner, hanging on to a lamppost.

"One time we picked up a couple of women at the bar in the Atlanta airport. We were in our early 20s, they looked like they were in their 30s. We go home to one of their condos and party. Nine-thirty the next morning the phone rings. My woman walks over to her phone. I hear her talking. Hangs up. She tells me it's her husband. Husband? She says, 'We're separated.' But he was on his way over. He and the other gal's husband. I went running upstairs to where Pete was, just as the two husbands are pulling up to the place. We knocked the screen out the back window and jumped from the second floor. A ten foot drop. The ground was soft. We hit the ground and rolled."

FOR MARAVICH, the drinking became an antidote to this basketball season gone haywire.

He had grown up believing that all his dreams could be fulfilled by Dr. Naismith's game. To the point when he had signed with Atlanta, his *had* been a storybook career. But as the complications of his rookie year piled on, that changed. And so did he. Stung by the reception given him by his teammates and by the media, Pete Maravich hardened. He kept largely to himself when on Hawks business—be it in airports or dressing rooms—and did not welcome strangers into his life. He'd become more suspicious of others' motives, even those who'd been his friends in the past.

"Pistol Pete had the Elvis Syndrome," said his old LSU teammate,

Rusty Bergman. "No matter where he went, people wouldn't leave him alone. He became very paranoid, even when he was around one of his old teammates. I felt it. He acted as though I had a hidden agenda any time I was talking to him or being around him. He just was never as relaxed around me as when he'd been at LSU. It was as though I was trying to take advantage."

The difficulties that their son encountered in his rookie year affected Press and Helen, too. When Howard Bagwell, Pete's Daniel High School coach and onetime neighbor, paid a visit to the Maraviches in Baton Rouge, he found that Helen had turned her home into a kind of shrine for Pete. Trophies and memorabilia so cluttered the place that Bagwell had to tread with care lest he trip or knock over one of these mementos. He also discovered that in her declining emotional state, Helen had become paranoid about black people.

"She was worried about Pete—afraid he'd be attacked by blacks," said Bagwell. "That was the reason she thought Pete should take karate. She was extremely proud of Pete. 'Pete's a star,' she'd say. As the Great White Hope, she was afraid that blacks would resent him. She mentioned it on numerous occasions."

For Press, who'd doted on Pete even through their often-contrary relationship, the lukewarm welcome his son had gotten from Hawks veterans, all of whom were black, apparently made him do a 180-degree turn on bringing black players to LSU. One Baton Rouge sportswriter said that at a time when the SEC color line was breaking down, Press suddenly became disinclined to recruit players of color after he'd brought in LSU's first, Collis Temple, for the '70–71 season. The same sportswriter remembered Press needling a rival coach who started four black players, saying, "Next year you'll have five black starters and then they'll run you out of this place."

Meanwhile, back in Atlanta, Maravich was coping with the tribulations of being Pistol Pete. His rookie season would set the tone for the rest of his NBA career, in Atlanta and beyond: personal success but unrelenting sniping that depicted him as more showman than winner. Nobody would suggest that he gave less than full effort or that he didn't provide prime entertainment value. But through the years the notion would persist that he was for Pistol Pete first and the team second. Critics would say that he had developed his game during countless solitary hours in the gym and that he still played as if he were the only one on the court. His admirers would counter that he never had the supporting cast of a winner. What the reality was depended on whom you asked.

Richie Guerin, Hawks coach: "Pete had a lot of growing up to do. Being away from his dad, who let him do things his way, he was now in a situation where he couldn't."

Herb White, Hawks guard: "Richie wanted him to take care of the big guys [i.e., play a slow-down game/work the ball inside]. Pete was always agreeable. But to Richie he'd try to make a case for opening up the throttle. He was depressed because he was trying to do what Richie wanted and it was hurting his game."

Bill Hosket, Buffalo Braves forward: "I had lunch with him that year, after I'd been traded from the Knicks to Buffalo. It was Bob Kauffman, Pete and I . . . at a hotel in Atlanta. And even with all the adjustments to the pro game he was trying to make, he still loved to entertain. At lunch, he was saying, 'I'll throw some passes tonight that people have never seen before.' He was just so flamboyant. That style today would fit right in. Back then it was abnormal. . . . Pete's ability was not appreciated as much because he was not on a winning team. We played in an era where, to be appreciated, you had to be part of a winner rather than a guy who just entertained the crowd."

Skip Caray, who broadcast Hawks games: "He was trying to adjust. It was hard because he'd always played one way. He knew he had to play the other way. . . . He was like a little puppy dog, trying so hard to please but not knowing how. He had to try to change his game, in a way he was not used to. The expectation was he'd save the franchise. He was 21, and his plate was awfully full. He knew he was in a mess."

Frank Hyland, beat reporter for the Atlanta Hawks: "I don't think race ever entered into play. A lot of people tried to make it out that way. I think Maravich was resented because he was arrogant on and off the court. He walks in, 'Here I am. Pete Maravich.' The others: 'Wait a second. We won a conference title without you.' The fact he was a white guy had nothing to do with it. A lot of people deep down resented him coming into a good ballclub and fucking it up, you'll pardon my language."

Tom McCollister, Hawks publicity director: "Pete felt like he was alone, on the court and off. They just wouldn't give him the ball."

Les Zittrain, Maravich's attorney: "Some of the animosity of his teammates was, like, 'We'll show this kid. . . .' And it manifested in their keeping the ball away from him."

McCollister: "There was a lot of jealousy. You could just feel it. You could just see it. Richie Guerin did the best he could with it. But it was no longer a team. Just a bunch of individuals."

White: "Hazzard wanted to call the team his own. He wanted the ball in his hands. A lot of times he might try to freeze Pete out—things of that nature."

McCollister: "The one guy that was more disruptive was Hazzard. He resented Pete more than anybody else. He wouldn't throw the ball to Pete very much. Unless there was nobody else to throw it to. Pete talked about it. Off the record, he'd say, 'This is bullshit. We can't do anything if they don't let me play.' It's not a direct quote, but it's close."

Hyland: "I don't think Pete ever got the rookie honeymoon he wanted. He was expected to be great and he wasn't. He dribbled too much. He could make brilliant passes except nobody ever saw them coming. He never understood that. He'd make ill-advised, bad plays."

McCollister: "Pete could throw the ball behind his back the length of the floor. And whoever was supposed to catch it, didn't—and Pete felt it was on purpose. He felt he was an upstanding guy and he wasn't treated fairly by his teammates. Except for Hudson. Hudson was the one black who didn't play favorites. If Pete was open he gave the ball to him."

Zittrain: "Pete truly tried his best to be one of the boys. And he got along with some of them. Others, he didn't. Sweet Lou [Hudson]—he was one of the good guys."

Caray: "I think he was a very lonely kid. He felt distanced from his teammates. He didn't know who to trust. He was 21—and a high-strung

21. Had a lot of money. But he was not the happiest. You'd see him a lot by himself."

Hyland: "Pete would say to me, 'What are you printing that shit about me for?' I'd say, 'Three-for-25. What am I supposed to say? You shot well? You haven't played defense in your life. You don't have to be a genius to say you played bad.'"

McCollister: "Cunningham and Hyland, the two beat reporters—both of them resented Pete . . . I felt they did that because they catered more to the Hawks team that was already there than to Pete. They felt if they treated him kindly, they'd have a hard time with the others. He was not well-liked by those two. . . . His reaction? There was some resentment from Pete because of that. He wondered, 'Why are they doing this to me?' And I had no answer to him."

Caray: "I did a halftime interview with him, the kind of thing he supposedly hated to do. I told him, 'Look, we can stop it at any time during the interview. If you say not to use it we won't. Deal?' He said okay. The first question I asked him was, 'How do you feel about life?' He started talking; it was the most animated I'd seen him. But in that interview, he told me that he'd painted, 'Take me' on the roof of his building. In case UFOs were passing by. I thought later: 'He's not happy. He wants out. Not just out of Atlanta but out of the NBA.' I'm not knocking Press. But I think he made a big mistake. His love for his son warped his judgement."

THE HAWKS' decision to sign Pete Maravich had been a business calculation.

And although Atlanta struggled on the basketball floor, Tom Cousins had been affirmed at the box office, as the *Wall Street Journal* reported in March 1971, as the regular season came to an end:

This year, 18 Hawk games were completely sold out, compared to only three sellouts last year when the team was in first place in its division.

Attendance this year leaped more than 20% to 245,910 from 202,847 the year before. Gate receipts rose even faster, to $930,833 from $632,518 the year before and $613,591 the year before that.

The team this season, despite its slump, appeared on national television five times, including one appearance on the ABC Wide World of Sports that paid the Hawk owners about $65,000. Last year the team appeared on national TV only twice during the regular season.

The team last season couldn't find a single buyer for its radio and television rights. It had to make its own arrangements with stations and advertisers, and it barely broke even. But this year there were several bidders, and the team made what [business manager] Gack terms "a substantial profit" on the rights. . . .

By March, as these figures were being tabulated, the Hawks' worst times were behind them. The team had come on strong, winning 13 of its last 17 games to squeeze into the playoffs in the Central Division of the NBA's Eastern Conference in spite of a 36–46 record. Atlanta became one of four eastern teams to make the playoffs.

During that 17-game stretch run, Maravich had been the dominant figure on the Atlanta team: He scored more than 30 points seven times and more than 40 three times. And although the Hawks would bow to the Knicks, four games to one, in the opening round of the playoffs, it did not alter the fact that under the most trying of circumstances Pete Maravich had proven he was a bona fide NBA guard.

He finished the regular season as the league's eighth-best scorer with 1,880 points in 81 games, an average of 23.2 ppg. Of the Hawks, only Hudson scored more—26.8 ppg. Maravich shot .458 percent from the floor, better than he ever had at LSU, and 80 percent from the free-throw line. He totaled 298 rebounds and 355 assists.

Those were solid statistics, particularly for a rookie. But the antagonism that his big-money contract had caused with teammates appeared to extend beyond Atlanta, affecting those writers and broadcasters who voted for Rookie of the Year. Geoff Petrie of Portland (24.8 ppg, 390 assists, 280 rebounds) and Dave Cowens (17 ppg, 228 assists, 1,216 rebounds) shared rookie honors, with Maravich finishing a distant third.

"It's a disgrace that Pete Maravich was not named Rookie of the Year," Guerin told newsmen. "Cowens and Petrie are fine players, but neither had a rookie year like Pete. . . . I put him in the same class as Oscar, West and Monroe when they came up. You know, it's difficult for a man Pete's age to handle the constant pressure that he was exposed to all year. He always impressed me the way he kept his cool—and through all the criticism and hostilities that he had to face. To do all that and still have a rookie year like he had, you gotta be some kind of ballplayer."

The kind of ballplayer he was had an artiste's need to delight, to constantly top himself. Although Maravich had the ability to soar up to the rim and although hours before games he would try various slam dunks with White—a renowned leaper at 6-foot-2—after opening tip the Pistol resisted the airborne gymnastics in spite of forever promising his friend Herb he would throw one down. For Maravich, the real thrill was to create magic with the basketball—improvised moves and/or passes that would bring the crowd to its feet.

But for all of his showman's urges, he remained a competitor, a player who, no less than he had in high school and college, still took to heart every loss. As his chaotic rookie year ended, he looked forward to proving that he need not be regarded as merely an entertainer on the court. Proud as he was of his ability to turn on a crowd, he wanted more. Pete Maravich was a player in search of legitimacy. As a winner.

THE PALACE intrigues of Maravich's rookie season were very much in the past as the 1971–72 season approached.

That the Hawks were now Pete Maravich's team was obvious even before the squad reported to its Jacksonville, Florida, training camp. In the off-season Atlanta management had traded Walt Hazzard (and Jerry Chambers) to the Buffalo Braves for 6-foot-3 guard Herm Gilliam and 6-foot-4 forward Don May.

That the team was being rebuilt to accommodate the Pistol was reinforced early on in the 82-game regular season when Bridges was dispatched to the Philadelphia 76ers for 6-foot-7 Jim Washington, and Davis was sent to the Houston Rockets for 6-foot-7 Don Adams.

The deals represented more than a purge of malcontents. The Hawks front office was opting for quickness up front rather than bulk and strength. In Washington, Adams, and May, and a rookie named George Trapp, the Hawks had acquired players who figured to fit better with Maravich's run-and-gun style. As for Gilliam—talented defender that he was—he offset the weakest phase of Maravich's game. Guerin could rely on him to clamp down on the other team's top guard.

What's more, the new bunch hadn't the past history—so brimming with divisiveness—that had undermined the Hawks in Maravich's rookie year. No wonder Pete approached his second pro season feeling upbeat, even after rookie complications that would have given most men battle fatigue. In a bylined article in *Sport Magazine*, published before the season began, his words underscored his eagerness for a fresh start:

> I think I'm ready, beginning with this year, to play my best basketball in the NBA. The shakedown is over. I think my teammates, after the way I came on toward the end of the season, understand me and accept me now. Since I signed, a lot of others have gotten big money like Artis Gilmore, who reportedly got twice as much as I did—so I am no longer *the* "millionaire rookie . . ." All I really want to do is play basketball, and I hope that now everybody is going to let me do it.

The experts figured that the reconstituted Hawks would soar. In its preseason issue, *Sports Illustrated* picked the Hawks to win the Central Division. But circumstances conspired against the Hawks and Maravich. A day before the team broke camp in Jacksonville, Maravich became ill.

"It started off," he said, "like a bad cold—fever, sore throat, and chills, and it got worse from there. They treated me at first for a throat infection, shot me full of penicillin and other stuff. Finally, they put me in a hospital in Jacksonville. One day I woke up with a breaking-out all over, and the doctors there thought I had scarlet fever. I checked out of the Jacksonville hospital and came to a hospital in Atlanta. Doctors there made tests for mononucleosis, but the results were negative. Finally, they decided it *had* to be mono and started treating me for that."

On October 5, an Associated Press story reported that team physician, Dr. Charlie Harrison, said that Maravich would miss the first two weeks of the season:

> Maravich, the floppy-haired sophomore whose absence in exhibition games lately has sparked angry crowd reactions, has been undergoing tests in an Atlanta hospital for more than a week. He was scheduled to be released Tuesday and confined to his apartment.
>
> The Hawks begin the regular season next Tuesday in Cincinnati.
>
> Herm Gilliam, a defensive specialist acquired from Buffalo this summer in a trade for Walt Hazzard, has been working the backcourt with Lou Hudson since Maravich's illness.

Recovery was slow and difficult. The mono sapped his strength, leaving him so exhausted that he had to have help climbing the stairs of his Atlanta townhouse. Maravich's weight dropped from 205 pounds to 169. To put the weight back on, he ate five or six meals a day. But it wasn't until late October, more than a month after he'd been hospitalized and with the season under way, that he was strong enough to practice with the team. By then, Atlanta's record was 3–6.

By November, Maravich was back in uniform. But neither he nor the team ever really fully recovered. Though there were nights when he looked as spry as ever—he scored 50 points on January 16 against Philadelphia and again on February 5 against the Cleveland Cavaliers—he hadn't the strength to sustain those big nights consistently. By February he weighed only 183 pounds and was now plagued by tendinitis and a bone spur in his toe. He finished the regular season averaging 19.3 ppg in 66 games, had 393 assists and 256 rebounds.

As Maravich put it: "I never regained my true form that year with my continual lack of energy. Doctors had even told me that I was foolish to come back to play as quickly as I did, because of the seriousness of the illness."

The Hawks finished the season with a 36–46 record and were beaten four games to two by the Celtics in the Eastern Conference semifinals of the playoffs. For Guerin it would be his last year as an NBA coach; he moved up to the front office as Hawks general manager at the season's conclusion.

To this day, beat reporter Hyland insists, "Maravich probably cost Richie his job. And my guess is that it was traumatic enough that he never wanted to coach again. It's purely my opinion, but I think after Guerin had Pete and saw his team crumble, he said, 'I don't need this any more.'"

IN HIS two years in the NBA, Pete Maravich had been diminished by matters largely beyond his control. But now, as the 1972–73 season approached, Maravich no longer felt restrained by in-house unrest and had prepared his body for the hard knocks of the pro game.

As Press wrote friends that August:

> . . . Pete called last nite. He hurt his leg, hip and jaw bone in karate group demonstration. He said he hadn't been to a karate class in 4 days because he's had to heal. He passed his purple belt. Now he's in the advanced stage and working on the blue belt. After that it is green, brown and finally black. He loves the damn stuff.

In a new building, the Omni, and under a new coach, Lowell (Cotton) Fitzsimmons, a Maravich looking suspiciously like the player who had lit up SEC field houses resurfaced, with all of those ingenious moves that even now, viewed through the prism of nearly three decades, qualify as state-of-the-art hoops improvisations.

See him as he glides downcourt on the fast break with those familiar loping strides, the ball yo-yoing from his fingertips, his shaggy hair flying up. There is no sense of urgency. The man is poker-faced and in command. The dark, haunting eyes take in the traffic. The moment belongs to Peter Press Maravich, who makes the play the way only he can.

Like this.

With a defender crouched before him, ready to spring right or left, Maravich chooses to give the moment a flourish. In a blink of the eye, he lets his dribble hang as he waves his hand sideways through the air, a phantom swipe at the ball that is a prelude to the real thing—a dead-on look-away pass that he throws with the same flicking hand motion in the very next beat, leaving the stun-gunned defender dead in his shoes and Maravich's teammate floating in for the easy layup.

It is done with Buster Keaton deadpan and executed so seamlessly— fake pass, real pass—that it leaves the hard-core fan momentarily breathless, delighted, and charged with the pleasure of the game's possibilities.

That was how it was in this '72–73 season. Maravich was scoring points in bunches again—better than 26 a game—and exciting crowds with the plays he made. At a time when the game was far more staid than it is these days, he could spin left or right with his dribble, go behind his back, through his legs, cross it over or do combination maneuvers—one from column A, one from column B—with a virtuosity that made the Globetrotters look conventional.

Maravich could step to the right and throw a bounce pass in that direction that would, with properly applied spin and cocked wrist, end up in the hands of a teammate racing down the left side of the floor. Maravich's "wrist pass" prompted Boston's Red Auerbach to say: "Some guys break the law of gravity, this guy breaks the law of physics."

Or, he could drive down the lane, as he did against the tenacious Mike Riordan, flip the ball behind his back, catch it while going airborne and then, resisting gravity as he drifted left, twist his body back to the right and scoop the ball underhanded with his right hand into the basket.

Amazing stuff, executed with a flair all his own. At a time of changing attitudes and cultural polarization—this was the era of Muhammad Ali and Joe Namath and the Vietnam War—Maravich was another of the elite free spirits in sports.

But with Fitzsimmons' Hawks, he had matured. He had learned to work his shimmy-and-shake opportunely. He had learned to view the game from a wider perspective than the me-first orientation he came into the league with—a legacy of three years of being Daddy Press' anything-goes *wunderkind*.

Pete's game had grown up. Or so it seemed. When he came to New York to play the Knicks, the *Times* spoke of a "new Maravich":

> In his third pro basketball season, Pete Maravich has a mustache, his hair is browner and he has matured as a player. He is no longer the Louisiana State University shooter who endeared himself to the ticket-holders with his shooting.
>
> The new Maravich has added many other essential facets of the game to his brilliant shooting, which made him the highest scorer in major college basketball history.
>
> "Pete is the guy who creates the action," said Cotton Fitzsimmons, the Atlanta coach. "He is becoming more of a complete ballplayer all the time. He has been moving the ball well, scoring like a gangbuster and has done a good job defensively."

When the team returned to Atlanta, Press came up from Boone, North Carolina, where he was coaching basketball at Appalachian State, to watch his boy play in the new arena that sportswriters had taken to calling "the house that Pete built." Press had lost his job at LSU after a 10–16 season in 1971–72, a turn of events that embittered Pete toward his alma mater for many years. In fact, when the Hawks were scheduled to play a preseason exhibition at the new Assembly Center on the LSU campus—ironically also referred to as "the house that Pete built"—Maravich boycotted the game, telling *Atlanta Journal* reporter Mike McKenzie: "They've got my jersey hanging in a trophy case in there, and it has a hole in it—right in the back, where they stuck the knife into my father."

Pete's bitterness was not an isolated instance. Even while the Hawks were winning for the first time in three years and Maravich was drawing praise for accommodating his teammates—nearly seven assists a game—he remained moody and withdrawn, a residue of the turbulent rookie year. Where once he had the boy's ingenuous love of game, now it was distorted by darker emotions.

Hal Blondeau: "Pro ball wasn't what he expected. It wasn't what he thought it'd be. I think he thought people had worked as hard as he to get there. It was his preconceived notion. He found out, hell, they were just bigger, stronger, meaner. I think that bothered him. He told me the pro game wasn't what it was cracked up to be. My perception is that he was disappointed by the lack of effort, and of giving back to the game. That's what he got from Press. You had to give back to the game. I know that's how Press felt. I think Pete never saw that once he got to the pros."

Mike McKenzie: "By '72–73, he was bitter and somewhat aloof. The rap on him was that he hadn't won and, as long as he did well and got his points, he didn't care. . . . Anybody that watched him knew it was garbage. He'd just die inside. He had a burning desire to win. But it was hard to know him. He wouldn't let you know him. He didn't trust the press. . . . He felt that the writers were not fair to him. The players— when he joined the team—started this thing, and the press jumped on it, ate it up and loved it. They fanned the flames. The broader picture was: the world against Pete."

Pat Williams, Hawks general manager: "He was very insecure despite all the fame. He was seeking solace in alcohol . . . and all the pleasures life had to offer, and finding nothing in it. He was a tormented man. So much acclaim. So much fame. But inwardly he was a frightened scared guy."

McKenzie: "At one point that season, Pete talked about the lack of support for the team in Atlanta. The fans that came to games were great, he said, but where were the others? I write the story, but I don't lead with that. It was just part of the story. Well, Lewis Grizzard, the executive sports editor of the *Journal*, calls me over and: 'Pete says this and you don't lead with it. . . .?' I say, 'It's in context.' He had Jim Huber rewrite the story and it became the lead. The lead in the final edition with a big headline. The next time I see Pete, he's on me for what I wrote. I explained about the editor. Pete called the paper and spoke to Grizzard. I got removed from the beat because of it. It was a sticky wicket—a situation that'd illustrate why he didn't trust the press. 'See what I mean?' he says to me. 'Anything I say they're going to make a big thing out of it. I know what I said and it didn't come out that way.' Sometimes that was true. Sometimes it was imagined."

Pete Maravich: "All my life I had tried to find satisfaction from other people and gain acceptance, but after years of searching for approval the energy to do so began wearing me down."

THE GAME took a toll on his body, too.

Dr. David F. Apple, Jr., Atlanta orthopedist and team physician to the Hawks, had treated Maravich for chronic heel bursitis, recommending rest and/or ultrasound.

In an interview with the *Medical Tribune*, Maravich said: "I've had bursitis in my heel since I was 15 or 16. It's worse at times. When my shoe rubs against it, it sends a terrible pain up my Achilles tendon and I can't run or jump. It's one of those things I've learned to live with."

Live with and play with. Playing with pain was common enough in the NBA. Although basketball was regarded as a noncontact sport, the truth was that it was a demanding game that often turned rough-and-tumble. Maravich was not unique among NBA players in coping with the nagging stresses that afflict a ballplayer's body.

But in New York to play the Knicks on November 9, 1972, he encountered a new dimension of medical travail. He awoke one morning and found that the whole right side of his face was paralyzed.

"I couldn't shut my eye—and that was scary because someone could stick a finger in there," he said.

Doctors diagnosed his problem as Bell's palsy.

"I also had Reiter's syndrome while I had Bell's palsy," Maravich said. "The palsy was on the right side of my face and the Reiter's affected my left jaw."

An Associated Press story a week later reported that Maravich had seen part-time action with the condition.

Suffering from Bell's palsy, Maravich tried to play last Saturday but lasted only six minutes. The condition prevents him from closing his right eye and triggers near constant headaches.

Coach Cotton Fitzsimmons said Maravich's ailment had improved and he would try again this weekend.

"Seems the same to me," Maravich said. "Some pain behind the neck and around the ear and I have to wear a patch or tape my eyes shut to sleep. Drives me crazy."

The high-scoring player also said, "I'm going to go back to playing anyway. I can't sit around forever."

He would miss six games. But after 32 days, the paralysis began to clear up. Maravich was back in action—a starter in his first All-Star game (eight points, five assists in 22 minutes) and the reconstituted backcourt leader of the Hawks. He would drive Atlanta to a 46–36 record—second place in the Central Division of the Eastern Conference—while averaging 26.1 ppg (fifth best in the league) and what would amount to a career-best 6.9 assists a game, sixth best in the NBA. Although the Hawks would be eliminated in the opening round of the playoffs, losing to Boston four games to two. Maravich was named to the All-NBA second team—a potent quintet of Cowens, Hayes, Barry, Frazier, and Maravich. First team: Abdul-Jabbar, West, Tiny Archibald, Spencer Haywood, and John Havlicek.

For Maravich the honors reflected acceptance, finally, by the public *and* the media. The turmoil that had sullied him as a rookie appeared to be receding into the past. The future looked bright. Under Fitzsimmons, Maravich had become a more complete player by expending his flashy skills more judiciously and by taking account of his teammates—by bringing them into the loop—and thus building a winner in Atlanta for the first time in his career.

It figured to get even better as the '73–74 season began.

Twelve games into the season, the Hawks had a one and one-half game lead in the Central Division, Maravich topped the league in scoring with a 29.6 ppg average, and *Sports Illustrated* had him on its cover with this blurb: "Pistol Pete Is on Target for Atlanta."

The magazine's Peter Carry would note:

> The current Pistol Pete is an improved model. Rarely does he drive at breakneck speed into the corner or wildly fling the ball up from mid-court. He usually concentrates on what his team is trying to achieve. Some of the original Maravich remains, but he does his between-the-legs, behind-the-back and over-the-shoulder passing and dribbling so fluidly that, along with his phenomenal quickness, they are now taken for granted.
>
> Still, in the last year he has proved that there are two things he does superlatively, perhaps better than anyone alive: handle the ball and shoot on the move.

Given that roseate picture, how did it come to pass that months later, a Hawks team that had looked so promising had turned into a tortured loser and once again the finger of blame pointed to Pete Maravich?

Well, with injuries to Gilliam and Hudson limiting their availability, with 34-year-old Bellamy rapidly declining as a force in the middle, and with the disappointing play of touted rookies John Brown and Dwight Jones, the team's chemistry changed. Where a season before Maravich felt confident that he could rely on his supporting cast, now he lost confidence and reverted to the me-first mentality that Fitzsimmons thought he'd exorcised.

"He put so much pressure on himself," said teammate Jim Washington. "If he didn't live up to his expectations, he really internalized. It was unfortunate because it wasn't necessary. He dealt with pressure by doing things to extreme. Like drinking."

Though Fitzsimmons tried to convince Maravich to distribute the ball to the others, he found that with each loss Maravich became more entrenched in the notion of winning games by himself.

"There was a lot of frustration," said Fitzsimmons. "Pistol was the greatest when it came to handling the ball that we had seen at the time. But he was a very emotional young man, an extremely emotional young man. When things didn't go right, he turned extremely unhappy."

On February 3, 1974, that unhappiness was expressed in Maravich's objection to a call made by referee Jim Capers in a game against Houston. When Capers subsequently hit him with a technical foul, Maravich became so angry that he had to be restrained from charging the referee by Hudson and Gilliam. In his agitated state, he inadvertently hit Hudson with an elbow and bloodied his teammate's nose. Maravich was ejected from the game.

"That night," said Fitzsimmons, "was where the parting of ways began. You see, Pistol was a guy who couldn't drink two beers without your having to peel him off the wall. At halftime, when we returned to the dressing room, he was sitting on the floor, not showered, with a couple of beer cans beside him. After the game, he showered, had a few more beers and created a disturbance at the hotel.

"I dealt with it, without the media finding out. Next day, when Pistol got on the plane, he'd been drinking. I told him, 'Go to sleep.' But he caused a problem on the plane and I took action."

"Hawks' Maravich Suspended 'Indefinitely' by His Coach" was the *New York Times* headline.

To reporters back then, Fitzsimmons was vague about what provoked the suspension, saying: "It was nothing big. Something occurred and Pete had to be suspended."

More than two decades later, Fitzsimmons would acknowledge that with the suspension—for two games, it turned out—the line of communication between Maravich and him went dead.

"From the point he returned from suspension, we had 33 games to play," said Fitzsimmons. "I started him every game but we never talked. I always spoke to him, but he would not acknowledge me.

"Pete idolized his father. You could tell there'd never be another coach like Press for him. You could never rise to that level. In Pistol's mind, you could never rise."

As the relationship between Maravich and coach turned icy, the

Hawks' general manager, Pat Williams—Guerin had departed for a job with a Wall Street firm—began to think about trading Maravich. Williams saw the incident in Houston as a reflection of a larger issue.

"Pete was living the wrong kind of life," said Williams. "Alcohol was an issue. He was out of control. He was going to do what he wanted to do on and off the court."

Earlier in the season, before Fitzsimmons began urging Williams to see what could be had for Maravich in a trade, the Hawks' GM had been contacted by Fred Rosenfeld, an attorney from Los Angeles. Rosenfeld was part of a group that had been awarded an NBA expansion franchise in New Orleans for $6.15 million, beginning with the '74–75 season, and he wondered what it would take to pry Maravich from the Hawks.

"At the time," said Williams, "I told him, 'You'd have to give up the whole French Quarter.'"

But once the point of no return was reached between Maravich and Fitzsimmons, Williams began to investigate other teams' interest in Maravich.

"Interestingly," he said, "Pete's market value was not very high. The feeling was you couldn't win with him; you had to turn everything over to him; he had not lived up to the hype, even if his numbers were amazing."

Maravich had finished second in scoring in the NBA, behind Buffalo's Bob McAdoo, with a 27.7 average, but his assists had dropped from 546 to 396. Meanwhile, Atlanta had finished second in the Central Division with a 35–47 record.

"The perception was," said Williams, "nobody was going to give up their great player for Pete except New Orleans. Except that New Orleans, as an expansion franchise, had no players. But all this time Fred Rosenfeld and I had dialogued regularly. Fred was a very aggressive, forthright kind of guy. Not til the end of the season did I indicate interest in a trade. I laid out an outlandish laundry list: 'Your number one pick this year, that year, etcetera etcetera.' At one point, when Fred kept saying yes, Tom Cousins told me, 'Don't take any more.' Because he was fearful New Orleans would go out of business."

The deal that the Hawks and the as-yet-unnamed New Orleans franchise struck—which came to be known as the Louisiana Purchase—was this: Maravich to New Orleans for its first-round selections in 1974 and 1975; second-round draft choices in 1975; an exchange of first-round choices in 1976 and 1977 if advantageous to the Hawks; the first guard and forward picked in the expansion draft; and the obligation to take the no-longer-desirable Bellamy in that expansion draft.

"Now we have a deal," said Williams. "And Fred Rosenfeld is in Atlanta. I've got to go tell Pete. Fred and I drive to Pete's apartment complex. I decide to have Fred wait in the car. I sat down in Pete's living room—I was very uncomfortable. But I explained what had happened—that we'd made a trade, to New Orleans. I explained that New Orleans had an intense desire for him. After his years at LSU, his presence in that market meant everything. There was a little pause. Pete looked at me and asked one question: 'What did you get for me?' I told him. There was another pause. He says, 'Is that all?' I said, 'Pete, that's the deal.'"

6

THE NEW ORLEANS franchise had been purchased by a group of wealthy men—several of them Los Angeles Lakers fans—who were drawn to the city by the ongoing construction of its multisports facility, called the Superdome.

That the Superdome would not be ready for the team's first season, 1974–75, was, it turned out, in keeping with the slightly unhinged spirit of the enterprise. That was not exactly a shock considering that the team's owners—Rosenfeld, the Beverly Hills attorney; Sam Battisone Jr., Santa Barbara-based owner of the nationwide Sambo's chain of restaurants; Fred Miller, an auto dealer from Van Nuys; Sheldon Beychock, a Baton Rouge attorney; and Andrew Martin, a New Orleans businessman—were new to pro basketball.

As a lawyer Rosenfeld had represented Lakers broadcaster Rod Hundley and a couple of the team's players, but that hadn't given him experience running a pro basketball operation. Yet it was Rosenfeld who took on the title of team president and worked through the expansion process.

There was much to do. Maravich, who signed a three-year contract worth $1.2 million, was the marquee name that the front office hoped would entice ticket buyers. But once the Pistol—hero to bayou fans all these years after his LSU heroics—was aboard, the Jazz, as the team would be known, had to acquire a coach and other players.

The coach turned out to be an unknown—Scotty Robertson, who had had success in the college ranks, guiding Louisiana Tech to a 165–86 record in 10 seasons.

In May, the league held an expansion draft to stock the New Orleans franchise. Each NBA team was allowed to protect 7 of its 12 players. The Jazz then selected one man—and one man only—from each organization's list of "exposed" players. As part of the Maravich deal, the first guard taken (Dean Meminger, New York Knicks) and the first forward taken (Bob Kauffman, Buffalo Braves) went to Atlanta.

That left New Orleans with the following players: Dennis Awtrey, 6-foot-10 center of the Chicago Bulls; Jim Barnett, 6-foot-4 guard from Golden State; Walt Bellamy, 6-foot-11 center, Atlanta; John Block, 6-foot-10 forward, Kansas City-Omaha; Barry Clemens, 6-foot-7 forward, Cleveland; E. C. Coleman, 6-foot-8 forward, Houston; Lamar Green, 6-foot-8 forward, Phoenix; Nate Hawthorne, 6-foot-4 guard, Los Angeles; Ollie Johnson, 6-foot-6 forward, Portland; Toby Kimball, 6-foot-8 forward, Philadelphia; Steve Kuberski, 6-foot-8 forward, Boston; Stu Lantz, 6-foot-3 guard, Detroit; Louis Nelson, 6-foot-3 guard, Washington; Curtis Perry, 6-foot-8 forward, Milwaukee; and Bud Stallworth, 6-foot-5 forward, Seattle.

Most experts viewed the Louisiana Purchase as dooming the Jazz to long-term mediocrity because of all the draft choices Rosenfeld had given up to the Hawks. Typical was what Joe Whittington would write in *The Sporting News*:

One thing seems certain. New Orleans went against just about every rule for building a successful expansion franchise. . . .

If The Pistol still has a grip on the sports fans of Louisiana, whom he once thrilled while at LSU, the new team should enjoy initial success at the gate as Maravich pounds away at the basket. It could be bleak after that. . . .

Buffalo is the prime example, making the playoffs for the first time after three seasons of 65–181 misery. It came about by drafting the Elmore Smiths, Randy Smiths, Bob McAdoos and Ernie DiGregorios.

Only after that are you in any position to work up through trades. For at least four years, the only thing New Orleans will have to trade is Maravich, and that starts a vicious cycle. . . .

Atlanta will be better off with just one man who has to have the ball, Lou Hudson, despite the fact that the Atlanta people say it wasn't a matter of "getting rid" of Maravich.

"How can we expect to do anything when Pete dominates the ball?" Hudson once asked a Houston player during a game.

On paper, the Hawks appeared to have snookered the Jazz by acquiring all of those draft choices. But the reality proved otherwise. In the '74 draft, Atlanta selected Tom Henderson, a guard from Hawaii, and Mike Sojourner, a forward from Utah. Henderson spent two and a half reasonably productive years with the Hawks before moving on to Washington. Sojourner lasted three unspectacular seasons in the league. In '75, through the Maravich deal the Hawks ended up with first-round selections David Thompson and Marvin Webster, both of whom opted to play in the ABA. So much for outwitting Rosenfeld and the Jazz.

Not that New Orleans hadn't its share of headaches. To begin with, many of the expansion players who reported to training camp were there grudgingly. To compound their displeasure at having to be part of a start-up franchise, some of these veterans were offended by the approach that Robertson took in training camp, running them through drills that they viewed as more suited to high school or college teams, like the one in which these old boys were asked to stand up to a player driving to the hoop and take the charge.

In fairness to Robertson, he was hamstrung by having too many bodies in camp, the result of other NBA teams breaking promises made to Rosenfeld. In lobbying NBA executives for the right to buy the New Orleans franchise, Rosenfeld had made tacit agreements to take certain players in the expansion draft, with the understanding that he would be able to move them later in trades. But in too many instances, the anticipated deals did not materialize.

As Bud Johnson, the former LSU sports information director who served as the Jazz's first publicity man, recalled: "Ownership thought it'd get three-for-one and two-for-one deals. They never pulled it off. It screwed up training camp. There were too many bodies. It wasn't a true training camp. Scotty Robertson was forced to work with too many guys. Bellamy played one game and was cut. He should have been cut the first day of training camp. But the front office was hoping that somebody on another team would go down and they could effect a deal for Bellamy."

The Superdome was a year away from opening its doors. And although that enclosed stadium, when completed, would seat 75,000 for the NFL Saints and, by shifting walls around, 19,203 for basketball—more when ticket demand might merit it—the team had to find another building in which to play.

The solution was to stage games in two nondescript arenas. One of them, the Municipal Auditorium, was a WPA monstrosity located in a run-down section of the city and seating 7,800. The building had only one dressing room, which meant that visiting teams would suit up at their hotels or brave it from behind a curtained-off portion of the arena's corridor.

With the Mardi Gras season in December, the Jazz would shift to the field house at Loyola, capacity 6,500. The Loyola field house had its share of quirks, most notably a court that was elevated three feet above floor level, an architectural peril in the eyes of the NBA Players Association. To avoid having its athletes topple off the court and suffer serious injury, the union insisted that the Jazz pony up $5,000 for a restraining net, an appurtenance that made the game resemble the caged environments in which 1920s teams often played.

In this makeshift atmosphere, Maravich & Co. were, as expansion teams tend to be, terrible. Only more so. In their gold-purple-and-green uniforms—the colors of the Mardi Gras—they lost their first 11 games of the season and were headed for another defeat against Portland when Maravich hit an off-balance jump shot from deep in the corner as he fell out of bounds with no time left. The shot gave New Orleans a 102–101 victory, its first win ever. Reporter Marty Mule would write in the *New Orleans Times-Picayune*:

> The roar and excitement from the 5,465 fans in attendance seemed to come from a crowd 10 times larger.
>
> "You'd have thought we'd won the world championship that night," Maravich said.

A week later, with the Jazz 1–14, Robertson—who would go on to be part of coaching staffs with other NBA teams—was fired.

THE DISMAL start that Maravich experienced in New Orleans was matched by what his father was going through as coach of Appalachian State.

In two seasons at the Boone, North Carolina, school, Press' teams had gone 6–19 and 5–20, and the '74–75 season would prove even worse.

But Press' problems were compounded by Helen's sickness. In the hope of reversing her deteriorating emotional health—she had threatened suicide on more than one occasion—Press had sent her to a clinic at Duke University. But as his assistant coach, former LSU player Rusty Bergman, recalled, the lengthy stay there proved fruitless:

"He'd spent $10,000 to $20,000 to help her at Duke. A clinic. Some type of rehab. One day, after she'd come back to Boone, he came into the office completely irate. He thought she was acting peculiar. He'd found four or five bottles of liquor, and poured every bottle down the drain. He was devastated because he spent all that money."

One day that October, Bergman and Press passed the afternoon on the 18-hole course of the Grandfather Golf & Country Club, 10 miles outside of Boone. As was his habit, Press needled the other golfers and improvised dime bets through the 18 holes. "Coach Maravich was," said Bergman, "a barrel of laughs."

On his return home, Bergman was surprised that his wife, Anne, wasn't there.

"Normally," he said, "she'd be fixing dinner. I'm waiting, waiting for her. Finally, I figure maybe she's visiting Helen—we lived four miles away from the Maraviches. I called down there. The man who answered identified himself as a policeman. I said, 'Is Anne Bergman there?' He said, 'No. She committed suicide. She shot herself.' I said, 'Are you sure? Anne Bergman?' He said, 'No. Helen Maravich.'"

With a 22-caliber pistol, Helen had shot herself in the head. Ten-year-old Diana, who was home at the time, had run to neighbors to get help. The neighbors had called Anne Bergman. Boone police, who had been summoned to the Maravich home before on occasions when Helen had threatened suicide, this time found her lying in a pool of blood, still breathing. It was approximately 6 P.M. Three hours later, Helen Maravich was pronounced dead at Catawba Memorial Hospital. She was 49 years old.

"Coach Maravich," said Bergman, "was totally shocked. Anne said he grabbed towels and threw them to Anne, saying, 'Here, clean it up, would you please?' Both he and Helen were clean freaks. He stood there, muttering, 'I don't know why she did it. It doesn't make any sense.'

"To be a coach at the college or pro level is so demanding, it occupies so much of a coach's time away from home. Press was totally eaten up with the game. His typical routine was after Helen and Diana went to bed at ten, he'd watch TV to midnight. Then he'd dream up new plays and read his bible. A lot of people thought Press wasn't religious 'cause he cussed. Anyway, he'd come to the office at ten the next day and: 'I got a new offense I want to show you.' Always Xs and Os. He was one of the greatest basketball minds.

"As for Helen, a coach's wife needs to be involved in other things so-cially. Or have a lot of family. She needs some kind of social outlet. Helen didn't have girl friends at Appalachian State. Or was involved some way socially. I felt she led a very lonely life."

Pete Maravich was doing stretching exercises alongside the Jazz's 6-foot-10 center, Neal Walk, when a Jazz official wandered onto the practice court at Tulane University and told him there was a phone call for him. That was how Helen Maravich's son would learn of her suicide. He left immediately to be with his family.

After his mother was buried in Aliquippa, a grieving Maravich returned to the team. In Cleveland, Walk recalled, Maravich talked about his mother while they sat in the airport there.

"It had a profound effect on him," said Walk. "He was carrying a big burden. He was very quiet, which was un-Pete. When Pete wasn't brooding or into his beers, he'd make jokes. He was the kind of guy who loved fast cars, and flashy things. He was bubbly most of the time. It was the way I knew him. That night, he wasn't like that. He said how sad, how unfortunate that his mother suffered for so long. I remember him shaking his head and wondering how his dad was gonna be."

Prior to that road trip, Pete's longtime girlfriend, Jackie Elliser—she'd begun dating Pete as a coed at LSU—had expressed her concern about Maravich to Walk, telling him, "Please take care of Peter Press." Walk, a former Florida University star who'd played against Maravich while in college and had developed a friendship with Pete during those years, understood her implicit fear—that her Peter would go off the deep end.

And indeed, in Chicago, Maravich succumbed to despair. After the Jazz played the Bulls there, and his teammates returned to their hotel and couldn't locate Maravich, Walk asked for volunteers to go looking for him.

"There were maybe five of us," said Walk. "We divided up. I told 'em, 'You take State Street. I'll take Rush. Look around. In bars.' We found him in a bar. He was real sloshed. We got him home. He threw up. We made him take a bath and put him to bed. In the morning, we had him take a shower and threw his gear in his bag. By the time we got back to New Orleans, he was all right."

"All right" only in a relative sense. For Maravich, the death of his mother would weigh on him through an expansion team's chaotic first season. The isolation that he had known in Atlanta would deepen, as would the void he had felt when he discovered that his success in basketball did not suffice as a life. In his quest for inner peace he had taken to dabbling in yoga, transcendental meditation, and the study of Eastern religions. But for all of his searching, the net result on the court after his mother's death was a conspicuous decline in his productiveness and, after Willem Hendrik (Butch) van Breda Kolff succeeded Robertson as coach, a certain ambiguity toward the new coach's demands on him.

Van Breda Kolff, 52, was an ex-New York Knick who'd played against Press and his Ironmen in the BAA and then gone on to coach in college (Lafayette, 1951–55; Hofstra, 1955–62; and Princeton, 1962–67) and the pros (Los Angeles Lakers, 1967–69; Detroit Pistons, 1969–71; Phoenix Suns, fired after seven games in the 1972–73 season; and the ABA Memphis Tams, 1973–74). He was a paradoxical figure—a man who had attended Princeton for a while and was sharp enough to do the *New York Times* crossword puzzle in ink, yet who had little of the refined air associated with alumni of Ole Nassau. Van Breda Kolff was rough-edged and blunt in his speech—a beer-quaffing ex-Marine whose sociability in the public drinking establishments of New Orleans—not to mention his sideline histrionics as a referee-baiting coach—quickly endeared him to the locals.

Companionable though he was when bellied up to the bar, as a coach he was not nearly so relaxed when it came to safeguarding his purist's approach to basketball. "The game," he would say, "is movement, cutting, passing, working together. I teach basics—see the whole floor, hit the open hand, move without the ball—the things that don't show up in the box score."

Those who failed to meet his old-school standards, even players with grand reputations, did not get off easy. Like Wilt Chamberlain, who played under van Breda Kolff with the LA Lakers in the 1968–69 season. The coach wanted his big man to operate at the high post to give teammates Elgin Baylor and Jerry West operating room. Wilt seemed unwilling or unable to implement van Breda Kolff's approach. A stormy coexistence followed.

In the seventh game of the 1968–69 championship series against

Boston, Chamberlain took himself out with more than five minutes remaining and the Lakers trailing by seven points. When the team rallied
and Chamberlain told his coach he was ready to return to action, van
Breda Kolff declined to put him back in. The Lakers lost in the title
game by two points. Van Breda Kolff was replaced as coach after calling
Chamberlain a quitter.

Given his firm ideas as to how the game was meant to be played and
his caustic tongue—he'd once called Lakers captain Baylor a "dum
dum"—it was inevitable that a freewheeling player like Maravich would
quickly run afoul of van Breda Kolff. The coach wanted a Maravich who
could operate as part of—not apart from—the rest of the Jazz. On taking
over from Scotty Robertson, he advised the Jazz's public address announcer that no longer did he want Maravich introduced as "Pistol
Pete," a name that proclaimed the egocentric quality that van Breda
Kolff thought needed muting.

"I did not enjoy watching Pete at LSU," van Breda Kolff would recall
years later. "This is a team game. You take good shots, play defense and
don't turn the ball over . . . When I came in, I thought Pete shot too
much. Too many bad shots and he tried to do too much with the ball. I
urged him to throw the ball to the first guy open rather than dribbling
in and out of two or three guys. On top of that, he wasn't very good on
defense."

Van Breda Kolff made his dissatisfaction plain, maligning Maravich
for being a "fucking ballhog" and, worse, sitting him on the bench for
his transgressions. For the prideful Maravich—by far the team's best
player—getting benched was tantamount to having his knuckles rapped
by the nuns in front of the class. He was not happy about it.

"Pete'd pout if he didn't think he should come out," said van Breda
Kolff. "I'd tell him, 'What? You got the pouts again?' Pete and I got along
fine except when I took him out when he didn't want to get taken out."

Unlike the impasse he'd reached with Fitzsimmons, Maravich kept a
dialogue going with van Breda Kolff. When hard feelings arose, the two
men would try to work things out in what the coach called "the occasional fireside chat"—conversation lubricated by a beer or two.

For both men, the season was one of unending flux, with more transients coming and going through the team's dressing room than through a hot-sheet Times Square hotel. Bellamy gone after one game. Toby Kimball lasting through three games. John Block, Jim Barnett, Stu Lantz, Neal Walk, Rick Adelman, Ollie Johnson dealt to other teams. In all, 26 players would suit up in Jazz uniforms at one time or another during the team's inaugural season. But so scarce was legitimate talent to complement Maravich that the team toyed with the idea of activating its 40-year-old assistant coach, Elgin Baylor, who had retired after the 1971–72 season but would fill in during team practices. The Jazz went so far as to order a uniform for Baylor but never did take the next step of placing him on the roster.

Even the front office got shaken up. Team president Rosenfeld soon departed in a dispute about money with the other owners, Battisone emerging as the majority owner. Battisone was not a hands-on boss, though, mostly staying put in Santa Barbara while leaving the daily operations to the team's general manager, Bill Bertka, and the marketing vice president, Barry Mendelson.

Through all of the early shake-ups, the only constant with the Jazz was that the team kept losing. Losing in the grand style: 1–15 became 3–30 (0–20 on the road) as the new year loomed and the Jazz threatened to become the worst-ever NBA team, surpassing for sheer incompetence the all-time patsy, the 1972–73 Philadelphia 76ers. That Roy Rubin-coached team had gone 9–73.

Though the Jazz floundered, the hard-core fans remained supportive, somewhat in the way New York Mets baseball fans had taken to heart that beloved loser. At $7.50 top price for courtside seats, those who showed up—an average of 4,954 per game—got to see NBA basketball and, stomping up and down the sideline while barking at the officials, the highly emotive van Breda Kolff. In earlier seasons in the league, he regularly incurred enough fines for the technical fouls called on him to keep an emerging Third World nation afloat. At New Orleans, it was no different. He railed at officials, punctuating his complaints with gestures broad enough—putting hands to head or outstretching arms or exhort-

ing his players on one knee like Al Jolson singing "Mammy"—to "play"
to the guy in the last row of the arena.

"Butch would get crazy out there," said season-ticket holder Richard
Katz, who sat directly behind the Jazz bench. "He'd get all disheveled—
a raving lunatic. Tie would come undone, shirt would come loose. I remember one time, one of the guys sitting with me said, 'Why didn't
so-and-so block out?' And van Breda Kolff turned around and said,
'Damn right he should have blocked out . . .' We all loved Butch van
Breda Kolff."

Maravich remained more equivocal about van Breda Kolff. At times,
he was peeved with the coach's blunt critiques. At other times he and
van Breda Kolff coexisted amiably enough, even, as the coach recalled,
playing racquetball together:

> The first time, we played at a racquetball club. The guy who ran it didn't
> want to let us use the facility. He told us, "It's only for members." Pete
> said, "I'm Pete Maravich." The guy said, "Okay, I'll let you play here
> once." Well, I beat him. And by the time I get home, the phone's ring-
> ing—it's Pete. He told me, "I drove home 70 miles an hour—I was so
> goddamn mad an old man beat me." He wanted to make sure to get me
> soon as I walked in the door. Get me for a re-match. Next day, we show
> up again. The guy running the club says, "I told you you could only play
> once." Pete says, "How much is a membership?" "Five hundred dollars."
> Pete says, "Okay, we'll join." That's how bad he wanted the re-match.
> That's how competitive he was.

But that competitive drive made Maravich sensitive to van Breda
Kolff's barbed assessments—and even to being too faintly praised. As
van Breda Kolff recalled: "Once, when we played Golden State, we beat
'em out there in a hell of a game. Pete went for 45 points. Bud Stallworth and our rookie, Aaron James, got 20 each. When I talked to the
press after, I didn't laud Pete enough . . . at least in Pete's mind. I'd
talked about James and Stallworth getting 20 each and the defensive job
that E. C. Coleman had done on Rick Barry. The next game, Pete laid

an egg and, when I talked to him, he said something about my overlooking him after the Golden State game. I told him, 'You played a great game. I just wanted to give credit to the others.'"

In their first season together, the two men had their ups and downs. In response to the familiar charge that he shot too much, Maravich ended up launching only eight field goal tries in a 101–94 loss to the Knicks on December 28 and afterward said, "I do what I'm told to do and play the way I'm told to play. That is what management and the coaches want, so that is what I do. I get paid the same no matter what.

"The type of game I'm playing is not my style, but I'm certainly trying to fit in. I can play any style of ball anybody wants me to play. I can fit into any team at any time in any way. Certainly I'd be better if I could run more, establish a running game. But the coaches want me to slow things down. They want me to run the so-called offense."

The subtext of Maravich's shot boycott was a to-hell-with-it contempt for not being allowed to be all the Pistol he thought he could be. The trick for van Breda Kolff was to resist overreacting to Pete's "pouts" while continuing to preach the team game and to hope that Maravich would find a happy medium with the Jazz.

But although Maravich made adjustments to satisfy his coach, he couldn't resist the occasional showtime flair. There were games when Maravich would swish the first of two free throws and then look to the bench and wink before intentionally banking the next one in. "I'd take him out of the game, but I loved it," van Breda Kolff conceded. "In the pros it's difficult to get respect through flashiness. You get it through bread and butter, and Pete, it wasn't in his makeup to be bread and butter."

As the Jazz shifted their home games to the Loyola field house, the team now was obliged to deal with the quirks inherent in the facility—a gym that, with no heating system, exaggerated the extremes of New Orleans' climate. When it was hot and humid, the floor took on condensation and turned slippery. When temperatures sank precipitously, the place was an icehouse—indeed, in the past when college teams played there, Abe Lemons, coach of Oklahoma City, had sat through one game in overcoat, ear muffs, hat, and gloves.

What's more, the tin roof covering the building magnified the sound of rain—wet weather resounded like a machine-gun attack—and, worse, the roof leaked, prompting custodial types to rush out pails to catch the spillage. More than once the team's player representative, Mel Counts, had to inspect the floor and decide whether it was passable for a game.

Meanwhile, van Breda Kolff tried to simplify the Jazz's offense, reducing the number of plays the team ran while encouraging a system of "organized confusion"—attacking other teams at their weak spots. But no matter what he did, the Jazz continued to lose, raising the pitch of the criticism the experts assayed. One writer called the New Orleans squad "one of the most uninspired undisciplined teams within memory . . . ."

Still, the team's fans continued to support the Jazz, whose coach proved more popular than any of his players except for Maravich. To a great degree, that owed to van Breda Kolff's theatrical extremes as a bench coach and to the public figure he cut in postgame French Quarter saloons like Pat O'Brien's, where van Breda Kolff and Rod Hundley, the team's broadcaster, not only were regulars but also were given to mixing easily with whomever was in the house.

Pat O'Brien's was famous for a sweet red drink, called a "hurricane"—served in a large tulip glass—that Hundley was known to consume while watching the beer-drinking van Breda Kolff chat up the patrons.

"People in New Orleans loved the man," said Hundley of van Breda Kolff. "Same for the sportswriters. He loved his beer. He loved to talk sports. He'd meet people so easily. Go into a bar in any city, and sit there for two minutes—Butch knew everybody in the joint. He'd strike up a conversation with anybody."

Van Breda Kolff's star player, Maravich, by now tended to keep to himself. The death of his mother sat like a weight on his conscience, and his heart ached for his father, who that January—in the midst of a 1–15 season—resigned his job at Appalachian State.

"Pete struggled after his mother passed away," said Don Sparks, the Jazz's trainer, who lived down the street from Maravich in Metairie, a suburb of New Orleans. "He kept so much of that to himself. And when his father quit at Appalachian, Pete became disenchanted because his father couldn't get a job in the NBA. Pete felt like his father was one of the best coaches there ever was. Press wanted to get in the pro game and for some reason couldn't."

New Orleans had a lively night life in which many of the Jazz players indulged. Not Maravich, who was conspicuous by his absence from those bars and clubs. Nor was he any more public when the team traveled. On the road he holed up in his hotel room, watching films on TV, his preference being for comedies, particularly those of the Marx Brothers.

But there was no escaping the critics' blunt ax. As the player the team had supposedly forfeited its future for, Maravich was a ripe target. With the losses mounting, more and more he took the hit when the experts leveled their guns on the team. In January 1975, Bob Wolf in *The Sporting News* wrote:

Rosenfeld, Bertka, et al. . . . would have been a lot better off if they had never thought of Maravich.

True, injuries have had something to do with Pistol Pete's disappointing showing—he is 10 points off his 27.7 average of last season—but there is more to it than that. Maravich has been playing as though he isn't the least bit interested in his work and his comments on the subject tend to support the impression.

After a particularly lethargic performance in Milwaukee recently, the young millionaire was asked if playing with such a ragtag team bothered him.

"It used to," he said. "But not any more. After a while, you have to rationalize things. It's such a broad question, I could talk for three hours about it. It's frustrating, but what can a guy do? There's nothing I can do. I signed a contract and I've got to honor it . . . ."

Adding to Maravich's frustration is the feeling that Coach Bill van Breda Kolff's system doesn't permit him to play his own free-wheeling type of basketball.

"How do they want me to play?" he asked. "Do they want me to play my style or do they want me to slow up all the time? There are so many different things I could say about this situation. But I just don't take a negative attitude any more. It's not worth it."

But even as Wolf was offering his observations, the old Maravich began to surface. Following the December 28 game in which he'd shot with conspicuous restraint—those paltry eight field-goal tries—Maravich, now sporting a mustache, went on a scoring tear. In the team's next seven games, he scored a total of 179 points on 45 percent shooting and had 53 assists.

"Got to give him a saliva test," van Breda Kolff told newsmen. "He's playing great, scoring, running the ballclub, taking the percentage shot and not throwing the ball away. Let's see what my man has done in the last three games. Thirty-eight points against Houston. Forty-two points, 17 assists, 10 rebounds, and 4 steals against Seattle and 40 points, 14 rebounds, and 13 assists Sunday night against Buffalo."

Down the stretch, the Jazz as a unit finally came together. By then only three of the team's expansion picks remained from the slew of players who had been drafted: forwards E. C. Coleman and Bud Stallworth and guard Louie Nelson. The other players to figure in the team's late-season surge—the Jazz would win 18 of its last 35 games—were rookie forward Aaron James and trade acquisitions Henry Bibby, Nate Williams, Otto Moore, and Counts.

The Jazz's closing drive put to rest those comparisons with the all-time NBA losers and sparked this *Sporting News* headline: "VBK Deserves Coach of the Year Nod for Jazz Job." Now, rather than being spoken of in the same breath with those earlier, pathetic franchises, the New Orleans team—finishing the season with a 23–59 record, worst in the league—was being bruited as a potential playoff team in the near future, a remarkable turnabout.

It put Maravich in a better light, too. After a season in which he averaged only 21.5 ppg (but 6.2 assists a game), he went from being a seemingly reluctant accomplice of van Breda Kolff to being a late-blooming team player. At least that's how many viewed him after the Jazz's productive finish. Maravich? He didn't buy the revisionist picture presented to the public, saying, "One man never has won nor ever will win a championship by himself. Yet people say, 'You can't win with Pete Maravich.' Win where? Lord knows, I came into the pros with a lot of pressure on me. No matter what I did it would never be enough. But put me on the Celtics and suddenly everyone would think I was the greatest player alive. 'Look, Pete Maravich has grown up.' Well, it would still be me, the same Pete Maravich playing the same way."

THE STRONG finish of the Jazz motivated Pete Maravich.

He resolved to show up for the 1975–76 season in the best shape of his life.

For a month that summer, he joined Press (and Diana) in Europe, where his father had arranged a series of basketball clinics in England, Spain, France, Italy, and West Germany.

After completing their tour, while Press remained behind to coach in Sweden, Pete headed for the training camp of the New Orleans Saints football team.

He and 7-foot rookie draft choice Rich Kelley had decided to put themselves through the grueling regimen that the Saints endured to prepare for the new NFL season.

Van Breda Kolff was impressed. "Kelley," he said, "lasted one week. Pete went through the whole training camp and came back 10 pounds heavier. Pete was a masochist. He didn't mind working, working, working. It's why he became such a great dribbler. To do those drills of his, it takes hours and hours of work. And he was always willing to do it."

Indeed, Pete went from the Saints' camp to the weight room after the NFL exhibition season began. He hefted weights regularly and, with Metairie neighbor and ex-Green Bay Packer Jim Taylor, ran miles along the levee on Lake Pontchartrain. In the weeks leading up to the Jazz's second year, he told a newsman: "I weigh over 200 pounds now, but I also have the strength to go along with the weight. I've put on muscle where I had fat before. I've been lifting weights and doing as many as 300 situps in an eight-minute period to increase my strength. When a basketball player gets tired in a game, it's usually because his stomach muscles are tired, so the more you develop these muscles, the more firm and tight they become and you don't get as tired. Also, because of the weights and exercises, I'm a lot faster and quicker than last year. The stronger your muscles are, the quicker they react and the quicker you are. I've noticed a tremendous change in my game."

Van Breda Kolff noticed other changes in Pete — the mustache gone, the trademark droopy socks abandoned, his jersey number changed from 44 to 7. What's more, Maravich as captain of the Jazz now seemed more willing to forego the fancy pass for the expedient one — to do whatever it would take to advance the team.

"Pete was, in his heart of hearts, a showman," van Breda Kolff said. "But that year he played the game. Players today play basketball. They don't play the GAME of basketball."

For van Breda Kolff, the distinction involved the nuances of winning basketball — of realizing that athleticism goes only so far and that a player who is mindful of team chemistry and able to enhance it is as valuable as any of his shake-and-bake counterparts.

"Pete," said van Breda Kolff, "could do both. He could play slam-dunk run-up-and-down basketball. And he could play the GAME of basketball — take advantage of what the other team gives you. That year he played the GAME of basketball."

The Jazz opened the season in the Superdome, a far cry from the funky home courts that had served as temporary facilities the year before. The Dome had cost $173 million to build and, though it was regarded as a state-of-the-art enclosed stadium, its very vastness — it sat on 52 acres — made it an often-confusing place to navigate. The Saints had had their players take preseason walk-throughs from the parking lot to the dressing room, and still some of them got lost.

"The first day," said Maravich, "somebody led me from the parking lot to the dressing room and I've been using that route since. I'd be afraid to try another way, I might not make it until halftime."

For all of its technological refinements, the new arena would require a shakeout period to overcome the glitches — scoreboards that failed to light up, ticket booths that had no hole in their windows to facilitate communication between ticket-sellers and the public, six 22-by-25-foot TV screens that played commercials at such a loud pitch that Saints quarterback Archie Manning petitioned for lower decibels. Observed van Breda Kolff: "The New Orleans school system isn't the world's greatest, but our fans all know at least one big word—'malfunction.'"

As a business proposition, the Superdome would prove to be less inviting to the Jazz than anticipated, once the dollars-and-cents realities sank in. For starters, the Jazz paid a per-game rental fee of $2,400 or 8 percent of the gate, whichever was greater, and ticket prices were subject to a nationally high 11 percent amusement tax. The team's deal with Dome management precluded it from sharing in fringe income—parking, souvenirs, game programs, and concession-stand items like the corned beef Domewiches, roast beef Poor Boys, and $1.25 Superdogs.

Yet at the outset, the Dome proved a happy place for the Jazz, who won five of their first six games and drew crowds nearly three times that of the previous year (13,000 per game). The Jazz fans saw a reconstituted home team, led by Maravich, who, though he missed the opening game of the season with a knee injury, returned with his leg wrapped and his heart in the game. For instance, in a double-overtime victory against New York, Maravich scored 45 points against Walt Frazier, considered one of the game's better defensive players.

By early November, the Jazz had become the city's hottest attraction this side of Bourbon Street. And when Kareem Abdul-Jabbar and the Lakers came into the Dome, the New Orleans front office fully expected the arena to be packed to capacity—and then some—for this seventh game of the season, since the Jazz were now exercising the option of opening a third-tier section of general-admission seats and offering these "terrace-level" tickets at $1.50 apiece. The vantage was so high up in the arena that from there Maravich looked like a swizzle stick and the ball like a raisin. But for budget-minded fans, it provided a chance to get in on the action.

That afternoon, though, the team's expectation of a box office bonanza dissipated under suddenly threatening skies: Eight inches of rain fell on the city and its suburbs, causing flooding in many areas. Out in Metairie, Maravich spent three hours bailing water from his lakeside home. While he did, the team's newly elevated executive vice president, Barry Mendelson, was contacting the Orleans Parish police for their help in transporting Maravich to the Superdome. The sheriff's department sent three jeeps to Maravich's address, but they were unable to get through the flooded streets.

A neighbor of Maravich stopped by in a boat and offered to ferry him to the game, but he politely declined the offer. By the time the authorities had dispatched a diesel truck, the rain had stopped and Maravich was in his Porsche and headed for the Dome. Much to his surprise, the crowd that was figured to have been diminished by the weather was filing through the turnstiles in what would amount to record numbers— 26,611, the largest paid attendance in NBA history. An advance sale of 18,000 seats had been supplemented by 8,000 walk-ins, most of them buying those $1.50 terrace seats.

"I'll never forget it," said van Breda Kolff years later. "I can still see the fans tromping into the place with their shoes in their hands. It wasn't much better inside."

Maravich and the Jazz did not disappoint the locals, beating the Lakers 113–110. The Pistol hit 13 of 28 field goal tries and four free throws— 30 points in all—and afterward said: "The incredible thing was that it might have been 30,000 if we hadn't had the greatest rain since Noah's Ark."

The victory made the Jazz 6–1 and put them at the top of the Central Division of the NBA's Eastern Conference, 48 games ahead of their expansion-year pace. Suddenly, the New Orleans team was being taken seriously, and the city sparked to its heroes, shelling out for reserved seats ranging from $3.50 to $7.50 and for those $1.50 bargain tickets.

For their money, fans were getting a Maravich who was scoring 23.1 ppg—sixth best in the league—while giving van Breda Kolff the more measured team-oriented game he favored. At the rate the Jazz were going, they stood a chance to be the first expansion team to qualify for the playoffs this early in their history. But on November 17, the team suffered a serious setback when Maravich was sidelined with a second-degree shoulder separation, brought about by a fall he took chasing down a loose ball during a practice scrimmage.

Not surprisingly, the Jazz slumped in his absence. As van Breda Kolff recalled: "Pete was out for twenty games; the team went six and fourteen."

The Jazz would regain ground in the standings on Maravich's return and end up with a 38–44 record—more wins than any expansion team had earned in its second season. And although that was encouraging to Jazz fans, and to van Breda Kolff, the team still failed to qualify for the playoffs. Yet it was tempting to think that had Maravich not missed 20 games with a shoulder injury, the Jazz might have made the cut.

Maravich, who'd married his college sweetheart, Jackie Elliser, that January, finished the year averaging 25.9 points per game—third best in the league, behind scoring champion Bob McAdoo (31.1 ppg) and Abdul-Jabbar (27.7)—and 5.3 assists a game. That all-round game elicited the praise of van Breda Kolff and made a profound impression on the writers and broadcasters who voted for the All-NBA team. For the first time in his career, Maravich was All-NBA, along with Rick Barry of Golden State, George McGinnis of Philadelphia, Abdul-Jabbar of Los Angeles, and Nate (Tiny) Archibald of Kansas City-Omaha.

Jazz fans could reasonably anticipate that under van Breda Kolff, the team would continue to improve. The coach and his star player had overcome earlier discord and seemed now to coexist as well as two strong personalities like them could expect to. When van Breda Kolff had coached at Los Angeles, Hundley recalled, Jerry West used to say, "He may not be the best coach, but I'd rather win for him than anybody else." By those words West was expressing the loyalty van Breda Kolff inspired and the deep personal regard in which West held the coach. Maravich hadn't anywhere near that strong an affinity for van Breda Kolff—in time theirs became a business arrangement, no more, no less, for Pete.

But it sufficed. Maravich had been All-NBA. The Jazz had won more than a second-year expansion team's share of games—and had gone 32–30 when Maravich had been in the lineup. Why wouldn't a Jazz fan count on a bright future? But what outsiders were blithely unaware of was that an internecine feud was brewing that would short-circuit van Breda Kolff's time in New Orleans.

THE '76–77 season was barely two months old when Butch van Breda Kolff was fired.

At the time the Jazz had a very respectable 14–12 record—a record that might have been even better had Maravich and an off-season acquisition, guard Gail Goodrich, been available to the coach full-time.

But both Maravich and the 33-year-old Goodrich, second in career scoring to John Havlicek among active NBA players, had missed a number of games with injuries.

Still, it wasn't that van Breda Kolff had suffered the unforgivable sin of losing, the usual pretext for firing a coach. The reason for his firing was his inability to get along with 33-year-old Barry Mendelson, a Jazz executive.

Mendelson had come to New Orleans with a background as a personal manager of sports stars—Jerry West had been a client—and a packager of TV sports shows. The Jazz hired him to direct the marketing and promotion of the club.

Mendelson created all sorts of gimmicky sideshows to Jazz games—from Frisbee giveaways to T-shirt nights. As season-ticket holder Richard Katz recalled: "Every night something was going on. Mendelson got a local Rolex watch dealer to give away a Rolex every halftime if you had the 'lucky number' in your program. The Jazz starters would be played onto the court by jazz musicians who'd be led by an old black woman, Ellen Tatum, carrying a parasol. Barry did a deal with Burger King—if the Jazz got 110 points, then there'd be free French fries for all ticket holders. So . . . games in which the Jazz were losing but had 105, 106 points, the people would be going nuts and the scoreboard would start blinking. People would be chanting, 'French fries, French fries, French fries.'"

Although Mendelson had come to New Orleans as a marketing man, once ensconced in the Jazz front office he set his sights on broader responsibilities. Mendelson wanted to make the basketball decisions that had been entrusted to the team's general manager, Bill Bertka.

As Jazz PR man Bud Johnson recalled: "After the '75–76 season, Mendelson sold the owners on the fact that a lot of the time Bertka was on the road with the team and business decisions needed to be made while Bertka was away."

Many of his Jazz colleagues resented Mendelson for his politicking and his overweening ambition. As Johnson put it: "The owners wanted somebody to be responsive to their questions and needs and I'm sure Barry Mendelson took care of himself."

The *Times-Picayune*'s Marty Mule stated that view more strongly: "Barry was a very amiable guy, but I always felt his ambition overshadowed everything about him. I think he was a guy that no matter what he had, there was always something more he wanted."

Mendelson became the Jazz's executive vice president, and Bertka was demoted to director of scouting and player relations. Whereas others in the Jazz organization derided Mendelson behind his back, only van Breda Kolff did it to his face. In part, the coach felt loyalty to Bertka, who had been instrumental in persuading the Jazz to replace Scotty Robertson with him. Beyond that, he regarded Mendelson as a poseur when it came to basketball matters. And whenever he could, van Breda Kolff would let Mendelson know it.

"Van Breda Kolff saw Mendelson as an interloper," said Mule, "and he wasn't polite about it. Once after Chiquita Banana had sponsored a promotion, van Breda Kolff said, 'The only promotion worth promoting is winning. Not Chiquita Banana.' It was a zinger aimed at Barry because Barry was always doing these things. He made it clear, early on, he had little regard for Barry Mendelson."

"Butch was a man's man and not very refined," said Johnson. "I remember that the summer between the first and second season there were supposed to be Jazz clinics out in the community. But the clinics couldn't go on unless a commercial sponsor would put up money AND van Breda Kolff's fee. Well, the clinics never occurred because Mendelson couldn't get anybody to come up with the money. And Butch couldn't resist sticking the needle to him: 'What's the deal? Weren't you the guy that . . .?'"

On December 14, 1976, as Maravich reported to practice at the Superdome, van Breda Kolff was leaving in his car. The coach honked his horn and waved and kept going. He had just been fired.

In a statement to the media, Larry G. Hatfield, a member of the Jazz's executive committee, said, "The board of directors of the team was simply unable to feel comfortable with Butch's view of a head coach's role. It appeared that Butch felt he had to take an adversary position each time the players and club philosophy were discussed. Under these conditions, it was decided that a long-term relationship was impossible."

Meanwhile, Mendelson was saying, "More or less, it was a collection of things that happened. Sometimes in general conversation, sometimes in meetings, maybe just a bull session, he would come in and it was always as if the owners were pitted against the coach."

When Maravich was asked whether he was surprised by van Breda Kolff's firing, he said, "The last time I was surprised was when I found out that ice cream cones were hollow."

The new coach was Elgin Baylor, the Hall of Fame player from the Lakers who'd been van Breda Kolff's assistant in New Orleans.

As assistant coach, Baylor had been the easygoing antidote to VBK, partaking of the locker room kibitzing and in-flight card games and backgammon, and even engaging in Jazz scrimmages.

"As assistant coach, he was, like, one of the guys," said Jazz center Rich Kelley. "Once he became coach, though, he felt it was important to become much more aloof. It never really fit."

Maybe. But by most accounts, Maravich welcomed the change in coaches.

Mel Counts, Jazz center: "Butch was very flamboyant, very direct. You knew exactly where you stood with him. He was an interesting man, very intelligent, at times overly intense. He'd get upset, but he didn't hold a grudge. You're talking about grown men playing a boy's sport. Trying to control them was not easy."

Bud Johnson, Jazz public relations director: "I think the players liked Elgin more. Butch would make fun of them. If somebody made a bad pass, he'd crack a joke about it. Elgin was more of a diplomat, more easygoing. Pete seemed to have a very deep feeling for Elgin. A definite bond there that wasn't there with Butch."

Rod Hundley, Jazz broadcaster: "I don't think Pete liked Butch so well as a coach. He never said such. It was just the way I read it. Butch didn't like behind-the-back shit. Pete went behind his back all the time. And took crazy shots. If you're a coach, you don't like that."

Marty Mule, *New Orleans Times-Picayune* sportswriter: "Elgin, being Elgin, was more easygoing in every way. Not just with Pete. He was a happy-go-lucky guy. Not a pusher in any way. He lets his knowledge and reputation talk for him. Pete liked him a lot. Elgin was one of his boyhood heroes."

Don Sparks, Jazz trainer: "Pete related to Elgin much better than to Butch. He had more respect for Elgin because of his stature as a pro player. As assistant coach, Elgin was one of the best players we had."

Dave Fredman, PR and sales assistant who succeeded Johnson as team PR director in midseason: "Butch was a brilliant guy, who marched to the beat of his own drummer. He'd come to practice with a cigar, wearing a T-shirt and shorts. His practice plan would be on a match book. A fun guy but a good teacher. He got a workable group of guys who knew their roles and how many minutes they'd play. Early on, the relationship between Pete and him was okay. One thing about Butch, he was not afraid to jerk Pete out of the game. Butch wanted to win. If Pete took a lot of bad shots, van Breda Kolff was not afraid to tell him. As for Pete, you could tell he never wanted to come out of a game. He had his pride. Elgin would play Pete 48 minutes a game. He pretty much let Pete go, wouldn't jerk him for bad shots as much, if ever."

Rich Kelley, Jazz center: "It was no secret that Elgin was not as strong a personality as van Breda Kolff. And not quite as eloquent. So Pete had a little more leeway in terms of pushing the envelope."

On the evening Bill van Breda Kolff was fired, Maravich, who'd averaged 38 minutes a game under van Breda Kolff, would play 47 1/2 minutes and score 51 points in leading the Jazz to a 120–117 victory over the Kansas City Kings.

Under van Breda Kolff, and now under Baylor, Maravich was scoring at a league-leading pace—better than 30 points a game. But Baylor had the misfortune of taking over the team at the precise juncture when the schedule—due to a boat show occupying the Dome—turned top-heavy with road games: 11 away games in January and only 3 at home. On the road, the team could not match its early season success and fell below .500.

Yet not for lack of production from Maravich had the Jazz slipped. In the final year of his three-year, $1.2 million contract—and as Goodrich went down with a torn Achilles tendon—the Pistol was making the case for an even better deal with his hot shooting. By February 25, he had scored 40 or more points six times—all on the Superdome court. As *New York Post* columnist Jim O'Brien, in New Orleans to cover the Jazz-Knicks game, would write: " . . . and he might just do it [i.e., score 40 points] again tonight against the Knicks."

In fact, Maravich exceeded those expectations. With attorneys Herskovitz and Zittrain in attendance at the Superdome, he lit up the Knicks for 68 points, the most ever scored by a guard in a single game. He did it against Walt Frazier, who had been named to the NBA's All-Defensive team seven years in a row. Yet on this night Frazier was at a loss to inhibit Maravich. The Pistol would recount to his friend, John Lotz, a former University of Florida coach, that at one point during the game Frazier had turned to teammate Earl Monroe and suggested switching defensive assignments. "Uh uh," said Monroe. "You're the defensive expert." On this night, Earl the Pearl saw discretion as the better part of defense.

For Maravich, the game had a life of its own.

"A thing like this catches you a little by surprise," Maravich said afterward. "I didn't know I was close to a record until one of my teammates told me during a time-out I needed only a few more."

The teammate, Jimmy McElroy, approached Maravich during a time-out with 6:50 remaining in the game and told him: "You better get a new firing pin, Pistol. 'Cause you're wearing that one out."

Before a crowd of 11,033, Maravich connected on 26 of 43 field goal attempts and 16 of 19 free throws as the Jazz won 124–107. He might have scored even more than 68 had he not fouled out on an offensive charge call with 1:18 to play.

In the history of the NBA, only Baylor, who had scored 71 points against the Knicks in 1960, and Wilt Chamberlain, who had scored 68 points or more seven times, had surpassed him for a single night's output.

Knicks coach Red Holzman was moved to say afterward, "It was a beautiful thing to watch for the fans here and you have to admire that kind of effort. We didn't play well, but he was phenomenal."

The Pistol's teammate, Fred Boyd, told newsmen: "If there was ever any doubt in anyone's mind, he erased it. The man proved he's the greatest offensive player in the game and even the doubters will have to recognize that now."

Said Maravich: "I could have scored more. I missed a lot of easy shots early in the game."

Zittrain, who with Herskovitz had come to New Orleans to initiate talks with the Jazz front office on Maravich's future—would he or wouldn't he stay with the Jazz?—recalled that after the record-breaking game, the local papers headlined: "Pete's Attorneys in Town / He Puts Money in the Bank."

A few weeks after his 68-point explosion, Maravich was center stage of an even more remarkable game. On March 18, the Jazz were in Phoenix to play the Suns. That evening, just prior to the start of the game, the Suns' public address announcer advised the crowd that the Jazz had suited up only seven players because the other five—Aaron James, Nate Williams, Bud Stallworth, Otto Moore, and Jim McElroy: all key members of the team—had been injured in a two-car collision earlier that day.

In the crowd that night was Hollywood producer Arthur Friedman ("Price of Glory") and his future wife, Barbara. Friedman, a hard-core baseball fan, had come to Arizona in March to check out major league spring training camps in Phoenix, Tempe, Mesa, and Yuma. Discovering that the Suns and Jazz would be playing that night, he took Barbara to the game.

"When I arrived I saw only seven guys practicing for the Jazz," said Friedman. "I wondered what the hell was going on . . . until the P-A announcer, prior to the national anthem, asked for a moment of silence for the five injured ballplayers. Like everybody else, I figured the Jazz, with only seven men, had no chance. But then Pete Maravich went off. I mean, he was unbelievable. He scored going to the right. Going to the left. Spin three times and shoot it up. It was as if he was possessed. It was one of the most spectacular performances I'd ever seen. And I've seen lots of Bird, Magic, and Michael. I mean the Suns were no pushover—what with guys like Alvan Adams and Paul Westphal, Garfield Heard and Ron Sobers. But they couldn't stop Maravich. Double- and triple-teaming him—couldn't stop him. The other four guys on the Jazz were setting picks for him and doing whatever they could to keep him going.

"Talk about a guy carrying a team. He was everywhere. Doing it all. Shooting and making these spectacular assists. At times he'd get exhausted and pretend to tie his sneaker laces rather than play defense, so he could catch his breath. Once the crowd realized what was happening, even though it was a Phoenix crowd, they began cheering for Maravich. One shooter against five guys. It was a surreal experience. Even Barbara, who didn't like basketball, was cheering for Maravich. On one drive, against a triple team, he dribbled along the baseline with his left hand and somehow managed to twist his body to the right and score. The crowd went crazy. Even the guys on the Phoenix bench were reacting. Like, 'Woa!' In the end, everybody was rooting for Maravich."

In the end, the Jazz—as the little team that could—took it to the Suns. Maravich hit 21 of 34 field goal attempts and 9 of 10 free throws for 51 points, the most points ever scored on the Phoenix court. What's more, he had 4 assists, 6 rebounds, 5 steals, and 2 blocks as the outmanned New Orleans team stunned and ultimately delighted the home crowd by beating Phoenix 104–100.

"That Phoenix game was really memorable," said Maravich years later. "When you look over at the bench and you want to come out, who were you going to bring in—Don Sparks, the trainer? There's nobody to go in."

Although the team remained sub-.500, even as Maravich was abusing opposition defenses, under Baylor the Jazz were a harmonious group. Although the coach no longer was a regular in backgammon games or the locker room kibitzing, he did allow himself to be drawn in to a challenge provoked by Maravich and others, revolving around the reputation that

E. C. Coleman had as a defensive stopper. Indeed, at the end of the '76–77 season, Coleman would be named to the league's All-Defense team, along with Bobby Jones of Denver, Bill Walton of Portland, Don Buse of Indiana, and Norm Van Lier of Chicago.

As Baylor recalled: "E. C. was talking about defense, about stopping guys from my era. Kidding around. Bertka, who was my assistant, said, 'There's no way E. C. could guard you.' Pete and the others were saying I'd never score. So we had a couple days off, and at a shootaround I agreed to play E. C. one-on-one, make-it, take-it."

What happened?

"Game was ten-baskets-win," said Jazz publicity man Fredman." Elgin got the ball out first."

Baylor: "I was driving, shooting from outside, whatever I could do."

Fredman: "E. C. never got the ball back."

Baylor: "Beat him 20-zip."

Although the team was comfortable with Baylor, months after van Breda Kolff was fired Jazz fans still bemoaned his demise. Some of them even made threatening remarks to Mendelson, who began turning up at Jazz games with police protection.

But although Mendelson's role in sacking van Breda Kolff made him unpopular with Jazz fans, it was his perceived underhandedness in the acquisition of Goodrich—who played only 27 games before tearing his Achilles tendon—that doomed him as the team's key executive.

"When Mendelson made the deal," recalled Fredman, "he said that he'd gotten Goodrich for a single draft choice. But the truth came out at the '77 All-Star game in Milwaukee. Some reporters were at the press table when an attorney for the Lakers revealed that Barry had given up TWO #1 draft choices, for 1978 and 1979. It led to a big media controversy. See, van Breda Kolff had told him if he was going to go after Goodrich, it was okay but not to give up more than one draft choice. And Barry never even told Butch about the two draft choices. By the way, the Lakers' 1979 #1 draft choice? Magic Johnson."

On March 23, the wire services carried this story:

Barry Mendelson, the general manager of the New Orleans Jazz, was dismissed today. Larry Hatfield, chairman of the National Basketball Association club's executive committee, said Mendelson had become a controversial figure because of his trade for Gail Goodrich, a guard with the Los Angeles Lakers.

Mendelson also had become the center of disputes with sportswriters and fans, particularly over the dropping of Butch van Breda Kolff as head coach last December.

The Jazz won-loss record was 14–12 when van Breda Kolff was let go. Under his replacement, Elgin Baylor, the club has compiled a 14–30 mark, and home attendance has shrunk considerably.

Goodrich was signed to a long-term contract, at more than $250,000 a year, before the season began. His acquisition cost the Jazz two No. 1 draft selections and a swap of draft positions with the Lakers. . . .

A few weeks later, the season was over, the Jazz finishing with a 35–47 record. Maravich would lead the league in scoring—a 31.1 ppg average—nearly five points better than Billy Knight (26.6) of Indiana and Abdul-Jabbar (26.2) of Los Angeles. He had 5.3 assists and 5.1 rebounds a game, a reflection of a fully rounded game. For the second year in a row, he was first-string All-NBA, along with Elvin Hayes of Washington, David Thompson of Denver, Westphal of Phoenix, and Abdul-Jabbar of Los Angeles.

During the season, the Pistol had taken to wearing a gold necklace that had the letters "M-E" and under that "1st."

"It stands for Me First and that's the way I feel," he told a newsman. "I learned long ago that nobody else is going to look out for you, you've got to take care of yourself."

Was that the sentiment of a survivor—few players had had to navigate the tricky straits Maravich did as a pro—or was it the sentiment of a spoiled-rotten star? Throughout his career, Peter Press Maravich would be confronted by the sneaking suspicion of many critics that he was more a traveling sideshow to the NBA's main stage—a man wired to

entertain with his prolific scoring and improvisational playmaking—
than a team player. Never mind the number of assists, the total rebounds, or the possibility that his defense was improving. For some of
these experts, Maravich was forever for Maravich.

Yet even as he might wear that provocative "Me 1st" necklace, in the
next paradoxical instant he was handing out cases of expensive cham-
pagne (Dom Perignon 1969) to teammates, front office workers, and
members of the media as a way of including others in his spotlit moment
as the NBA's leading scorer.

Maravich the paradox. More and more, he seemed a man of contrary
impulses—a flamboyant player on the court but guardedly private off the
court; a vegetarian who espoused the virtues of alfalfa sprouts and
whole-grain bread but continued drinking alcohol to excess; a critic of
negative press who was full of negative emotions about his own life.

ONE MATTER that Maravich was entirely positive about was the stateside return of his father during the '76–77 season.

Yes, Press was back, and reaching out to old friends of his, in letters
that detailed what life had been like after Helen had died:

> Time flies, doesn't it? My daughter Diana will be 13 on her next birthday
> in September [1977]. She is almost 5-foot-7, 105 lbs. Doing well in
> school. She is an honor student.
>
> We spent a year (almost) in Sweden. I coached a club in Div I, which
> is the top league there. They let 2 Americans play—preferably a center
> 6-8 or better, and an outstanding playmaking, shooting guard. Most of
> the 12 clubs in the league had 2 blacks—those rejects from the NBA.
> Sorta a proving ground for them. I had the only all-white team. My team
> played well. We were runners up in the Swedish Cup tournament. The
> team, Hogsbro, beat me by 9. We beat them by 7. I thought there would
> be a third game, but the secretary of the basketball federation in Stock-
> holm gave the title to Hogsbro because they beat me by the point differ-
> ence. We were 28–9 overall.

I even enrolled at the University of Lund, an institution some 800 years old. I studied the Swedish language. I can still read it altho I lost my ability to speak it since there are no Swedes here. Also studied the Socialistic system of government. I told my professor to shove it up his butt. I told the class of 15 people from Germany, Hungary, Poland, yes even Yugoslavia, that they were all slaves. Every time I said something about Democracy the class would yell in unison, "You lie!" I told my professor that was typical of brain-washed individuals. Diana too went to school. She studied Swedish from 8:00–12:00 and picked up her classes in the afternoon. I went to college for six months. Studied my butt off. I joined the Swedish Library Circle and read 27 novels while I was there. Diana did well in Swedish. Everytime I would say something to her in Swedish she would laugh.

We spent Xmas in West Berlin. I also had a General whom I knew from previous trips to set me up a tour in East Berlin. I showed Diana the entire Berlin Wall. We also spent lots of time in Denmark, too. We spent a couple days in England, too.

Pete and I put on basketball clinics two years ago in Spain, Italy, Sardinia, Sicily, Germany. Over 15,000 came out to see Pete. . . .

About the only thing left for Pete is the 20,000 point club of which only 8 former NBA players distinguished themselves. That plus the world championship.

He'll play 7 or 8 more years. He's only played 7 yrs after this season and has almost 13,000 points.

In L.A., where all the Hollywood stars go, he damn near beat L.A. by himself one night. He hit for 46. Jack Nicholson from "Cuckoo's Nest" went crazy at the game. He told Pete, "Past, present or future, no one will ever be able to carry your jock."

I have been scouting basketball games for different colleges. Also doing talent scouting for the Jazz. The Jazz sent Diana and I to Hawaii for 10 days, St. Pete, Fla., for 6 days, Kansas City for 5 days. I guess I have scouted and seen 110 games all total.

I live in Mandeville, Louisiana, which is about a mile north of Lake Pontchartrain. It is a new development. I live on the 7th green. We have a 18 hole golf course, million-dollar clubhouse, 6 tennis courts and an Olympic type swimming pool. My home cost me $80 Gs, but I covered half of it. The other half I borrowed from the bank at 8 and 3/4%. I still have a whole yard 100 feet by 200 feet to fix up—grass to grow, shrubs, etc. The furniture, etc is in place. Can't do everything because I have to cook every night when Diana comes home from school. On top of that— wash clothes, clean house, dishes, etc. My job is never done.

Pete lives on the south side of the Lake. We are 35 minutes by car from each other. I have to cross a bridge that is 24 miles long (world's largest) across the lake.

I am 45 minutes from the Dome.

Ronnie works at the French Quarter. He is the mayor down there. He lives next door to Al Hirt. He is a manager for Jim Moran's million-dollar Riverside Restaurant. He manages 3 bars there. He's a real street man.

My brother Mark visited with me recently. He still lives in Aliquippa. Also Sam, my other brother, lives in Midland, about 10 miles from Aliquippa. That's it—you have the latest dope on the Maraviches.

THROUGHOUT the '76–77 season, there had been rampant speculation in the media about whether Pete Maravich would re-sign with the Jazz once his contract expired at the end of the season or instead opt to go elsewhere and play for a title contender.

The Pistol had made no secret about wanting a championship ring, the only objective as a basketball player that he had yet to attain. On more than one occasion he had pointedly remarked that if he were to re-turn to the Jazz, he expected management to acquire a capable big man.

Several times in his pro career, it appeared that Maravich was about to be teamed with that capable big man, but on each occasion his franchise's attempts to secure that player—Julius (Dr. J) Erving in Atlanta and Moses Malone and Sidney Wicks in New Orleans—had been foiled, either by a directive from the league to lay off ABA stars Erving and Malone or, in the case of Wicks, by the player refusing to report to New Orleans.

With Maravich's success as the league's leading scorer came the belated recognition by his peers and the media. Sure, there were still crit-ics who questioned whether Maravich could, if he had to, mute his game to be part of a winner. But increasingly he was getting the respect that had been denied him earlier in his career, when the burden of his LSU heroics had been compounded by his being the white boy with the big-bucks contract.

Nothing like the antagonism he had encountered in Atlanta, from teammates and the media, existed in New Orleans. In the hearts and minds of his teammates, and Jazz fans, Pete Maravich was *the man*. As Jazz center Rich Kelley put it: "Nobody was close to Pete as a talent or attraction. We were all comfortable with him as #1. We were a team of castoffs. There weren't a lot of strong personalities in terms of people de-manding respect or jockeying for power in the locker room or on the court. Guys here were role players and kind of comfortable in that. We reveled in the chance to play ball and be doing it with Pete, who created on the court. It was a rollicking good time."

Yet the joy of the game sometimes escaped Maravich. As the honors piled on and the spotlight brightened, he continued to feel a void. He filled the void by drinking to excess, even inviting his brother Ronnie and friends to join him in alcoholic binges at the home he shared with Jackie—no boon to a happy marriage. Success at the game that had been his obsession since grade school did not compute to the happiness he had imagined. When earlier in the '76–77 season the Celtics' Dave Cowens had taken a leave of absence from the team, saying he needed the time off to regenerate his enthusiasm for the game, Maravich told newsmen, "I was thinking about doing the same thing last year [1975–76]. I had lost my enthusiasm and motivation."

By placing his diminished enthusiasm for the game in '75–76, he seemed to imply that all was A-OK in this season as the league's leading scorer. But that was not the case. For instance, the morning after he scored 68 points, he would later say, he awoke with the desire to escape the pressure of having to top himself. The perceived necessity to do more and be more was eroding the pleasure he'd once taken in the game. With his obsessive personality, Maravich was consumed by the tacit bargain he'd long ago made—to give all that he could of himself. It was how he was wired, but the recognition of it now weighed on him. As he would say, "What once was my god and provider became the thorn in my side, and I couldn't help but become disillusioned."

Escape from the pro game's hurly-burly was a note he had sounded from his earliest tortured days in Atlanta, and his being the main man for the Jazz did not deter him from sounding that note again. He continued to imagine a refuge beyond this earth, a place in which he could find the serenity that eluded him as the Pistol.

"Do you know what I think?" he told *Sport Magazine*'s Robert Ward. "I think some day a space ship is going to come down and take me away from all this . . . stuff. My idea of heaven is a place just beyond space. I mean, the heavens are going to open up . . . and then beyond that will be heaven, and when you go inside, then the space closes again, and you are there . . . definitely a wonderful place . . . everyone you ever knew will be there. Great."

Meanwhile, in the here and now, Maravich carried on. That August, assured by the new Jazz general manager, 34-year-old Lewis Schaffel, that the team would bring in a big man to complement him, Maravich signed a five-year, $3 million contract that either matched or fell just short of what Abdul-Jabbar, the league's highest-paid player, was making—depending on which news service report you believed.

Either way, Maravich had committed his future to the Jazz.

In turn, Schaffel, a former players' agent and attorney, delivered on his promise to provide the muscle the team had lacked. Atlanta free agent Leonard (Truck) Robinson, a 6-foot-7, 225-pound forward, suited up with the Jazz, who sent Ron Behagen to the Hawks as compensation.

Maravich's experience in Atlanta regarding his so-called exorbitant salary had been chastening enough to prompt him to research the money made by high-profile celebrities in other enterprises, the better to cope with whatever hubbub there was this time about his deal.

"Nobody," he said, "says anything about actors, TV newsmen making a million a year, a rock star like Peter Frampton grossing $50 million a year. I don't see anybody harping on the Grateful Dead or Elton John.

"There's an actor who turned down two million for three weeks' work. He wanted three million for two weeks. Yet I'm always being harped upon, because I'm there on the sports page every day.

"Man, the basketball player WORKS. The travel is really hard. We're extremely specialized, the most specialized people in the world probably. More so than a heart or brain surgeon. We SHOULD get paid.

"There's no difference in me playing ball and Lavar Burton playing Kunta Kinte in 'Roots.' It's all entertainment. You're trying to draw an audience. It's all one big conglomerate."

With Robinson at forward, the hoops conglomerate New Orleans Jazz entered the new season with a player whose knack for rebounding accelerated the game, enabling the team (read: Maravich) to run. That made Truck, at first blush, a fortuitous addition, and Maravich was quick to praise him as "exactly what this team has never had." The team won 10 of its first 18 games, as Maravich—averaging 27 points a game—vied with Denver's David Thompson for the league scoring lead.

But after that early success, the Jazz slumped, the hammer of discontent dropping once again on Maravich. Early into the '77–78 season, he heard whispers that Schaffel was bum-rapping him as selfish to newsmen and, worse, floating his name as trade bait with other teams.

"From day one," said Jazz publicity man Fredman, "Lewis didn't like Pete, didn't like the way he played. There was immediate conflict. Without the permission of Sam Battisone, the team's owner, he started checking out trades, investigating what he could get for Maravich, word of which got out to the media."

And got out to Maravich, too, who said, "Whenever things aren't going well, they blame the white boy making the most money."

Suddenly, a season that looked as though it could be the Jazz's best ever became fraught with complications. Maravich, who wanted to believe that the backbiting to which he had been subject in Atlanta was forever past, found himself under siege again. Trouble ensued.

As John Papanek would write in *Sports Illustrated*:

... At 29 he has still not gotten over his occasional bratty habits of crying to officials, ignoring open men to shoot from 25 feet or screaming at less talented teammates when his often miraculous passes bounce off their faces.

Last week, during a 123–108 laugher over Indiana, Kelley stunned everyone on the floor by yelling at Maravich after he carelessly threw a pass out of bounds, "Run the goddamn play through, Pete."

Paranoid even in good times, Maravich grew more so when an unnamed teammate was quoted in the local press as chastising him for "not making sacrifices."

Maravich responded by telling newsmen after one loss: "Gimme a Jabbar or a Baylor. It takes a team to win and we only had a few guys who wanted to play tonight."

Early in November, when the Jazz played the Knicks at Madison Square Garden, he reacted to Robinson's published comment that the Jazz "didn't have enough ball movement" by refusing to shoot in the fourth quarter as New Orleans lost by three points to New York. It occurred during a troubling road trip in which the Jazz went 0–5.

Back in the Superdome against Seattle, Maravich remained in Shot Withdrawal Mode, taking only five shots (of which he hit four) even as he passed up uncontested layups. Although he handed out 15 assists in the Jazz's 127–116 victory, his self-denial disturbed the home crowd, which booed him for being un-Pete.

Afterward, Maravich told reporters, "This is the way management wants me to play. I shot like [Portland Trailblazer Dave] Twardzik does. He leads the league in percentage. Anyway, I didn't pass up any good shots."

It was, ultimately, an act of rebellion, passive aggression aimed at the naysayers—Schaffel, his own teammates, the critics who insisted he was a ballhog and poison to the chemistry of any club. The reference to Twardzik was calculated. Twardzik, a starting guard, had been but a cog in Portland's championship season in '76–77, a player who hustled on defense and worked the ball to better scorers like Bill Walton, Maurice Lucas, and Lionel Hollins while settling for the occasional high-percentage shot. Over the course of that championship season, Lucas had fired up 1,357 shots, Hollins 1,046, and Walton 930. Twardzik had attempted only 430 field goals and made 61 percent of them, many of them layups. He was content to be a spear carrier.

Maravich, everybody knew, was no Twardzik and never had been. He was, and always would be, the Show. It was what drew Jazz fans to the Dome. As Rod Hundley put it: "Pete was the local hero. You wouldn't have sold a ticket without him. He was idolized. People had been trained from the Pistol's days at LSU. They didn't give a damn if the team lost as long as Pete got his 30 and made the fancy plays."

And there was no question that Maravich still had the showman's gift. Hundley cited a game against the Philadelphia 76ers: "Pete did something really different. He slapped the ball over on the fast break, and then he slapped it back with the other hand going the other way and they called him for walking. And Pete yelled at the ref, 'How do you know if that's walking? You've never seen anybody do it before.'"

One game after emulating the selfless Twardzik, Maravich reverted to character, scoring 39 points on 19 of 33 shots (including the winning basket) against the Houston Rockets. But his anger at being depicted as a player whose ego subverted the team's chances rode through his postgame comments to the media: "I have had a lot of disappointments in my career. It's very difficult to be happy in this business. When you win, you're the happiest guy in the world. When you lose, you're in the coldest business you could imagine. It doesn't matter to me if I score one point or 100. I get the same paycheck twice a month. Everybody has to make certain sacrifices. If you lose a game, it's your fault. You're making the most money so it's your fault. If some kid comes up to me for advice, I'd tell them to take up an individual sport like tennis or golf. Then, if you lose, it really is your fault."

On December 16, during a home game against Phoenix, when Baylor substituted for Maravich at 6:09 of the third quarter, a Jazz season-ticket holder, Henry Rosenblatt, shouted at Pete from his front-row seat.

Maravich rose up from the bench and walked over to where Rosenblatt sat. Pointing a finger at him, he screamed, "I want everyone to know that you are not a fan. You are an asshole."

Security guards and team officials quickly intervened, ushering Maravich back to the bench. He would return to the game in the fourth quarter, score eight points for a game total of 34 as the Jazz lost 126–113.

Rosenblatt, a season-ticket holder since 1974, later told newsmen that he was upset because Maravich was not providing leadership.

That echoed the line that Schaffel was putting out, and Maravich was not about to offer himself up as a free target to the GM, either. To one newsman he said that Schaffel was "a lying, backstabbing sonofabitch who's been out to get me from the start." To another, *Times-Picayune* columnist Peter Finney, he said that the team would be better off if Schaffel went on a scouting trip to Iran, a country that at the time was holding American citizens captive.

The next day, accompanying Finney's column with the Pistol's barbed words about the team's GM, was a photo of Schaffel that had been touched up so that Lew appeared in a sheik's turban. The photo provided a few laughs for Jazz players and some of Schaffel's front office colleagues.

But it was no more than a moment's comic relief in a season that threatened to come unhinged practically before it had begun. Over the years, his Jazz teammates had found playing with Maravich a roller-coaster ride along uncharted tracks. On any given night, they would tell you, it was hard to say which Maravich would show up—the bubbly extrovert who'd talk a mile a minute about the virtues of organically fed turkeys and raw milk or kibitz about drag racing teammates on the way back from the Dome to Metairie in his Porsche or the other Maravich, the withdrawn, profoundly glum soul—the Maravich who holed up with wife Jackie in a house full of burglar alarms and electric sensor pads and rarely joined teammates for postgame drinks at Pat O'Brien's or live jazz at Rosey's. That Maravich would write in his diary: "With all the trophies, awards, fame and money, I am not at peace with myself."

Rod Hundley: "I'd never seen a guy like Pete. One day talking and laughing, the next day in a shell—wouldn't talk to anybody."

Andy Walker, Jazz guard: "Like Dr. Jekyll, Mr. Hyde."

Rich Kelley: "I wouldn't be surprised if you go back and find that Pete was a manic-depressive."

Neal Walk: "I'm not a doctor, but I think he might have been bipolar. Highs and lows. Like the tides. Gregarious yet at the same time a loner."

Paul Griffin, Jazz forward: "After all those years, he had a built-in defense mechanism for strangers. He wouldn't give them the time of day. He'd turn his back and walk away . . . be it in an airport, hotel lobby, or after a game."

Elgin Baylor: "As a person, he was a great guy. A wonderful person. Pete had a big heart. There was nothing he wouldn't do for teammates. He'd give them money if they needed it. In talking to players, they'd tell me, 'Pete did this. Pete did that.'"

Mel Counts: "He was a very gentle, very caring individual."

Dave Fredman, Jazz publicity director: "Pete was a sensitive guy. A lot more than people thought because of his flamboyance on the court."

Walk: "One Thanksgiving in New Orleans, he invited me over to his house for a holiday dinner. He was very attentive to the fact that I was a vegetarian. He had every kind of bean and grain. I was touched by his thoughtfulness."

Butch van Breda Kolff: "He was fun to be around. He had a good sense of humor. He liked to kid. But he was never a wise guy. Or fresh. There's a way of zinging a coach. And Pete never crossed the line."

Kelley: "When not in formal practices, guys'd play h-o-r-s-e or two-on-two. The games would be physical and kind of funny. A lot of trash talking. The object was to embarrass somebody. Pete would do it with his mouth and by making outrageous predictions and shots."

Andy Walker: "When he was upbeat, he was one of the fellas. He had a little swagger. He could play the dozens. Or laugh and joke and clown around. He didn't act like he was better than us."

Counts: "His mind was racing a mile a minute. Like a Machine-Gun Kelly. He'd go into things—his views, his philosophical beliefs. He was an interesting person to be around."

Walk: "I'd listen to his thoughts and feelings about diet, and martial arts. The martial arts had led him to yoga and New Wave kinds of things that gave him a better perspective. Pete was exploring other options."

Don Sparks, Jazz trainer: "He became health-food conscious. He read and studied up on this pill, that pill."

Baylor: "All the time talking about eating habits. Not eating hamburgers and so on, taking a lot of herbs."

Counts: "Interests? Well, he liked video games, particularly this one called 'Pong.'"

Kelley: "Pong was the first big video game. It's one where the ball bounces around and you have paddles to hit it with. He had that thing installed. Whenever you'd go over his place, you'd be locked into that sucker for two hours. Pete's was a very addictive personality in terms of competition. There were four, five players who lived where he did, in Metairie or in Kenner, the next town over: Aaron James, Bud Stallworth, James McElroy, Nate Williams, and Paul Griffin. Once a week in the locker room, you'd hear a story of some sick drag racing. Somebody who'd been racing Pete. Pete would start it and then make the other guy tell it. That was part of the punishment for losing to him."

Walk: "He loved riding in that Porsche. Me, I thought his foot was too heavy when he drove. Guys on the team called him 'Speed Racer,' or 'Speed' for short. He liked fast stuff. And chrome and glass. Pete was like a kid. He was excited to have stuff and show it to you. Like a new stereo. With the other guys he'd talk cars. Didn't interest me. But when he was talking about something he was into, he was very enthusiastic."

Kelley: "For months at a time he'd be a joy to be around. But then he had very dark periods. The manifestations were very obvious. No bounce in his step. Little interaction with the rest of us. To be quite honest, it'd throw the team into a funk and we'd lose more than when he was 'up.' Guys would say, 'Oh shit, Pete looks like he's in one of his moods. We got to suck it up.' Sometimes one of the guys would tease him: 'Pete's not feeling good. Let's pack it in.' Pete might laugh a little but continue in that state of mind. I'm no psychologist, but I pretty firmly believe those moods of his were chemically driven. By no means am I licensed to give a diagnosis on the subject, but that's my layman's look at things 20 years later."

Walker: "When he was in one of his moods, he played as though he was in a deep fog. His eyes were in a daze. I thought it tended to happen more often in the lower NBA markets—Kansas City, places like that. L.A., Boston, New York—he was focused and ready to kill. He'd be pumped. I think a lot had to do with the crowds and the media attention. In other markets, he didn't focus in.

"I remember a play he made in L.A. that brought the house down. He drove with his right hand along the baseline and, when Abdul-Jabbar came over to stop him, without breaking stride or jumping, he flipped the ball over his head up to the top of the backboard, above the box, a beat before Jabbar could get at him. Flipped it up without even looking at the basket. When the shot went in, Jack Nicholson jumped out of his seat and threw up his arms in excitement."

Sam Battisone, Jazz owner: "I liked him a lot. But there were tremendous pressures as soon as he put that uniform on . . . and self-expectations—he felt responsible for winning and losing. He took that pressure on himself."

Kelley: "Pete loved to talk basketball. I spent my share of nights, drinking beer with him and talking. He could talk a wonderful game. A team game. But it wasn't the game that happened on the court. In truth, he was kind of frustrating to play with. He felt so much need to create on every play, be involved on every play—you can't do that in the pros. Even Michael Jordan, even HE realized sometimes you need to be moving without the ball.

"I played with a lot of guys who could score. Adrian Dantley. Alex English. Pete. As a general rule, most guys that play with scorers like that don't like playing with them. I don't know whether I'm being charitable or not, but I always thought that guys like Pete and Dantley and English shoot a lot because they think they're doing it for their teammates. In their minds, it's the best way to win. I know that's what Pete had in his heart and mind—that the best chance for the team is for him to do spectacular and creative things. He felt it was his burden."

THROUGH HIS years as coach of the Jazz, Baylor had sought to refine Maravich's hell-bent game, his objectives much the same as those of van

Breda Kolff and Fitzsimmons and Guerin—hit the open man and work hard on defense.

Somehow, amid all the tumults of the '77–78 season—the infighting with Schaffel, the occasional complaint from Robinson about Maravich's firing up long-range shots before ol' Truck had crossed half-court, the confrontation with the courtside fan—amid all that suddenly emerged the Maravich of a purist's dream. Even as he confided to his diary that his knees hurt badly from patella tendinitis, beginning that December Pete Maravich passed, shot, rebounded, and defended— played with a purpose that delighted his coach and teammates. To this day, nobody can explain wherefore and why—it just happened.

As Rich Kelley recalled: "He started doing less. Less shooting. Less dribbling. Less spectacular passing. More basic passing. More rebounding. He was only shooting it 18 times a game, his percentage was up. He was really, really good."

Good on the level of an Oscar Robertson or Jerry West?

Kelley: "For that two month period, easily. He controlled ballgames without being flamboyant, or wasteful. There are not many guards that can do that."

Baylor couldn't have been more pleased either, saying: "For that period he was the best all-round, he was playing terrific. Everybody was enjoying playing with Pete."

By January 31, 1978, the Jazz had won eight straight games, were one game over .500 with a 25–24 record, and were looking very much like a playoff contender. The city of New Orleans was rocking with excitement, the Jazz drawing an average of 13,459 fans a game at the Dome. Maravich? He was leading the league in scoring with 28 points a game, was sixth in assists and eighth in steals. In the Jazz's eighth straight victory, he had generated 35 points, 11 assists, and 5 steals and had thrilled to the crowd's chant of "Pistol, Pistol, Pistol." But on the night of January 31, against the Buffalo Braves in New Orleans, in his most productive period as a pro, the often-turbulent NBA career of Pete Maravich took another hit.

It was the fourth quarter, with the Jazz headed for their ninth straight victory (114–95), when Maravich took the ball near midcourt and, as a defender tried to jam him, jumped into the air and whipped a pass through his legs to Aaron James breaking to the basket for the slam-dunk layup. A sweet pass—one of thousands of crowd-pleasing maneuvers he'd executed through the years. But this one would cost him.

"Pete came down awkwardly," recalled reporter Marty Mule, "and you could hear the snapping sound from his knee and then Pete's yell of pain."

He fell hard on the right knee and writhed in pain on the court until a time-out was called moments later. Maravich would be carried from the floor, grimacing while fearing that his career was over. He'd heard the popping sound and guessed that he'd torn tendons in his knee.

But early prognoses suggested a less worrisome outcome. After examining the knee, Jazz trainer Sparks told newsmen: "It looks like a strained ligament just below the knee on the outside part of the leg."

Days later, Maravich canceled out of the league's annual All-Star game, to which he'd been named an Eastern Conference starter. A news report said that he would be sidelined "at least a week" with his knee injury.

But two weeks after incurring the injury, he had missed seven games, and the pain remained sharp enough and the knee swollen enough to prompt his having an arthroscopic examination done.

On February 19, a UPI report indicated that Dr. Kenneth Saer, the team doctor, said the injury—characterized as minor damage to the inside margin of knee cartilage—would heal without surgery. The story continued:

. . . Saer said he had performed an orthoscope examination on Maravich yesterday and had found an injured ligament intact. Previous examinations had indicated that the ligament might have been torn. Saer said Maravich should be able to run by next week.

On February 24, Press wrote friends:

Pete has been working hard rehabilitating his knee. He is riding a stationary bike, massaging, exercising, walking. Maybe next week he'll jog some. The Jazz are still in the thick of the race for a playoff spot. We broke an 8-game losing streak last nite beating Golden State Warriors, 115–91. Without Pete we don't fast break or aren't much of a threat. But every victory counts. We have five games at home and, hopefully, we can win all five but that is a big order.

On March 21, 52 days after incurring his injury, Maravich returned, playing 12 scoreless minutes against the New Jersey Nets with his leg taped and afterward saying: "Being back for the first time I didn't want to go full blast and make change of direction moves that might have hurt. But my timing was off and I found it hard to coordinate my brain with my body. I couldn't make certain moves I'm used to.

"In all fairness to the Jazz, coach Baylor and myself, if I'm only going to play 12 minutes a game the rest of the year, there is no sense in playing. This isn't going to get me in shape and I'll just be what I am now when the playoffs start. Getting in shape is my main concern. Offense is timing and having your legs under you. Right now I don't have my legs."

The reason was that there was more to the injury than previously thought. When Maravich went to the Jobe-Kerlan clinic in Los Angeles, it was determined that, besides the stretched anterior cruciate ligament, his lateral meniscus cartilage had been torn. That meant that the knee would require an operation.

It also meant that Pete Maravich's season was over. He had played 50 games and averaged 27 ppg and 6.7 assists a game. The injury may very well have cost him another scoring title. Although George Gervin (27.22 ppg) of San Antonio just edged out David Thompson (27.15) as the league's scoring leader, had Maravich been healthy it was not hard to imagine his generating enough points to surpass both men. But with a league requirement of a minimum of 70 games or 1,400 points, Maravich did not even qualify with his 50 games and 1,352 points.

When he went down with his knee injury, the Jazz seemed a shoo-in for a playoff spot. The team would have to lose 20 of its final 30 games to blow its chance. Well, without Maravich, it did precisely that. Needing a win in the final game of the season to qualify for the playoffs, New Orleans lost to Houston in a "home" game that was played in Biloxi, Mississippi, because the Dome was not available. It left the Jazz with a 39–43 record. With Maravich in the lineup the team had gone 26–24; without him, 13–19.

A cruel finish to a season that had promised to be Maravich's finest as a pro. Cruel and, to a degree, ironic. Because just as he had injured the knee at LSU executing a showman's flourish, so it had happened again here in New Orleans.

"It symbolized a lot of the complications of his life," said Kelley. "With the team so far ahead, he probably shouldn't have been in the game to begin with. But there he was, in a game already in hand, trying to juice the crowd. And he did do something other-worldly before collapsing in a heap. But the whole franchise was never the same after. And neither was he."

SURGERY would be followed that summer by rehabilitation of the damaged knee.

When Pete Maravich reported to training camp for the '78–79 season, his knee was encased in a cumbersome Lenox Hill knee brace—a two-pound steel protective device that had been worn by Joe Namath on returning from his knee injury.

But as Maravich would concede later, although the knee brace gave him psychological security, and perhaps helped stabilize a knee he was still rehabilitating even as he was playing, it created certain other problems. As a result of wearing the brace he would incur lower back problems and be forced to miss part of the exhibition schedule. And by relying on the knee brace to support his moves, he would devalue the muscles surrounding the knee, a classic case of use it or lose it.

By December, those muscles around the knee were atrophying; Maravich also began to suffer from tendinitis in his knees. It left him in a no-win situation: The weakened knee required strengthening exercises; tendinitis gets better with rest.

All of this was reflected in significantly reduced statistics. By early December Maravich was averaging 23.3 ppg on .408 shooting and was behind his normal pace in assists and steals. As Curry Kirkpatrick would report in *Sports Illustrated*:

> As a result of all this, the real Pistol Pete has been seen only for brief, shining moments. Maravich hasn't been able to drive to the basket much nor has he been effectively penetrating. He can't spring off the knee for his jump shot nor can he go high for layups. Maravich's quickness and lateral mobility have been severely limited; he is practically a statue on defense. Moreover, the Pistol's entire game, so dependent on slashing inventiveness, has suffered terribly.

As if the Jazz weren't hit hard enough by having a diminished Maravich, the team's relationship with its other star, Truck Robinson, became terribly strained. Prior to the new season, Robinson's in-house advocate, Lew Schaffel, had been dismissed as general manager. But Truck was confident enough of his output in '77–78 — he'd led the league in rebounding with 1,288 while averaging 22.7 ppg — to feel he could get management to give him more of his deferred salary up front. After all, the Jazz's season-ticket slogan, "You can bet on the fire of the Pistol and the power of the Truck," appeared to give him special status. But when Robinson's agent, Don Cronson, tried to renegotiate his man's deal, he was turned down by Jazz management. The team's refusal to renegotiate sent Robinson into a snit. He did not report to training camp and missed several exhibition games.

Meanwhile, Cronson dragooned Maravich into the controversy when he told newsmen: "The Jazz has two sets of rules. One for Pete and one for the rest of the players."

Predictably, Maravich was not happy at being used as a negotiating tool by Cronson.

The result was that the Jazz soon had two unhappy stars and, not surprisingly, a record that reflected it. And as the team sank deeper into the standings, Robinson and Maravich grew increasingly alienated, both men pushing to be traded elsewhere.

And by now the thriving coexistence that Maravich and Robinson had had at the outset had diminished. "There was," said Paul Griffin, "an ego thing going on with Pete and Truck. Truck came in and came in scoring a lot. It created a little animosity—like, who was the big dog on the team. They didn't get in each other's face. But Pete was used to being the big dog—he won the scoring championship. And Truck took a little of the spotlight from him.

"So there was often a competitive thing going on between them. It could get a little nutty. Like Truck woud tip a waitress, pulling out a lot of bills that he'd flash. A roll of, say, 100-dollar bills. And Pete would say, 'That's nothing. I got $1,500 in cash in MY wallet right now.'"

By early January the team had lost 14 of its last 17 games, and Baylor was quoted as saying that management would have to take steps to end the quarrelsome atmosphere or else risk even more "disgusting basketball."

Meanwhile, Larry Hatfield, the head of the team's executive committee, was telling newsmen, "Obviously we're not very happy about the situation. We have a real chemistry problem. We are not getting 100 percent from our talent.

"There was a time we would never have thought of trading Pete. He's in the second year of a five-year contract, but he has asked to be traded. We would accommodate him if we could improve our team. But now that everyone knows Pete wants to be traded, the telephone has not exactly been ringing. There's a lot of talk, but it's just talk."

The talk was limited because NBA general managers would not make substantive offers for Maravich on account of his $600,000 salary and the questionable status of his knee.

"About that time," said Jazz publicist Fredman, "we had to take a team picture in the French Quarter. The day turned out to be quite cold and Truck Robinson, who'd been making life miserable, said, 'I'm not going.' Well, it was the straw that broke the camel's back."

On January 12, the Jazz, who had acquired Spencer Haywood from New York days before, traded Robinson to the Phoenix Suns for Ron Lee, Marty Byrnes, two first-round draft picks, and $500,000 in cash. At the time, Robinson was averaging 24.1 ppg and 13.3 rebounds a game. Lee (9.8 ppg) and Byrnes (6.8 ppg) were Phoenix substitutes.

In a parting shot, Robinson said, "I came into a situation where Maravich was all the people knew. Pete, Pete, Pete. You couldn't name five players on the Jazz before I got there. It was 'Pete and the rest of the Jazz.' All of a sudden I come in—a black player in the South—and it's Pete *and* Truck. A lot of people didn't care for that."

Regardless, Truck was gone, and a month later so was Maravich. By February, his knee had become too painful for him to continue playing. After 49 games and with the season doomed, he and his doctors decided that his taking the rest of the campaign off would allow the knee to heal properly. In retrospect, Maravich, who finished with a 22.6 ppg scoring average and 4.9 assists, came to believe that he had returned to action prematurely, a conclusion with which Baylor agreed.

"Pete was a competitor," said Baylor. "He wanted to play. But there's no doubt in my mind he came back too soon. He was favoring his knee. He was not the same player."

And the Jazz, it was clear, were not the same team they had been a year earlier. The club was headed nowhere—at least in the standings. But a plot was now afoot that would get the team moving, literally, in another direction—northward to Salt Lake City, Utah.

"By now," said Fredman, "we were playing before sparse crowds. At the same time, we were fighting with the Superdome over dates. Every January, February, we had trouble getting dates for home games because the boat show or the Mardi Gras crowded us out. Sam [Battisone, Jazz owner] was losing money with the team at the same time his Sambo's chain was having problems."

In 1979, Battisone sold the Sambo's chain.

"Sam decided if we can't get the dates from the Superdome and we don't have more than 2,600 season tickets sold, as we did that year—the best we'd ever done in New Orleans—he was going to move the team," said Fredman.

The low season-ticket base, Battisone said, owed to the capacious nature of the Dome. Jazz fans believed—and rightly so—that with the Dome's ability to expand its seating to accommodate customer demand there was no reason to worry about getting shut out of a ticket.

"People thought if you wanted a ticket, you just walked up to the gate day of the game," said Battisone. "Which made selling season tickets difficult. We drew great crowds in New Orleans, but only for select games, and with a lot of $1.50 discount tickets. Besides, the city really wanted a baseball team more than it wanted the Jazz. They had us, but the Superdome people were always talking about what would be done when baseball came in."

There were other factors—that deadly 11 percent amusement tax, an 8 percent rental tax, lack of corporate support in New Orleans and, as Marty Mule would write:

> . . . To this day, there are Jazz staff, coaches, players and fans who believe Battisone, a rare visitor to New Orleans, simply wanted to shift his team closer to his Santa Barbara, Calif., home, to Salt Lake City, spiritual epicenter of his Mormon faith, and found reasons to justify it.
>
> Barry Mendelson, who was executive vice president of the Jazz . . . said he believes there was an unspoken agreement among the owners in the last year in New Orleans that they would pull up stakes and move the team 'somewhere more friendly to us.'
>
> "'More friendly' meaning geographically," Mendelson said. "Sam was from California and decided the team should be closer to him."

Whatever the reason, the Jazz had played their final season in New Orleans. When *Times-Picayune* reporter Jimmy Smith wrote the story announcing the move, he quoted Maravich as saying. "I'm still going to get paid."

"The next morning," said Smith, "I get a call from Pete, who says, 'Jimmy, Pistol. You misquoted me.' I told him, 'I thought you never read a paper.' He said, 'I check it every now and then to see if we're in the middle of a nuclear war.'"

THE RECONSTITUTED Utah Jazz were barely recognizable as the squad that had preceded them.

Truck Robinson, of course, had been traded while the team was still in New Orleans. Others moved on after the '78–79 season—Jimmy McElroy to Detroit, Rich Kelley to the New Jersey Nets, Ron Lee to Atlanta, Spencer Haywood and Marty Byrnes to Los Angeles, and Paul Griffin to San Antonio. Aaron James, Tommie Green, and Gail Goodrich retired.

The new faces that Utah fans—more than 5,000 of them season-ticket holders—would greet included Adrian Dantley and Ron Boone, who came over from Los Angeles, Allan Bristow (San Antonio), Ben Poquette (Detroit), Mack Calvin (Denver), Bernard King (New Jersey), and rookies Donald Williams and Paul Dawkins.

The housecleaning also brought a new coach, Tom Nissalke, and new general manager, Frank Layden.

What was not new to the Jazz was Pete Maravich, who was 31 and had knees of a man far older. The Pistol was a reluctant arrival in Utah. With his wife and infant son Jaeson, he was comfortable in Louisiana, where he was, after all, an icon. It was there he planned to live after his NBA career was finished.

By the start of the '79–80 season in Utah, Maravich had shed his Lenox Hill knee brace and, like it or not, was gainfully employed in Salt Lake City. The knee was still tender enough that Jazz trainer Sparks would wave him off the practice court when he detected the hint of gimpiness in Maravich's stride.

"When he came to Utah," said Sparks, "Pete was having a problem with the knee. He couldn't go through a full practice. We worked out in a high school gym that had a hard floor. As soon as he came out of practice, he'd sit with an ice bag on his knee for the rest of the practice."

In 17 appearances with the Jazz, Maravich played 30 minutes a game and averaged 17.1 ppg and three assists. Although they were hardly vintage Maravich numbers, they did not appear to reflect a "shot" player. Yet by late November, with the Jazz at 2–18 and having lost 14 straight games, Nissalke decided that Maravich was no longer of any use to him.

The events that shaped the coach's decision to sit Maravich began on November 27, 1979, when Maravich did not play against Magic Johnson and the Los Angeles Lakers. Three nights later, against Golden State, Maravich did not play because of illness, and Utah broke its losing streak with a 112–104 win. The victory apparently persuaded Nissalke that Maravich's 17 points a game weren't worth the perceived problems the Pistol created by dominating the basketball. When Utah played its next game, against Seattle, a healthy Maravich was on the bench again.

And there he would remain through December and into January, as Nissalke made it clear that he had no intention of ever playing him again.

To add insult to injury, GM Layden told newsmen: "I'm going to get rid of the losers. There's no future for Pete here, and it's better to move the guy this year before he's established an identity in Utah. There are several owners who would love to have a gate attraction like Pete, but the coaches are afraid of him. I wouldn't be surprised if he just packed it in if he can't get on with a contending team in the next few weeks."

Some 20 years later, Nissalke would say, in defense of his benching the Pistol: "Pete was a shadow here. He just couldn't get up and down the floor."

Nissalke, who'd coached at Tulane and in the pros at San Antonio in the ABA and Houston in the NBA, would claim that the decision to put Maravich in the deep freeze was a collective one—"a joint decision with the owners and management." But Battisone's recollection differed: "I remember it as Tom's decision to sit him. I was not happy about it."

Neither were many Jazz fans, who came to the 12,500-seat Salt Palace, the team's home court, carrying placards that read: "Release the hostage," a takeoff on the hostage crisis in Iran faced by the administration of President Jimmy Carter.

Even Dave Fredman, the Jazz publicist, questioned Nissalke about the move. "He decided," said Fredman, "that Pete just couldn't play any more. My point was neither could the other guys. Pete still had some games in him. He wasn't what he was, but he still could play. I don't know if they thought he would quit. But Pete still had a substantial part of his contract in effect. I told Nissalke, 'I don't think it's right.' He said, 'What has Pete Maravich ever done for you?' I said, 'He's always been nice to me and I still think he could make the plays.' I later found out that when Nissalke had been an assistant coach at Tulane, at the time Pete was at LSU, he devised a game plan to stop Pete. Well, Pete—with a bad ankle and tape on the outside of the shoe and around the sole—went out and scored a whole lot of points. And embarrassed him. There might have been some hard feelings from that."

Regardless, it became obvious that the Nissalke/Layden plan was to embarrass the superstar into taking his big-buck contract and retiring, at a considerable savings to the franchise. But Maravich had no intention of doing that. He maintained a stony silence when asked about his future by the media, but to Fredman he said, "They're saying I'm old and washed up. We'll see. I'm not quitting."

To the outside world, he presented a picture of an athlete unperturbed. But the evidence was that away from the public eye, he was hardly serene about being treated so contemptuously. As he languished on the bench, he ceased working out on his own, as he had done for years. The compulsive fitness addict gave way to an angry, self-pitying man who, cliche of cliches, drank to drown his sorrow.

In Seattle, a drunken Maravich, confused about what floor his hotel room was on, pounded at the door of a room he mistakenly believed was his. When the door opened and a bishop of the Mormon church looked out, Pete Maravich collapsed onto the floor. The Mormon official recognized Maravich and phoned a Jazz official staying in the hotel. The official contacted the house doctor. Maravich was taken to a local emergency room and treated without the incident being made public.

Meanwhile, Maravich's attorney, Les Zittrain, was looking for a way to end the sticky situation in which his client found himself.

"I remember," said Zittrain, "calling Sam Battisone from Pittsburgh and saying to him, 'Isn't this absolutely ridiculous—your superstar sitting on the bench?' To Pete, I had said, 'Just sit and take it. If you don't, they could have legal cause to break the contract.' Anyway, Sam said, 'What should we do?' I said, 'Come to Pittsburgh.' Which he did. And we worked out a deal."

On January 17, the Jazz waived Pete Maravich. He had not played in

28 straight games. In announcing the transaction, the Jazz's Larry Hatfield said that the $1.8 million that the club still owed Maravich for the three years remaining on his contract would be paid out over an unspecified longer period — 10 years, as it turned out.

Once he was waived by the Jazz, there was a 48-hour waiver period during which any team could claim Maravich. None did, knowing that to do so would make them responsible for picking up his substantial contract. After that 48-hour period, Maravich became a free agent and could be signed for far less money — as little as the $30,000 NBA minimum. That sum would be in addition to what Utah was obliged to pay him.

Maravich was eager to join a contender so that his last goal as a basketball player — of winning a championship ring — could be realized.

At first blush, it appeared that the Philadelphia 76ers had an inside track on the Pistol's services. Indeed, a headline in the January 22 *New York Times* read "Maravich Becomes Free Agent; Likely to Sign with 76ers." The Sixers believed they had assurances that Maravich would come aboard and had even printed his name on the back of a jersey.

At the time, the 76ers were in the thick of an Eastern Conference battle with the Boston Celtics. The team needed a guard who could score: It had lost Doug Collins' 13.8 ppg contribution to an injury after only 36 games. What remained of the 76ers was high-caliber: Julius (Dr. J) Erving, Darryl Dawkins, Bobby Jones, Steve Mix, Maurice Cheeks, Henry Bibby, and Caldwell Jones. It was not hard to imagine that group, bolstered by Maravich, being capable of winning an NBA title.

The general manager of the Philadelphia team was Pat Williams, whose last transaction with Maravich had been the none-too-pleasant one, as GM of the Hawks, of telling him he'd been traded to New Orleans.

"Pete flies to Philadelphia," recalled Williams. "I was a little apprehensive because of our last encounter. But he arrives in good spirits and takes a physical at Temple University Hospital. Then we put him on a plane to Boston. The next day we hear: Pete Maravich has signed with the Celtics. It was not a pretty scene. Our owner, Fritz Dixon, was very angry: 'You guys screwed it up. How did you screw it up?'

"Later, the word was that our doctors had given Pete a full physical, including the finger test up you-know-where. Which apparently really angered Pete. That was what went out over the grapevine. And the other thing was: the ghost of the Celtic past. He saw all those championship banners and thought he could get one."

THE CELTICS' championship tradition had gotten badly scuffed up toward the end of the '70s.

Two sub-.500 seasons in '77–78 and '78–79 embarrassed devotees of that franchise. As *Time* magazine put it:

> It was not just defeat: 103 losses against only 61 wins, the worst record in the league. It was the way the games were lost: Curtis Rowe dribbling endlessly; Bob McAdoo shooting 20 times a game; Sidney Wicks driving into a wall rather than passing to an open teammate. It was not, in short, the Celtic way, the kind of team play that brought 13 championship banners to Boston, including eight straight titles between 1958 and 1966.

But a year later, the Celtics had executed as radical a turnabout as the league had seen. From a team that had finished dead last in the Atlantic Division of the Eastern Conference in '78–79 with a record of 29–53, Boston was transformed in '79–80 to a contender, largely owing to the addition of a high-priced rookie forward named Larry Bird.

Bird did what great players do: He made his teammates better. He was a catalyst for victory, fearless in the clutch, savvy and unselfish in his surgical disassembling of opposition defenses. The combination of Bird, Cornbread Maxwell, a rejuvenated Dave Cowens, Tiny Archibald, Rick Robey, Chris Ford, and M. L. Carr battled the 76ers for supremacy in the East.

The Celtics viewed Maravich as insurance—a backup player with the ability to provide instant offense. What's more, he had the range on his jump shot to take advantage of the league's new three-point arc. And even with his defective knees, he could do what many players could not—he could create shots off the dribble, a virtue come playoff time when defenses stiffened.

But the flip side of Maravich was the reputation he had for occupying the basketball at the expense of team function. The bugaboo word that had haunted him through the years persisted: *selfish*. It was a word that cast a shadow over his accomplishments and in some quarters had marked him, indelibly, as the anti-Christ of team harmony. Former NBA player and future coach Pat Riley had said of him: "Maravich is the most overrated superstar who ever came down the pike. Every guard in the league wants to send a limo to pick Pete up at the airport and play against his soft defense. I not only don't think Pete could play any other way, I don't think he wants to."

Riley's was hardly the definitive statement on Maravich's capacity to fit his unique skills into a team situation. Although many agreed with Riley's barbed assessment, just as many took a brighter view of Maravich, such as Portland coach Jack Ramsay, who said, "He could adapt to whatever was necessary to win."

Boston, many thought, would test Maravich's ability to work within a strictly team context and provide the last word on his basketball sociability. But in truth, the partial season in Boston offered too spare an opportunity from which to draw eternal truths about the player.

To begin with, he arrived in Boston uncharacteristically out of shape—the result of the cold war that Utah management had played—and immediately went on the injured list with a slight groin pull. The Celtics shunted him off to a practice facility separate from the one the rest of the team used and told him to work himself back into shape. Maravich found this isolation somewhat unnerving, as if he was a kind of basketball leper, in quarantine.

Nor were his expectations met concerning the opportunity he thought he'd been promised. Signing for a reported $80,000, he had expected to play 24 minutes each night out but averaged only 17 minutes through his 26 games with Boston. There were nights when he delivered the firepower the Celtics had hoped he could. On February 8, when guard Chris Ford left the team to be with his ailing mother, Maravich started, playing 42 minutes and scoring 31 points against Indiana. Two nights later, against Detroit, he started again and scored 20 points in 28 minutes. Boston won both games.

But when Ford returned, Maravich went back to the bench. And although he understood that Celtic coach Bill Fitch did not want to jar team chemistry by suddenly featuring the new guy, it left him feeling like odd man out. In fact, he had gone practically overnight from fabulous phenom and league's leading scorer to a veteran scarred by a game that he had once regarded as the glory of his life. A whiff of sadness trailed him now in his twilight quest for a championship ring. He was a man who seemed haunted by could-have-been, as Carrie Seidman would write in the *New York Times* that March 19:

> . . . His hair was a frenzy of curls where once it had been straight. His speed on the court had diminished and he was like someone in suspended animation. Thin lines of fatigue marked a face that had once grinned with alacrity. Even his trademark—a pair of socks that flopped around his ankles—was gone, replaced by a set of white socks with green stripes that stood at attention halfway up to his battered knees.
>
> The last year had taken a toll on Maravich; it was a year in which he fell out of favor when the New Orleans Jazz moved to Utah, was waived, and then picked up by Boston when just about everyone had expected he was on his way to Philadelphia. And though he is resigned to his fate, Maravich still thinks about what might have been. . . .
>
> "My career has probably been stifled since day one," said the former Louisiana State all-American. . . . "If I'd have come out with Boston or New York, my whole career, my whole life, would have been changed. I would have been Pete Maravich, 'winner'—as society puts it—not Pete Maravich, 'loser.'"

Leigh Montville, writing in the *Boston Globe*, would note:

> This was a last chance to bring back the joy of the game, to light the lights he couldn't light by himself anymore. He was the child prodigy grown old. Where had the time gone? He was 32 years old, but at the same time he was 100. Where were the championships? He could make a basketball walk and talk and play the piano, but somehow the words and direction and songs never had been exactly what he wanted them to be.

Maravich had come to Boston seeking a champion's luster, seeking to repudiate the chronic slanders that made him out a loser. By the end of the regular season, it appeared as though he'd made a wise move. The Celtics finished the 82-game schedule with the best record in the NBA—61–21.

Maravich had played a bit part in Boston's winning the Atlantic Division: an average of 11.5 ppg and one assist per game in that foreshortened run of 26 games. But his decision to seek his championship ring with Boston—the NBA team most associated with a winning tradition—would suddenly, and shockingly, backfire when the 76ers—irony of ironies—knocked the Celtics out of the playoffs, four games to one, before losing in the championship round to the Los Angeles Lakers.

But Maravich was so fixated on his goal of an NBA title he would remember Philadelphia's playoff destruction of the Celtics in a distorted way. How else to account for his stating in his autobiography that the Sixers, not the Lakers, won the NBA championship that year?

In the Philadelphia-Boston series, Maravich saw limited playing time and scored 31 points, making only 14 of 33 shots. Afterward, he wondered whether he would have felt vindicated even had the Celtics won another title if his role in their championship drive had been as minimal as it was in this season. It was a short, straight line from that notion to the notion of retirement.

Yet although he entertained the thought of retiring, he went ahead as though he meant to play again by putting himself through rigorous workouts on Nautilus strength-building machines and on free weights and by running wind sprints. When the Celtics reported to training camp that September, Pete Maravich was there with them—in body but not, it turned out, in spirit.

After an intrasquad scrimmage in which he scored 38 points and then was told by newsmen that the team's coaches said he had a ways to go before becoming a true Boston Celtic, he felt ambushed by the assessment and weary of the years of Maravich-bashing. In his time, he had been a unique figure in the game, a player whose ingenuity with the basketball was unsurpassed. Basketball had been his obsession, but all these years later he found it no longer served. There was a hole in Pete

Maravich, a hole that the game did not fill. He was worn down by the tumults that his presence provoked. Worn down and, he hoped, ready to move beyond the borders of the 94-foot wooden floor on which he had chased his dream.

"There was a certain aura that was gone," said Dave Cowens, who'd known Pete from college days. "Maybe not an aura, but a . . . I'm not sure of the word. Something was missing. He had been consumed by basketball as a kid, absolutely consumed, and I think after a while that feeling had gone. No one had played more basketball than him. No one. Not the number of games. Summer and winter. From the time he was a kid."

On September 20, 1980, after playing 10 seasons in the NBA and despite being offered a contract by Boston, Pete Maravich up and quit the game.

The Celtics team he ran out on went on to win the world championship.

7

FROM CHILDHOOD ON, Pete Maravich had always taken defeat personally.

That was not so unusual. Many young boys invest deeply in sports, viewing it as a proving ground, a first chance to stake their place in a competitive world.

In Maravich's case, the urgency was compounded by the heightened involvement of a charismatic father whose approval he very much sought.

And maybe the boy used basketball to compensate for the uneasiness he felt about a mother who was not quite like other mothers. With a basketball he could create a world apart.

However, that world ultimately came to haunt him. Unlike other paid professionals, Pete Maravich was not able to treat the losses his teams suffered and the controversies that swirled around his style of ball as strictly business. For him, the game was his be-all and end-all, and the price he paid was a deep and corrosive hurt. Through his 10 seasons in the NBA, he became a brooding figure whose mood swings—heightened by too much alcohol and, some say, occasional drug usage—made him a puzzle to teammates and coaches.

In retirement, the ill feelings he harbored did not suddenly go away. The Pete Maravich who left the NBA because he'd lost his passion for the game was a wounded man. What was he to do with the rest of his life?

That summer—July 1980—Press wrote friends:

> . . .The family is well. Pete's son Jaeson is now 14 months old. I don't know what he (Pete) will do . . .

The future remained a clouded subject to Pete as well, as he disappeared from public view. For two years, he lived far from the spotlight, in a life so unsatisfying that he continued to blur it with alcohol and morbid thoughts.

At times when he would nudge his Porsche up to 130 miles an hour on the causeway over Lake Pontchartrain, it would occur to him that with a slight turn of the wheel the wrong way, he could disappear from his dismal life and nobody would be the wiser. An accident, they would say. What a tragedy.

In those first two years out of the NBA, he remained in Metairie, in the five-bedroom, $300,000 house that was furnished with bleached pine furniture and Jackie's quilt collection and was located on the lake. He turned down requests for interviews and looked after his small construction business while renovating for his family a nearly 100-year-old Victorian, gingerbread-style home in rural Covington, 45 miles away.

He had always been guarded about his private life. Attorney Zittrain remembered the time, back in 1970, when he suggested using Jackie in a TV commercial for Vitalis hair cream—a commercial in which an attractive woman looks admiringly at Maravich. But Pete quashed the idea, saying, "Absolutely not. Our lives are going to be private."

More than a decade later, he remained determined to keep his personal affairs no one's business but his own. But by late 1982 that life with Jackie, Jaeson, and infant son Joshua still was a dark and inhospitable existence. The refuge he had hoped for away from basketball had not materialized. His efforts to explore alternate paths—reincarnation, mysticism, astrology, astronomy, UFOs, and survivalism—just doubled back on his own deep unhappiness.

On a night in November 1982, as he tossed and turned in bed and again thought of suicide, he could not quiet his mind. "I kept thinking of the perverted things I had done, the alcohol I had consumed," he said. "I kept thinking of the letters I had torn up from people who loved me, the people I had hurt. I was crying out within my spirit that November night in Metairie in 1982. I was crying out in my spirit, 'God, you're going to have to raise me; I can't raise myself.'

"It was about 5:50 in the morning, and I heard God speak to me. 'Be strong and lift thine own heart' were the words I heard. They shook the whole room, reverberated through it. People ask me why would God speak to me and not Billy Graham. Well, they'll have to ask God that."

Maravich woke Jackie and asked had she heard God's voice, as he had. She shook her head and said no, then went back to sleep. But for Maravich the moment would define the rest of his life and take him along a new path—that of a Born-Again Christian.

HE HAD never done things halfheartedly. His religious awakening would, it turned out, consume him.

As once he had dedicated himself to the nuances of basketball, now he dedicated himself to spreading the gospel. The reclusive Pete Maravich stepped back in public view again, this time in the service of his Lord, Jesus Christ.

In basketball clinics for youth, he would dazzle the children with his legerdemain and then recruit them for Jesus, using his own life as an object lesson.

"I've experienced just about everything you can experience," he would say. "I've been wealthy. I've had material things everybody always wants. I've had popularity. I've broken over a hundred [scoring] records in high school, college, and the pros. I've been given keys to cities, been named the honorable mayor of a few others, given admiral status in the Navy. I've flown around the world in a Lear jet and given clinics, I've met with kings. But I was having a problem with my life. All those things would only give me pleasure for a moment or two. I wanted something more."

He conveyed the same message to hardened criminals in a tour of Florida prisons, through the prison ministry of Bill Glass, the former Cleveland Browns football player. From church pulpits, before TV cameras and radio microphones, in basketball clinics and camps, in psychiatric hospitals, and once to a crowd of 35,000 at the Billy Graham Crusade in Columbia, South Carolina, he delivered the word that through Christ he had turned his life around and so could you. Visitors to his home in Covington were given religious tracts. Dave Fredman, still working for the (Utah) Jazz, received literature about Jews who had converted to Christianity, germane to him as a member of the Judaic faith. When radio/TV interviewer Larry King underwent heart bypass surgery, Pete sent him a leather Bible with King's name embossed in gold on the cover and this letter:

> Dear Larry: I'm so glad to hear that everything went well with your surgery. I want you to know that God was watching over you every minute and even though I know you question that, I also know that one day it will be revealed to you. My prayer is that you remain open and God will touch your life as He has mine. Once I was a disbeliever. When I could not fill my life with basketball, I would simply substitute sex, liquid drugs or material things to feed my internal shell-like appearance. I was never satisfied. I have finally realized after 40 years that Jesus Christ is in me. He will reveal his truth to you, Larry, because He lives.

Slowly but surely old acquaintances became aware of the change in Maravich—that the brooding, tortured soul had found a way out of his abyss. Some were startled that Maravich, the ultrahedonist, always so self-absorbed, was capable of reversing course. Bud Johnson, the sports information director at LSU and first publicist with the Jazz, remembered: "I called him one night to do some charity event. Pete started questioning me about what the money was for, where it was going. Then he started telling me about his work with kids and that his whole focus was Christianity and being a good father and husband. This wasn't the Pete I'd known from the Jazz. The person I remembered from back then wanted a freebie from the YMCA in Metairie. THAT Pete always thought of himself first, last and always. As we had this conversation, I started crying. That he really cared about these kids—well, that was the most touching moment I can remember. 'You really changed,' I told him."

Johnson was added to the list of folks to whom Maravich sent Bibles and religious literature. Not all were as receptive as Bud, but Maravich was not put off. As he told one reporter: "Guys I know who were good buddies while I was playing run when they see me coming now. They don't want to hear it. But that's OK. I'm just spreading the message. I can't change them. But there is nothing you could trade me for the inner peace I feel now."

Cotton Fitzsimmons got a sense of Maravich's newly found serenity when he ran into him at the Los Angeles Forum. "The Pete I had known with the Hawks was a very emotional guy," said Fitzsimmons. "He didn't have his life straight . . . That period during our final year when he wouldn't speak to me—now at the Forum he came up to me and apologized for it. Hugs and an apology. I told him, 'You don't have to apologize.' He'd gotten his life straightened out."

His old LSU teammate, Rusty Bergman, saw the change in Maravich, too. "He felt good about himself," said Bergman. "He no longer felt everybody was out to use him or get him. Now he had no problem talking to me or being around me. He had a genuine interest in Rusty Bergman. He asked, 'How's the family?' Before it was, 'What do you want from me?'"

LSU team manager David Tate was also cheered by Maravich's religious awakening. "I keep a picture of Pete in my Bible and use it as a bookmark," he later wrote an acquaintance. "Daily as I open my Bible and see Pete's picture, I'm reminded of how God changed Paul in Biblical times, how God changed Pete in modern times, and that He can change friends of mine today who still haven't accepted Jesus as Lord and Savior."

Times-Picayune reporter Marty Mule, who had covered Maravich when he played with the Jazz, interviewed Pete after he had been elected to the Louisiana State Hall of Fame. "We sat poolside at a hotel in Natchitoches, 300 miles from New Orleans," Mule said. "To make conversation, I asked him what he had been up to. That opened the floodgates about his finding the Lord. An hour later, I had to say to him, 'Pete, I have to write a story.' He was like that with a lot of people. Pete had an obsessive personality."

On the mahogany front door of his home in Covington, Pete had a verse of scripture—"Commit thy works unto the Lord"—carved. In 1983 in Clearwater, Florida, he founded a Christian basketball camp at which he gave testimony of his experience and had the youngsters eat natural foods that reflected his own diet: freshly squeezed juices, fruits, grains, salads, bottled spring water, and no red meat. Purity of body and spirit.

Pete lived it as he talked it, giving up alcohol and one time fasting for 25 days, taking in only freshly squeezed juices—a regimen by which his weight dropped 25 pounds to 170 pounds.

Every Thanksgiving, through a black church, he arranged to hand out 100 turkeys to the poor and elderly in Baton Rouge. "Anybody can write a check," said Alfred Young, pastor of the Christ Temple Church. "But he would load the turkeys in his car and we'd go around handing them out."

His objectives had shifted. Where once he sought fame and fortune, now he looked beyond himself, wanting to be of service to others. He resolved to be a good husband and father and a worthy friend.

In stumbling onto his midlife vocation, he was guided and encouraged by John Lotz, an assistant athletic director at the University of North Carolina. Lotz, a devout Christian who had played varsity basketball at East Texas Tech, heard Maravich speak at Campbell College and was "shocked" by the power of his words. Shocked because the words did not jibe with the image that he, like so many others, had of Maravich as the ever-so-flashy "Pistol Pete."

"In reality," said Lotz, "Pete was a very humble guy. And he was one of the most powerful speakers. God touched him. From the point where I first heard him, we spoke to each other every day."

The two men buoyed one another with their faith. A special friendship developed, which Maravich affirmed with cards that underscored that very point:

> *In God's perfect time,*
> *in God's perfect way —*
> *He gave me a friend*
> *like you!*

Then, in a handwritten postscript, Maravich added: "My love to you, brother, and to Vicki (Lotz's wife) and the girls. [Signed] Peter / The "Pistol."

On another occasion he sent Lotz a poem written by Roy Lessin:

> *Friendship*
> *is a special gift —*
> *It adds fragrance to life,*
> *It creates love and trust.*
> *Most of all it brings*
> *an awareness*
> *of what it means*
> *to be blessed by God.*

In his Covington home, Maravich had built a basketball half-court in his attic. Every day he would work out there, honing the ballhandling drills that he now used to attract listeners to his Christian message. The awards and memorabilia from his basketball career were given away or stored. He did not need to be, or want to be, reminded of that past, living as he was in a present filled with religious feeling. "Pistol Pete Maravich died," he would say. "I am Peter Maravich and we are two different lives."

In time, though, he became more relaxed about his NBA past and began playing in the annual Legends game that was part of the league's

All-Star weekend. Recalling the Maravich who appeared at those exhibitions, the *New York Times'* George Vecsey would write:

> He would show up for . . . old-timers' gatherings, lean, almost scrawny, the result of lengthy fasts and limited diets. His eyes looked haunted above the ancient mariner mustache, but he could still look one way and flick a soft lead pass the other way.

But even at these basketball occasions, Pete would bring his passion for Christ. At one NBA All-Star chapel, he recited this prayer that he had written:

> Heavenly Father, we have gathered here this morning before thy presence with thanksgiving and praise. We sing in our hearts for joy to you, O Lord, and we that know you shout joyfully because you are the rock of our salvation. Father, your word says that "man is like a mere breath; his days like a passing shadow." Make us realize the shortness of our days here upon this earth, so that we will begin to utilize the precious time you give to each of us for the winning of souls to the kingdom. Give to us that know you the desire and power to boldly and confidently witness what Christ has done in each of our lives. Your word also says in Matt. 16:26, "For what will a man be profited if he gains the whole world, and forfeits his soul; or what will a man give in exchange for his soul." What upon this earth is worth the eternal loss of one's soul? Father, there is no amount of money that one can have, or material things one can possess, nor prestigious awards one can receive, or even power that one can own which will ever fill the void and godly-shaped vacuum that is present within the hearts of all people who have said no to the Savior. For all that is external and physical is but for a fleeting, temporary moment, compared to the inexplicable joy when the truth of Jesus Christ comes home into one's heart, and a lasting peace which is permanent and eternal. My prayer this morning, Father, is for the light of the gospel of Christ to penetrate the darkness here this weekend; the deceived and even the stupid for your words say in Psalms 149:10, "The senseless and stupid shall alike

perish." I also pray for an injury-free game and travel mercies to all as they leave for home. I pray for all of these things in the magnificent, wonderful name of Jesus, Amen.

Whereas once he had holed up in his Metairie home like a recluse, now Maravich traveled the country, and beyond, even agreeing to make a six-game tour of the Far East with other ex-NBA players like Earl Monroe and Rick Barry.

In May 1985, he joined Press in Israel, where the two men ran clinics for 225 Israeli coaches. By now, Press was moving toward becoming a Born-Again Christian like his son and was following Pete's lead in heeding a diet devoid of red meat and dairy products. Indeed, when Press' old North Carolina State assistant, Charlie Bryant, encountered him at the annual basketball camp at Campbell College in Buie's Creek, North Carolina, Press' newest passions were apparent.

As Bryant recalled: "I stopped by Press' room at Campbell College. I hadn't seen him in two or three years. It was a warm night. Press was sitting at the edge of his bed, drawing plays and talking to a former player of his. I walked in and I had one of those tennis elbow wraps. Press looked up and said, 'I know a doctor in Alabama can cure that.' No hello or nothing. And then: 'And I know what caused it,' he says. And me, I knew what was coming next, so I teased him: 'Yeah, I been eating too many vegetables.' He said, 'You stupid sonuvabitch. You ain't been eating vegetables. You've been eating that damn red meat.'

"The same night, he told me he and Pete were going to this doctor in Alabama to have their blood flushed. They would get hooked to some damn machine and have their blood run through the machine and back into their body. He and Pete were both on that jag and Pete was into the religious bit. THAT kind of surprised me—somebody gets into religion who hadn't been on that path before."

In February 1986, Press wrote friends:

. . . Pete has been flying and making speeches (giving his testimony) all over the country. On top of that he is playing basketball again, believe it or not, with the Hollywood Shooting Stars, a splinter group that fell away from the Globe Trotters. The Shooting Stars are run by Meadowlark Lemon and other Globies. Pete hadn't played a game since 1980, and in the first game in La Cruz, Mexico he bombed the nets for 22 points in 15 minutes playing time.

The Shooting Stars mixed basketball with religion. When the team came to Baton Rouge to play at the LSU Assembly Center, Maravich led a pregame open chapel service to which the 700 fans who turned out were invited. As Joe Planas of the *Baton Rouge Morning Advocate* would note:

> He held his Bible, spoke eloquently, quoted Romans, John, Ephesians. It was a strange talk from a fellow who used to booze it up in college, was considered a ladies' man, rebelled against authority and teachers, and was ultimately dropped from the university. He was Devil-may-care in those days. Now it's Devil, Beware!

As close as Press and Pete had been, they seemed to draw even closer through their shared faith. As they had for years, they would work together that summer in clinics that the older Maravich arranged in Atlanta, Georgia, for Reverend Nelson Price of the Roswell First Baptist Church; in Kenner, Louisiana; and in Houston, Texas. Press would also work at Pete's camp in Clearwater.

Absent from the family circle was Ronnie, about whom Press would say this in his correspondence:

> Ronnie still lives on Bourbon St. He is a lost soul and we (Pete and I) are trying to save him. We pray nightly and I'm sure the Lord will answer us. By the way, I became a Born Again Christian at the First Baptist Church. Even got immersed in water. I don't want any part of Satan. No way.

Soon after, Press got the news that he had prostate cancer.

"He went to see a doctor in New York," said Rusty Bergman. "This doctor told him to eat a certain diet and pray, rather than have surgery. At the time, his cancer was 90 percent curable. Press was very hard-headed. Him and Pete both. He told me, 'Rusty, I'm going to prove to you that by eating this diet in a year I'll be okay.'

"In a year, he came back with Pete from doing clinics in Europe. He landed in Raleigh, and he was urinating blood. The cancer had spread elsewhere."

Bone cancer, the doctors said. In December 1986, Pete flew to Clearwater, where his father now lived, and took him back to Covington with him. There, weakened by radiation treatments, Press came down with walking pneumonia at Christmas. Desperate to reverse the cancer, Pete flew with his father to Hanover, Germany, drawn there by the pioneer research of an oncologist. For 11 days, Press took treatment while he and Pete read together from the Bible. The son's prayers went unanswered. Press' cancer had spread to his lungs.

That March, with the NCAA finals in New Orleans, Rusty Bergman stopped by the Covington hospital where Press was confined: "He was skin and bones. He told me, 'If God is good enough to give me another few years, I'll praise Him all over the world.'"

On April 5, 1987, as Pete held his hand, Press Maravich passed away. In his autobiography, his son would write:

Dad handed me something beautiful and precious and I will always be indebted to him. He gave me his life full of instruction and encouragement. He gave me hope in hopeless situations and laughter in the face of grim circumstances. Dad gave me an example of discipline unequaled, dedication unmatched. He gave me the privilege of seeing an unwavering faith when the darkness of life and death surrounded him.

At his father's funeral, in Aliquippa, Pete recalled sitting at Press' bedside in his final hours and whispering into his ear, "I want you to know, Dad, that I will be with you soon."

As Press Maravich had stipulated, his son placed a basketball in his coffin.

A MONTH after his father died, in May 1987, Pete Maravich was inducted into the Basketball Hall of Fame in Springfield, Massachusetts, along with Walt Frazier, Rick Barry, Bob Houbregs, and Bobby Wanzer.

The 39-year-old Maravich couldn't help but feel melancholy as he conjured up memories of the unique odyssey that he and Press had undertaken. In this city where Dr. Naismith had invented basketball in 1891, and before a crowd that had come to see him honored, he spoke of the man who'd imbued him with the passion—not to mention the tools—for basketball.

But the heartbreak that went with the glory he knew as a professional player would keep Pete from indoctrinating his sons into the game. Only after Jaeson came home from school one day and asked him, "Daddy, did you used to be Pistol Pete?" did he show his boys NBA highlight tapes of their dad the Pistol.

In time his sons would play in schoolboy competitions, but Maravich would not push them as Press had pushed him. Yet he wanted his boys to know what his father and he had shared, those decades of their connection to a game and what it had wrought. For that reason, he undertook to write his autobiography as well as to develop a film that would explore, in a sanitized version, the relationship between Press and him through his high school years. Finally, in May 1987—working 12-hour days—he shot a videocassette series entitled *Homework Basketball* that would show him, at age 40, deftly performing the drills that had transformed a skinny boy into a ballhandling genius.

All the while, he continued to travel the country, speaking about his Christian faith—to national broadcast figures like Larry King ("I used to get life-extending drugs from Eastern Europe."), to the Christian Broadcast Network ("I was temporarily happy but it wasn't true joy."), to the ink-stained wretches of the fourth estate ("Children are taught that they originated with primordial slime. When you're told you're a monkey, you're going to start acting like one.").

In October 1987, Frank Schroeder, executive producer and director of *The Pistol: The Birth of a Legend*, the feature film on Maravich's formative years, watched the aging athlete work out in a gym. As he told the *Los Angeles Times'* Scott Ostler: "He hadn't shot a basketball for three months but he wanted to sharpen up because he had promised Mead-owlark Lemon he would play a game with Meadowlark's team. Pete told me, 'Shooting is something I don't have to practice. I did it all my life and you never lose your eye.' He bet me he could shoot from 30 feet out for a solid half hour and never miss two shots in a row.

"We had two balls. I would rebound and feed him as soon as he would shoot the other ball. He shot for a half hour, never inside 30 feet and never missed two in a row."

Wrote Ostler:

I don't know how good a judge of distance Schroeder is.

But I believe he is honest, and allowing him an error factor of 10 feet, it's still an amazing story.

A month later, Maravich came through Savannah, Georgia, to play in a charity game. Charley Rosen, coach of the Savannah Spirits of the Continental Basketball Association and a published author as well, re-called: "He was playing with one of those God squads. He was out of shape, plopping his way up and down the court, missing shots, mishan-dling the ball but having the time of his life. Before the game, he had told me he was off drugs, pills, booze and that for the first time in his life he was happy. He didn't give me a God-rap or anything like that. He said that playing ball had never been fun. He was very friendly, very out-going. He wasn't bullshitting. He looked content."

In December, he ended the long grudge he'd borne against LSU when he made a tear-filled speech during the unveiling there of a portrait of Press and him. Later that month, Maravich was in Raleigh, where his Broughton High jersey number was retired at halftime of a schoolboy basketball tournament. "I'm glad they are doing it now while I can enjoy it," Maravich told newsmen. "Usually they wait until you are dead."

Friends from his distant past remarked on how serene he now ap-peared and how he had changed.

"Earlier in the day, before his jersey was retired, there were a number of receptions for Pete with teammates, press and the community," recalled Olin Broadway, who'd coached Pete at Broughton. "Pete took each one of my children off and spent 15 to 20 minutes talking. He told them, 'I want you to know I really did enjoy my relationship with your dad. Listen carefully to him. And pay attention to what dad says.'

"Through the years, you heard a lot about his selfishness and for a time his experimenting with drugs. But Pete put himself on the right track. He was a very unusual kid. An extraordinary kid."

On January 4, 1988, Maravich flew to Los Angeles to consult on the script for *The Pistol: The Birth of a Legend*. But prior to huddling with the screenwriter, Darrel Campbell, he had agreed to an interview on a Christian radio program, *Focus on the Family*, hosted by Dr. James Dobson, who held a Ph.D. in child development.

At the time, *Focus on the Family's* organization was headquartered in Pasadena. There, three times a week, Dobson and several colleagues worked up a full-court game at the local First Church of the Nazarene gym. Maravich was invited to join the group and, though he had been pained in recent months by neuritis in his neck and shoulder, he accepted.

On January 5, Gary Lydic, Dobson's director of ministry services and a former backcourt man at McPherson College in Kansas, drove by a motel in San Demas, California, and picked up Maravich and film producer Schroeder. It was 5:45 A.M.

"As we drove out to Pasadena, Pete and I talked—we shared our relationship with Jesus Christ on the way to the church," said Lydic. "It was the first time I'd met him. But it was only a matter of minutes before I knew his belief was real. It was so transparent his love of Jesus. You knew how deeply, deeply he felt about Christ changing his life. Certainly he got into God's words. He must have spent tons and tons of time with the Bible. For on the ride over he was sharing scripture with me—he knew things backward and forward.

"The gym at the First Church of the Nazarene is in the basement. It's a full court, glass backboards. Among the group of guys was 7-foot-2 Ralph Drollinger who'd played for UCLA and then the Dallas Mavericks [1980–81, six games, 2 ppg average]. As we played, Pete certainly was not trying hard. He was hardly working up a sweat playing with a bunch of fat old men. But like the rest of us, he was having a good time. There was a lot of laughter. I loved watching him dribble between his legs. We played three games of 11 baskets. And after the third game, some of the guys stepped out to get a drink of water.

"At that point, Dr. Dobson said to Pete, 'How could you give the game up?' Pete said, 'Til today, I didn't know how much I missed it. Two weeks ago, I couldn't move my right arm above my shoulder, and the pain was so great.' And then Dr. Dobson said, 'And Pete, how do you feel today?' Pete took a shot, I rebounded it. Pete said, 'Never better.' At that moment, I turned toward him, in time to see his head and body hit the floor. He fell face forward. Pete had a great sense of humor. I thought he was putting us on. I walked over, thinking he'd jump up in our faces. But his face was pale. He was jaundiced and his eyes rolled back in his head. About thirty seconds after the seizure he stiffened and quit breathing. Dr. Dobson did CPR. I called out to the guys to dial nine-one-one. All of us in the gym began praying. Crying out, 'Lord, save his life!'

"The paramedics arrived and worked on him for 30 to 40 minutes. I remember I helped wheel the stretcher out. I remember the doors closing in the ambulance. We followed in cars to St. Luke's Medical Center in Pasadena. Two things hit me. The ambulance is not going very fast and the red light is not on. That means he's dead or in deep trouble. Twenty minutes later, in the emergency room, Dr. Dobson told us, 'Sorry, Pete's gone home.' We held hands around Pete's body. Never before or since have I seen a more peaceful face."

HIS HEART had given out — a heart that had never been standard-issue to begin with.

An autopsy determined that the 40-year-old Maravich had died of deterioration of the tissues in his heart because he was born without the most important artery system that supplies the heart with blood. People normally have two systems. He had only one. As Allan Parachini of the *Los Angeles Times* would write:

Maravich, the autopsy found, had no left coronary artery complex, one of the two systems of pencil-thick arteries that nourish the heart muscle with a continuous supply of richly oxygenated blood. The coronary arteries are the vessels on which bypass surgery is performed after the coronaries become clogged with fatty plaques that impair blood flow.

A diagram in *USA Today* would show that Maravich's right artery, which was much larger than normal, compensated by "wrapping itself around the back of the heart and opening up on the front, where the left coronary artery should have been."

Medical experts afterward said that this rare condition usually precluded strenuous activity and that those born with it rarely lived past 20.

"This [type of episode] is characteristic of the 16-year-old who collapses during a football game," said Dr. Paul Thompson, a sudden death expert at Brown University in Rhode Island. "But for a guy to go 10 years in the NBA and have a congenital anomaly like that is, to say the least, very unusual. How could a guy like that run up and down the court for 20 years?"

THE GAME had changed in the eight years since Pete Maravich had left it. Like it or not, pro ball had become more disposed toward flash than it had been in the '70s.

As *San Francisco Chronicle* columnist Art Spander put it: "Now everyone's a hot dog—or a Polish sausage. We get 360-degree spins, over-the-head dunks and enough slapping of palms to create a percussion section for a marching band."

In a decade when marketing would make icons out of NBA players like Magic Johnson and Larry Bird, when sneaker commercials celebrated the trick moves of the game's stars, the NBA shifted into entertainment mode. FAN-tastic was reserved for the look-away pass, the slam dunk, the crossover dribble that leaves a defender standing slack-jawed in his tracks.

By the '80s, they were playing Pete Maravich's basketball, a trend intensifying as the Magics and Isiahs were succeeded by the likes of Kobe Bryant, Allen Iverson, and Sacramento's Jason Williams. The great purveyors of the scene, ESPN SportsCenter and Fox Sports Net, celebrated every shimmy and shake that Kobe and his NBA brothers perpetrated, which certainly didn't discourage future generations from putting the ball between the legs or behind the back.

Oh, he would have been a treat in this jazzed-up game, Pistol Pete. As his contemporary, Walt Frazier, noted: "He was a great showman. If he was playing today, he'd be the most popular player in the league."

But it was Maravich's fate to be in advance of his time and to be the sort who took the slights and slanders about his kind of basketball to heart.

PETE MARAVICH was laid to rest in Baton Rouge on a cold Saturday in January.

A youngster he had befriended in Clearwater arrived after his parents' all-night drive. When the boy laid a rose atop the coffin, a witness said, "It sent a shiver through you."

Across the country, in Decatur, Georgia, an old teammate, Herb White, although not a poet, was moved to write these words on hearing of his friend's death:

> *He came rushing at us with floppy socks and hair,*
> *doing things on the court no one else would dare,*
> *shooting out of the bayou like a meteor rising,*
> *and in a short time we were all realizing*
> *that as he did those things in his own special way,*
> *we were seeing a whole new style of play.*
> *He could do it all, and then some. With an artist's grace*
> *he was one of those treasures we can never replace.*
> *He had hard times and troubles, maybe more than his share,*
> *yet somehow he always seemed to hang in there.*
> *Pistol Pete: forever showtime.*

In 1997, 50 years after Press Maravich had played for the Pittsburgh Ironmen, his son Pete was honored for being among the league's 50 greatest players. At the time, he was the only one of the group not still living.

APPENDIX

COLLEGIATE RECORD

Season	Team	G	FGM	FGA	Pct.	FTM	FTA	Pct.	Reb.	Ast.	Pts.	Avg.
FRESHMAN YEAR												
66–67	Louisiana State	17	273	604	.452	195	234	.833	176	124	741	43.6
VARSITY YEARS												
67–68	Louisiana State	26	432	1022	.423	274	338	.811	195	105	1138	43.8
68–69	Louisiana State	26	433	976	.444	282	378	.746	169	128	1148	44.2
69–70	Louisiana State	31	522	1168	.447	337	436	.773	164	192	1381	44.5
	Varsity totals	83	1387	3166	.480	893	1152	.775	425	549	3667	44.2

GAME-BY-GAME TOTALS

Freshman Year, 1966–67

Game	FGM	FGA	Pct.	FTM	FTA	Pct.	Reb.	Ast.	PF	Pts.
LSU 119, Southeastern 70	19	41	.463	12	15	.800	14	11	3	50
LSU 83, Baton Rouge Hawks 79	9	31	.290	16	20	.800	22	8	2	34
LSU 74, Loyola 72	13	32	.406	8	12	.667	8	3	3	34
LSU 96, Tulane 78	15	38	.395	6	10	.600	12	9	2	36

Freshman Year, 1966–67 (*cont.*)

Game	FGM	FGA	Pct.	FTM	FTA	Pct.	Reb.	Ast.	PF	Pts.
LSU 113, Miss. State 80	13	30	.433	9	10	.900	9	9	4	35
LSU 97, Ole Miss 76	15	31	.484	13	16	.813	8	4	1	43
LSU 88, Auburn 73	17	28	.607	10	12	.833	6	5	3	44
LSU 98, Bordens 68	17	30	.567	6	9	.667	11	18	1	40
LSU 97, Southern Miss. 82	-	-	-Did not play.			-	-	-	-	-
LSU 69, Tulane 68 (OT)	13	39	.333	5	7	.714	8	6	4	31
LSU 111, Baton Rouge Hawks 84	26	51	.510	14	16	.875	9	9	3	66
LSU 105, Loyola 59	20	36	.556	10	10	1.000	14	4	3	50
LSU 136, St. Mark's 89	15	38	.395	20	21	.952	11	7	3	50
LSU 108, Auburn 71	21	41	.512	15	18	.833	7	4	4	57
LSU 94, Southern Miss. 86	15	29	.517	12	12	1.000	11	4	2	42
LSU 106, Miss. State 71	19	32	.594	15	17	.882	5	8	2	53
LSU 110, Ole Miss 98	14	41	.341	17	21	.810	15	9	4	45
LSU 74, Tennessee 75	12	36	.333	7	9	.778	6	6	4	31

Sophomore Year, 1967–68

Game	FGM	FGA	Pct.	FTM	FTA	Pct.	Reb.	Ast.	PF	Pts.
LSU 97, Tampa 81	20	50	.400	8	9	.889	16	4	1	48
LSU 87, Texas 74	15	34	.441	12	16	.750	5	5	2	42
LSU 90, Loyola 56	22	43	.512	7	11	.636	9	4	2	51
LSU 94, Wisconsin 96	16	40	.400	10	13	.769	9	6	5	42
LSU 100, Florida State 130	17	41	.415	8	10	.800	5	9	3	42
LSU 81, Ole Miss 68	17	34	.500	12	13	.923	11	3	4	46
LSU 111, Miss. State 87	22	40	.550	14	16	.875	8	3	2	58
LSU 81, Alabama 70	10	30	.333	10	11	.909	6	5	3	30
LSU 76, Auburn 72	20	38	.526	15	17	.882	9	1	2	55
LSU 90, Florida 97	9	22	.409	14	17	.824	10	8	5	32
LSU 79, Georgia 76	14	37	.378	14	17	.824	11	5	3	42
LSU 100, Tulane 91	20	42	.476	12	15	.800	5	8	4	52
LSU 104, Clemson 81	14	29	.483	5	6	.833	6	2	5	33
LSU 95, Kentucky 121	19	51	.373	14	17	.824	11	2	3	52
LSU 91, Vanderbilt 99	22	57	.386	10	15	.667	6	3	4	54
LSU 96, Kentucky 109	16	38	.421	12	15	.800	8	3	4	44
LSU 67, Tennessee 87	9	34	.265	3	3	1.000	6	0	5	21
LSU 69, Auburn 74	18	47	.383	13	13	1.000	6	1	1	49
LSU 93, Florida 92 (OT)	17	48	.354	13	15	.867	7	3	4	47
LSU 73, Georgia 78	20	47	.426	11	18	.611	4	2	4	51
LSU 99, Alabama 89	24	52	.462	11	13	.846	12	3	2	59
LSU 94, Miss. State 83	13	38	.342	8	12	.667	7	7	4	34
LSU 99, Tulane 92	21	47	.447	13	15	.867	5	0	3	55
LSU 85, Ole Miss 87	13	26	.500	14	16	.875	4	8	2	40
LSU 71, Tennessee 74	7	18	.389	3	4	.750	3	1	5	17
LSU 86, Vanderbilt 115	17	39	.436	8	11	.727	6	9	3	42

Junior Year, 1968–69

Game	FGM	FGA	Pct.	FTM	FTA	Pct.	Reb.	Ast.	PF	Pts.
LSU 109, Loyola 82	22	34	.647	8	9	.889	7	11	1	52
LSU 86, Clemson 85	10	32	.313	18	22	.818	4	4	3	38
LSU 99, Tulane 101 (2OT)	20	48	.417	15	20	.750	7	2	4	55
LSU 93, Florida 89 (OT)	17	32	.531	11	15	.733	8	5	3	45
LSU 98, Georgia 89	18	33	.545	11	16	.688	10	5	3	47
LSU 84, Wyoming 78	14	34	.412	17	24	.708	6	2	2	45
LSU 101, Oklahoma City 85	19	36	.528	2	5	.400	8	7	2	40
LSU 94, Duquesne 91	18	36	.500	17	21	.810	2	6	3	53
LSU 82, Alabama 85	19	49	.388	4	4	1.000	10	5	4	42
LSU 92, Vanderbilt 94	15	30	.500	8	13	.615	4	3	3	38
LSU 71, Auburn 90	16	41	.390	14	18	.778	5	5	3	46
LSU 96, Kentucky 108	20	48	.417	12	14	.857	11	2	3	52
LSU 68, Tennessee 81	8	18	.444	5	8	.625	4	2	5	21
LSU 120, Pittsburgh 79	13	34	.382	14	18	.778	8	11	3	40
LSU 81, Ole Miss 84 (OT)	11	33	.333	9	13	.692	11	5	4	31
LSU 95, Miss. State 71	14	32	.438	5	6	.833	11	10	3	33
LSU 81, Alabama 75	15	30	.500	8	12	.667	5	6	1	38
LSU 94, Tulane 110	25	51	.490	16	20	.800	10	1	4	66
LSU 79, Florida 95	14	41	.341	22	27	.815	6	2	2	50
LSU 93, Auburn 81	20	44	.455	14	15	.933	3	5	3	54
LSU 83, Vanderbilt 85	14	33	.424	7	8	.875	8	8	3	35
LSU 89, Kentucky 103	21	53	.396	3	7	.429	5	2	4	45
LSU 63, Tennessee 87	8	18	.444	4	8	.500	3	7	3	20
LSU 76, Ole Miss 78	21	39	.538	7	11	.636	3	1	2	49
LSU 99, Miss. State 89	20	49	.408	15	19	.789	4	5	2	55
LSU 90, Georgia 80 (2OT)	21	48	.438	16	25	.640	6	4	4	58

Senior Year, 1969–70

Game	FGM	FGA	Pct.	FTM	FTA	Pct.	Reb.	Ast.	PF	Pts.
LSU 94, Oregon State 72	14	32	.438	15	19	.789	5	7	1	43
LSU 100, Loyola 87	18	36	.500	9	10	.900	6	6	4	45
LSU 109, Vanderbilt 86	26	54	.481	9	10	.900	10	5	1	61
LSU 97, Tulane 91	17	42	.405	12	19	.632	4	5	3	46
LSU 98, Southern Cal 101	18	43	.419	14	16	.875	6	4	3	50
LSU 111, Clemson 103	22	30	.733	5	8	.625	6	9	3	49
LSU 76, Oregon State 68	8	23	.349	30	31	.968	1	8	3	46
LSU 84, UCLA 133	14	42	.333	10	12	.833	4	7	4	38
LSU 80, St. John's 70	20	44	.455	13	16	.813	8	1	2	53
LSU 94, Yale 97	13	28	.464	8	11	.727	5	8	4	34
LSU 90, Alabama 83	22	42	.524	11	18	.611	7	2	4	55
LSU 70, Auburn 79	18	46	.391	8	11	.727	6	2	4	44
LSU 96, Kentucky 109	21	44	.477	13	15	.867	5	4	4	55
LSU 71, Tennessee 59	12	23	.522	5	7	.714	4	9	3	29
LSU 109, Ole Miss 86	21	46	.457	11	15	.733	5	12	3	53
LSU 109, Miss. State 91	21	40	.525	7	9	.778	3	6	4	49

LSU 97, Florida 75	20	38	.526	12	16	.750	9	7	1	52
LSU 104, Alabama 106	26	57	.456	17	21	.810	5	4	3	69
LSU 127, Tulane 114	18	45	.400	13	15	.867	4	6	3	49
LSU 94, Florida 85	16	35	.457	6	10	.600	6	8	2	38
LSU 99, Vanderbilt 89	14	46	.304	10	13	.769	5	3	2	38
LSU 70, Auburn 64	18	46	.391	10	15	.667	8	4	4	46
LSU 88, Georgia 86	17	34	.500	3	6	.500	2	6	3	37
LSU 105, Kentucky 121	23	42	.548	18	22	.818	4	7	4	64
LSU 87, Tennessee 88	10	24	.417	10	13	.769	7	6	2	30
LSU 103, Ole Miss 90	13	43	.302	9	14	.643	9	4	3	35
LSU 97, Miss. State 87	22	44	.500	11	13	.846	2	8	4	55
LSU 99, Georgia 88	16	37	.432	9	10	.900	3	11	2	41
LSU 83, Georgetown 82	6	16	.375	8	12	.667	...	...	...	20
LSU 97, Oklahoma 94	14	33	.424	9	13	.692	...	...	...	37
LSU 79, Marquette 101	4	...	...	12	16	.750	...	...	...	20

While LSU's athletic department provided Maravich's composite statistics for his senior year, it was unable to locate his statistical lines for his final three NIT games. Partial statistics from those games were assembled from newspaper reports.

NBA REGULAR-SEASON RECORD

Records: Shares single-game records for most free throws made in one quarter—14 (November 28, 1973, vs. Buffalo)—and most free throws attempted in one quarter—16 (January 2, 1973, vs. Chicago).

Honors: All-NBA first team (1976, 1977), All-NBA second team (1973, 1978), NBA All-Rookie team (1971).

Season	Team	G	Min.	FGM	FGA	Pct.	FTM	FTA	Pct.	—REBOUNDS—			Ast.	PF	Dq.	Stl.	Blk.	TO	Pts.	Avg.
										Off.	Def.	Tot.								
70–71	Atlanta	81	2926	738	1613	.458	404	505	.800	...	...	298	355	238	1	...	...	...	1880	23.2
71–72	Atlanta	66	2302	460	1077	.427	355	438	.811	...	...	256	393	207	0	...	...	...	1275	19.3
72–73	Atlanta	79	3089	789	1789	.441	485	606	.800	...	...	346	546	245	1	...	...	...	2063	26.1
73–74	Atlanta	76	2903	819	1791	.457	469	568	.826	98	276	374	396	261	4	111	13	...	2107	27.7
74–75	New Orleans	79	2853	655	1562	.419	390	481	.811	93	329	422	488	227	4	120	18	...	1700	21.5
75–76	New Orleans	62	2373	604	1316	.459	396	488	.811	46	254	300	332	197	3	87	23	...	1604	25.9
76–77	New Orleans	73	3041	886	2047	.433	501	600	.835	90	284	374	392	191	1	84	22	...	2273	31.1
77–78	New Orleans	50	2041	556	1253	.444	240	276	.870	49	129	178	335	116	1	101	8	248	1352	27.0
78–79	New Orleans	49	1824	436	1035	.421	253	277	.841	33	88	121	243	104	2	60	18	200	1105	22.6
79–80	Utah – Boston	43	964	244	543	.449	91	105	.867	17	61	78	83	79	1	24	6	82	589	13.7
Totals		658	24316	6187	14026	.441	3564	4344	.820	...	...	2747	3563	1865	18	587	108	530	15948	24.2

NBA PLAYOFF RECORD

Season	Team	G	Min.	FGM	FGA	Pct.	FTM	FTA	Pct.	Reb.	Ast.	PF	Dq.	Pts.	Avg.
70–71	Atlanta	5	199	46	122	.377	18	26	.692	26	24	14	0	110	22.0
71–72	Atlanta	6	219	54	121	.446	58	71	.817	32	28	24	0	166	27.7
72–73	Atlanta	6	234	65	155	.419	27	34	.794	29	40	24	1	157	26.2

Season	Team	G	Min.	FGM	FGA	Pct.	FTM	FTA	Pct.	—REBOUNDS—			Ast.	PF	Dq.	Stl.	Blk.	TO	Pts.	Avg.
										Off.	Def.	Tot.								
79–80	Boston	9	104	25	51	.490	2	3	.667	0	8	8	6	12	0	3	0	9	54	6.0
Totals		26	756	190	449	.423	105	134	.784	...	...	95	98	74	1	3	0	9	487	18.7

NBA ALL-STAR GAME RECORD

Season	Team	Min.	FGM	FGA	Pct.	FTM	FTA	Pct.	Reb.	Ast.	PF	Dq.	Pts.
1973	Atlanta	22	4	8	.500	0	0	...	3	5	4	0	8

Season	Team	Min.	FGM	FGA	Pct.	FTM	FTA	Pct.	—REBOUNDS—			Ast.	PF	Dq.	Stl.	Blk.	TO	Pts.
									Off.	Def.	Tot.							
1974	Atlanta	22	4	15	.267	7	9	.778	1	2	3	4	0	2	0	0	...	15
1977	New Orleans	21	5	13	.385	0	0	...	0	0	0	4	0	1	4	0	...	10
1978	New Orleans	Selected, but did not play—injured.																
1979	New Orleans	14	5	8	.625	0	0	...	0	2	2	2	1	0	0	4		10
Tottas		79	18	44	.409	7	9	.778	...	...	8	15	8	4	0	4		43

INDEX